IMAGES
of America

KINGSPORT

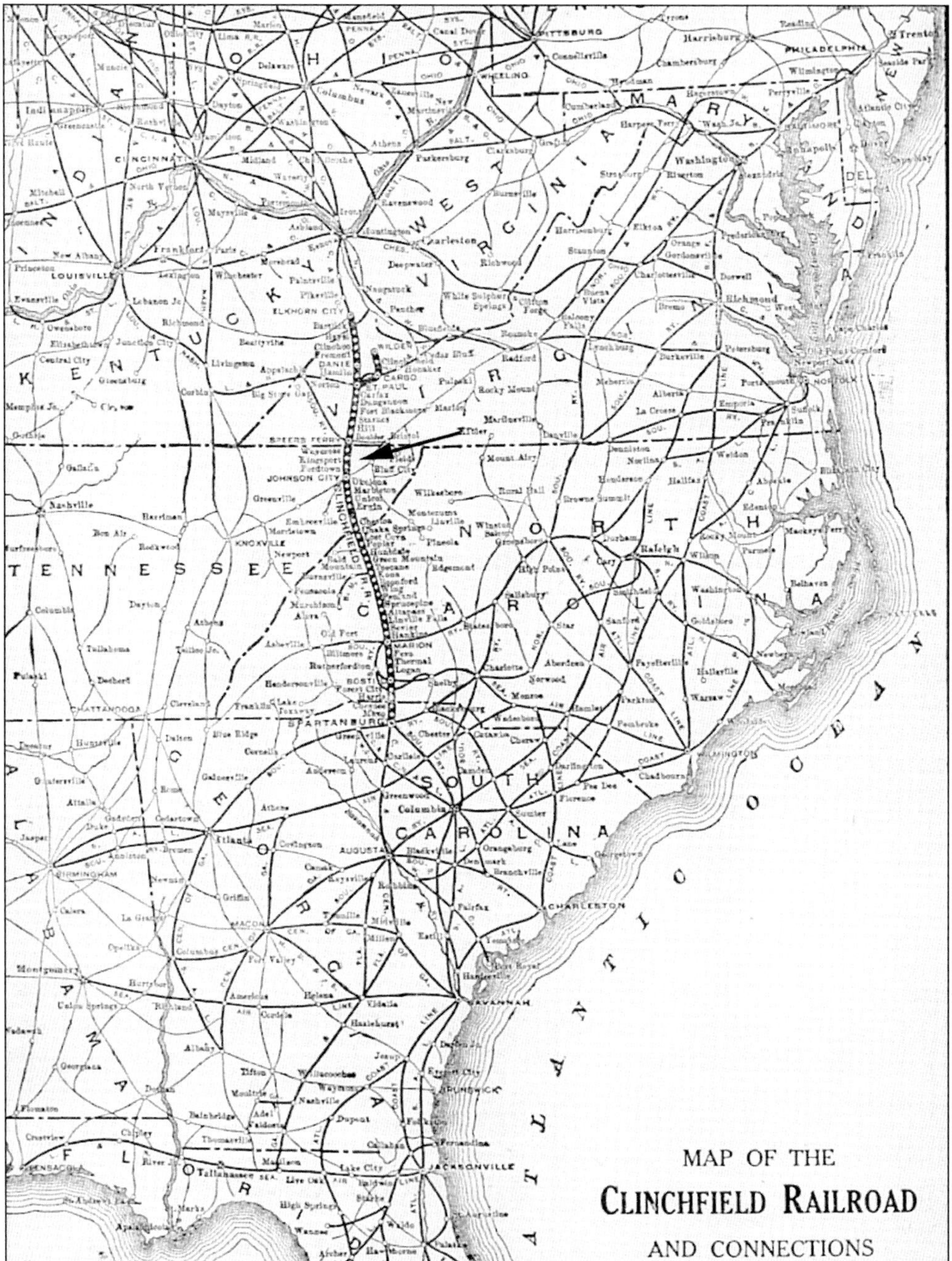

In the post-Civil War era, the establishment of railroads in the Appalachian South contributed to the development of its towns and cities and fostered economic growth. Between 1906 and 1916, the construction of the Carolina, Clinchfield and Ohio Railway across the ridges of the Southern Appalachians led to the creation of modern Kingsport in northeast Tennessee. During this era of economic transformation, the New South philosophy became evident in the fashion by which the railroads were realized—the cooperation of Northern businessmen allied with a new middle class of ambitious, Southern Appalachians.

IMAGES
of America

KINGSPORT

Martha Avaleen Egan and Nellie McNeil

ARCADIA
PUBLISHING

ISBN 978-0-7385-8985-3

Published by Arcadia Publishing
Charleston, South Carolina

Printed in the United States of America

Library of Congress Catalog Card Number: 98-87138

For all general information contact Arcadia Publishing at:
Telephone 843-853-2070
Fax 843-853-0044
E-mail sales@arcadiapublishing.com
For customer service and orders:
Toll-Free 1-888-313-2665

Visit us on the Internet at www.arcadiapublishing.com

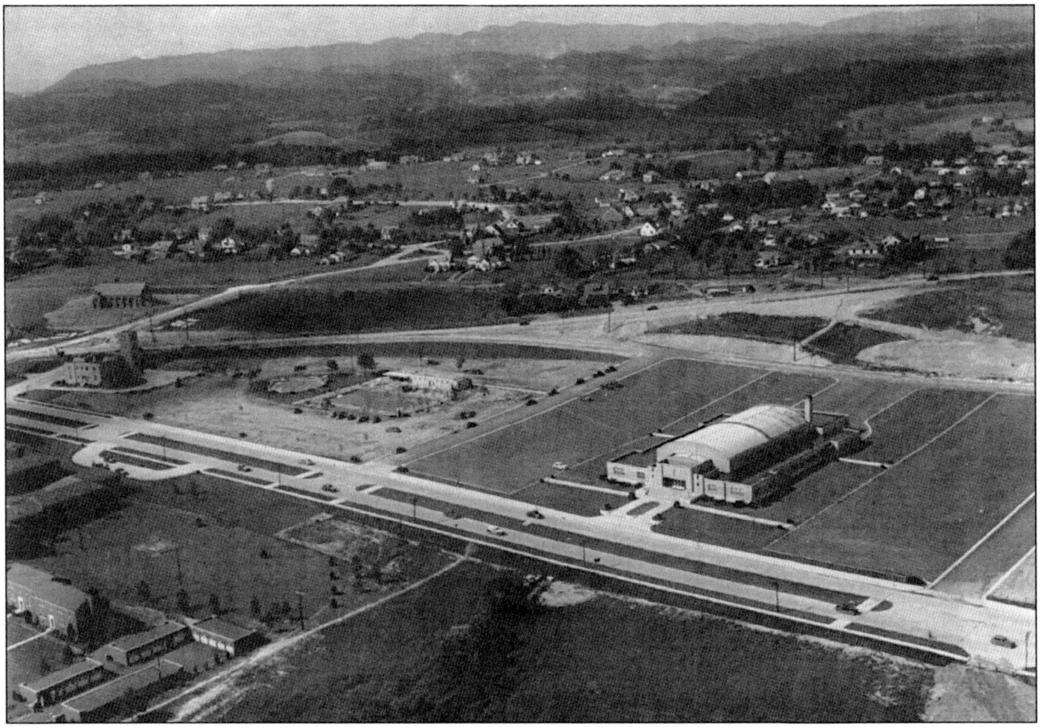

During World War II and into the post-war years, recreational and cultural activities in Kingsport centered around the Civic Auditorium. Under the direction of the Kingsport Department of Recreation, the members of the newly created Recreation Commission oversaw the initiation and development of a myriad of activities in the facility, including the Rotary Club's annual exposition, well-known bands in concert, grand opera programs, athletic activities, art classes, art exhibits, lecture series, graduation exercises, theatrical presentations, and banquets.

Contents

ACKNOWLEDGMENTS

The creation of this book is made possible by an extraordinary group of people who are unfaltering in their belief that history matters. The Friends of the Archives of the City of Kingsport and its predecessor, the Kingsport Archive of History, led efforts to collect and preserve the heritage of Kingsport and to establish an archives as part of the J. Fred Johnson Memorial Library. It is this group's sense of Kingsport history that has guided their strong commitment to their community. Its members are all longtime supporters of library programs.

All author royalties from the sale of this publication will go to the Friends of the Archives to benefit its programs of public education, community outreach, and historic preservation.

The archives enjoys strong community support. Notable among the many supporters who advanced its establishment and continued growth are the Eastman Chemical Company and the King Foundation (E. William King, John R. King, and Margaret King Norris), as well as the City of Kingsport, retired Congressman James H. Quillen, and the National Historical Publications and Records Commission.

Serving as the 1997–98 officers and board members of the Friends of the Archives of the City of Kingsport are Nellie McNeil, president; Ann Morison, secretary; Robert Harvey, treasurer; Thomas Gannaway; Nancy Gideon; Valda Page; David Shivell; and Jean Spencer. This group selected the photographs from the Archives of Kingsport and reviewed the final manuscript.

It is the good fortune of any project to have the counsel and professional expertise of Nellie McNeil. Valuable suggestions have been provided by Dr. William J. Wade, professor of history, and Dr. John S. Gaines, professor of education, both of King College. Julie Roberson and Aaron Cowan, King College Archives interns, helped with research. Special thanks are extended to Margaret McNeer and Elizabeth Alvey. I wish also to thank Celia Bachelder, Jill Ellis, James Stallard (Holston Defense Corporation), Mike Mills (Holston Army Ammunition Plant), Lt. Paul Bowman (Kingsport Police Department), and Mr. and Mrs. William S. Todd. Kim Crowder-Vaughn, of the East Tennessee State University English department, provided her time and skill in the proofreading of the manuscript.

The primary photographic collections of the archives represented in this book include Mattie McDowell; Thomas McNeer Jr.; Richard Alvey; Guy and Carl DeVault; Ellis Binkley; JPS Converter Textiles; Mason and Dixon, Inc.; Kingsport City Schools; and Nancy N. Pridemore. It should be noted that prior to the creation of the archives in 1994 numerous individuals donated photographs to the library. These photographs are gathered together in what is called the Palmer Collection, housed in the archives. Many of them are reproduced in this book.

For the initiation and support of the library's archives, thanks are extended to Library Director Jud Barry, the Kingsport Public Library Commission, and Leisure Services Director Tom Bowman. The good wishes of the Kingsport Library staff are appreciated.

Fundamental to the creation of this book are Arcadia Publishing Senior Editors Sarah Maineri and Mark Berry. Their expert publishing and editing skills are matched by their patience and kindness.

—Martha Avaleen Egan, archivist

INTRODUCTION

by Mayor Ruth C. Montgomery

The Archives of the City of Kingsport is the only municipal archives in Tennessee. It was created in 1994 and serves as a division of the Kingsport Public Library. The mission of the Archives is to preserve for consultation and for study the documentary heritage of the city of Kingsport. It houses historical materials generously donated by area citizens, businesses, industries, and organizations.

The Archives is supported in its mission by the Friends of the Archives, an organization of volunteers dedicated to preserving our heritage. *Kingsport, Tennessee* results from the efforts of this non-profit organization. In nearly 200 carefully selected photographs, the book depicts the history and heritage of our region from its earliest beginning to the 1950s.

The theme of the 1998 Tri-Cities Tennessee/Virginia Economic Summit was "From strong roots, building tomorrow," and that theme reflects the essence of this region and the city of Kingsport. Those early settlers who came to the region with their hopes for a better and brighter future gave the city strong roots, enabling the community to adapt and progress. Kingsport was first settled in the 1750s along the Holston River in northeast Tennessee. King's Mill Station, which was later called King's Port, was established on nearby Reedy Creek by Colonel James King. Kingsport became a natural stopping point for pioneers heading upstream, including the flatboats on their way to Fort Nashborough and Daniel Boone, who blazed the Wilderness Road to Cumberland Gap. Netherland Inn served as an inn and tavern for these travelers and stands today as an historic site on the edge of the Holston.

The completion of the Carolina, Clinchfield and Ohio Railway early in the 20th century enabled Kingsport to develop as an industrial town with industries located along the Holston River and the railroad. Nearby coal mines made it possible to manufacture products for the eastern United States. Early foresighted industrialists engaged Dr. John Nolen, an eminent city planner, to design the city which came to be known as "the Model City." The city was chartered in 1917 and was the first city in Tennessee with a city manager form of government. Its school system was planned by educators at Columbia University.

The planned industrial town clustered residential neighborhoods within walking distance of the work place with commercial areas closeby. The plan included wide streets and distinctive traffic circles, or roundabouts. The preservation of John Nolen's "Model City" has become an important citizen goal, and the privately funded Kingsport Regional Interactive Design Studio in partnership with the University of Tennessee's College of Architecture is entrusted with that mission.

Important historical sites include Netherland Inn and the Exchange Place. The downtown is anchored by the Main Street Historical District on one end and area churches and a traffic roundabout known as Church Circle on the other. The Downtown Heritage Trail was dedicated in the summer of 1998, and a printed guide gives residents and visitors information on the downtown historical sites.

Kingsport today is a thriving industrial city with 41,000-plus citizens and is home to the world headquarters of the Eastman Chemical Company and AFG Industries, Inc. Other large industries include a division of Willamette Industries, Quebecor Printing, Holliston Mills, and JPS Converter Textiles. The city continues to operate under the city manager form of government, and the school system remains one of the best in the state. It has funded a modern library, a senior center, 6 miles of a "Greenbelt" walking trail, and Bays Mountain Park, the largest municipal park in the United States. An added emphasis on tourism with the 1996 opening of the MeadowView Conference Resort and Convention Center reflects the ability of the "settlers" of today to adapt to changing needs.

Today,the region and Kingsport are referred to as "the First Frontier." The heritage left by those faces in these pages is echoed by the citizens of today, and the "first frontier" is now the areas of science, medicine, and technology. The strong roots vividly portrayed in this book remain the foundation of our tomorrows and an even better and brighter future in the 21st century.

One

Early History

In the late 18th century, beyond the barrier of the Appalachian Mountains, permanent white settlements began to develop along the Holston and the Watauga Rivers. Following the Wilderness Road carved out by Daniel Boone in 1775, families traveled through the Cumberland Gap into Kentucky. After the America Revolution had ended, large numbers of settlers crossed over the mountains into an area which was home to the Shawnee and the Cherokee. In 1783, only 12,000 Caucasians lived west of the mountains and south of the Ohio River. By 1790, the census documented more than 100,000 residents of the future states of Kentucky and Tennessee. Long Island, near present-day Kingsport, was centrally located on the route of the "Great Indian Warrior Path" traveled by Cherokees, early settlers, and traders and later traversed by wagons and stagecoaches.

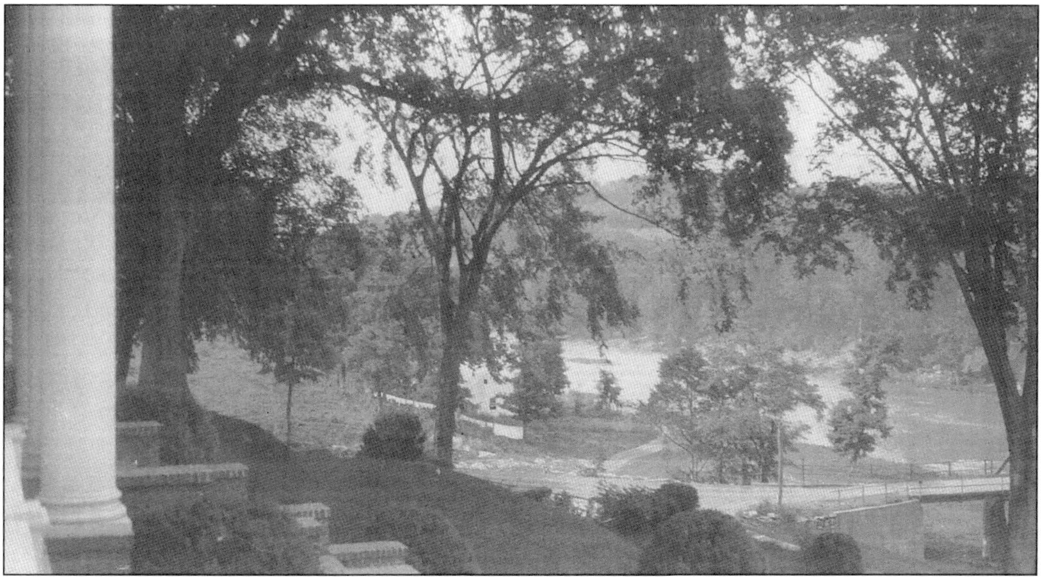

This view of the Holston River from the porch of an antebellum mansion, Rotherwood, shows the region as it existed in an early era. Before becoming a commercial port town in the 19th century and a New South industrial center in the 20th century, the area now called Kingsport was the sacred land of the Cherokee nation. Located upriver from the convergence of the north and south forks of the Holston River, the Long Island of the Holston was the location of ancient Native American villages. Later, during the era of the Cherokee, many tribes held "talks" and made treaties with one another on the island, which was considered to be a holy place where nothing was to be killed.

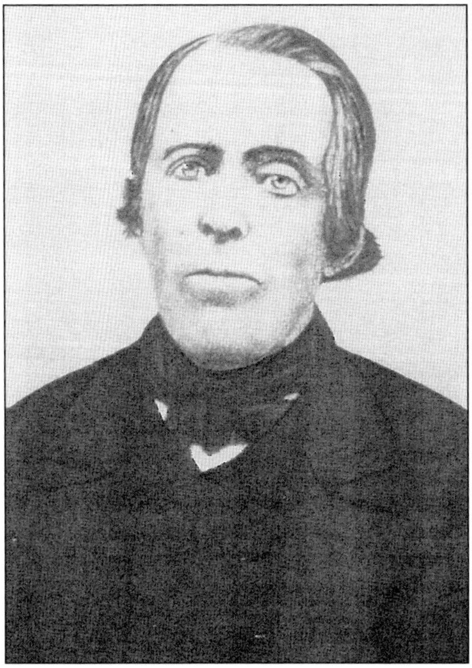

The prominent King family shaped the history of Sullivan County in the 18th and 19th centuries. Instrumental in the early development of the area which became Bristol, Colonel James King (1752–1825) established an iron works at the mouth of Steele Creek. A fleet of wagons carried the iron products to the Kingsport shipping point on the Holston River. First known by the names of Island Flats, Fort Robinson, and Fort Patrick Henry, the area came to be known as Christianville for Gilbert Christian, a local landowner. In the early 1800s, William King (1752–c. 1840) of Washington County, VA, a cousin of Colonel James King, purchased a 2.5-acre tract in Christianville and established King's Boat Yard. After expanding his business interests, he became one of the wealthiest men in east Tennessee and southwest Virginia. Reverend James King (1791–1867), a son of Colonel James King, is known as a Bristol founder and was involved in the beginnings of King College.

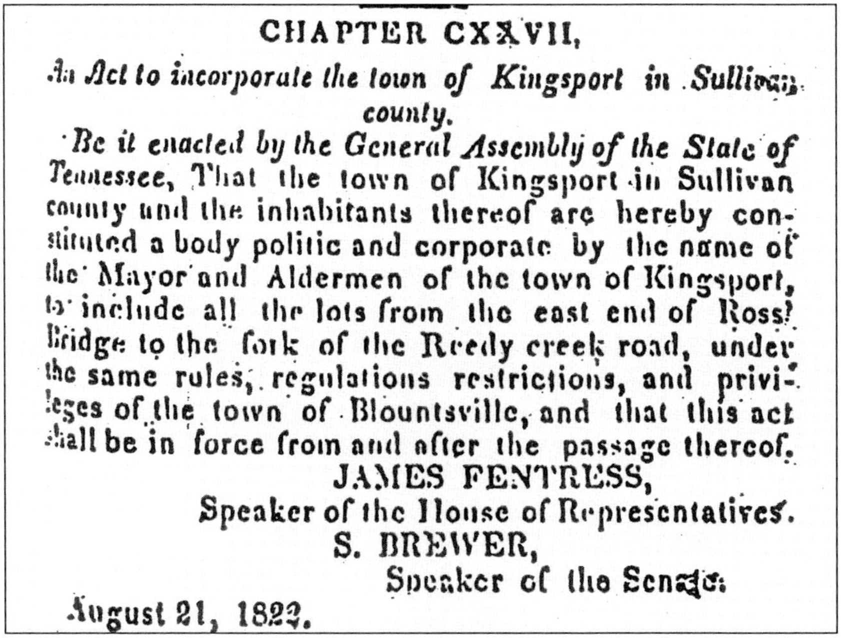

CHAPTER CXXVII,

An Act to incorporate the town of Kingsport in Sullivan county.

Be it enacted by the General Assembly of the State of Tennessee, That the town of Kingsport in Sullivan county and the inhabitants thereof are hereby constituted a body politic and corporate by the name of the Mayor and Aldermen of the town of Kingsport, to include all the lots from the east end of Ross' Bridge to the fork of the Reedy creek road, under the same rules, regulations restrictions, and privileges of the town of Blountsville, and that this act shall be in force from and after the passage thereof.

JAMES FENTRESS,
Speaker of the House of Representatives.
S. BREWER,
Speaker of the Senate.

August 21, 1822.

On August 21, 1822, the Tennessee General Assembly passed an act which officially incorporated the area as Kingsport. At this time in Sullivan County, there were two incorporated towns, Blountville and Kingsport. Nineteenth-century Kingsport operated with a board, consisting of a mayor and aldermen, and the city's boundaries were from Rotherwood Bridge east up the Holston River to Reedy Creek, up Reedy Creek to the forks of present-day Bloomingdale Pike and West Sullivan Street, to the west along Sullivan Street and Fort Robinson Drive to the north fork of the Holston River and down the river to Rotherwood Bridge.

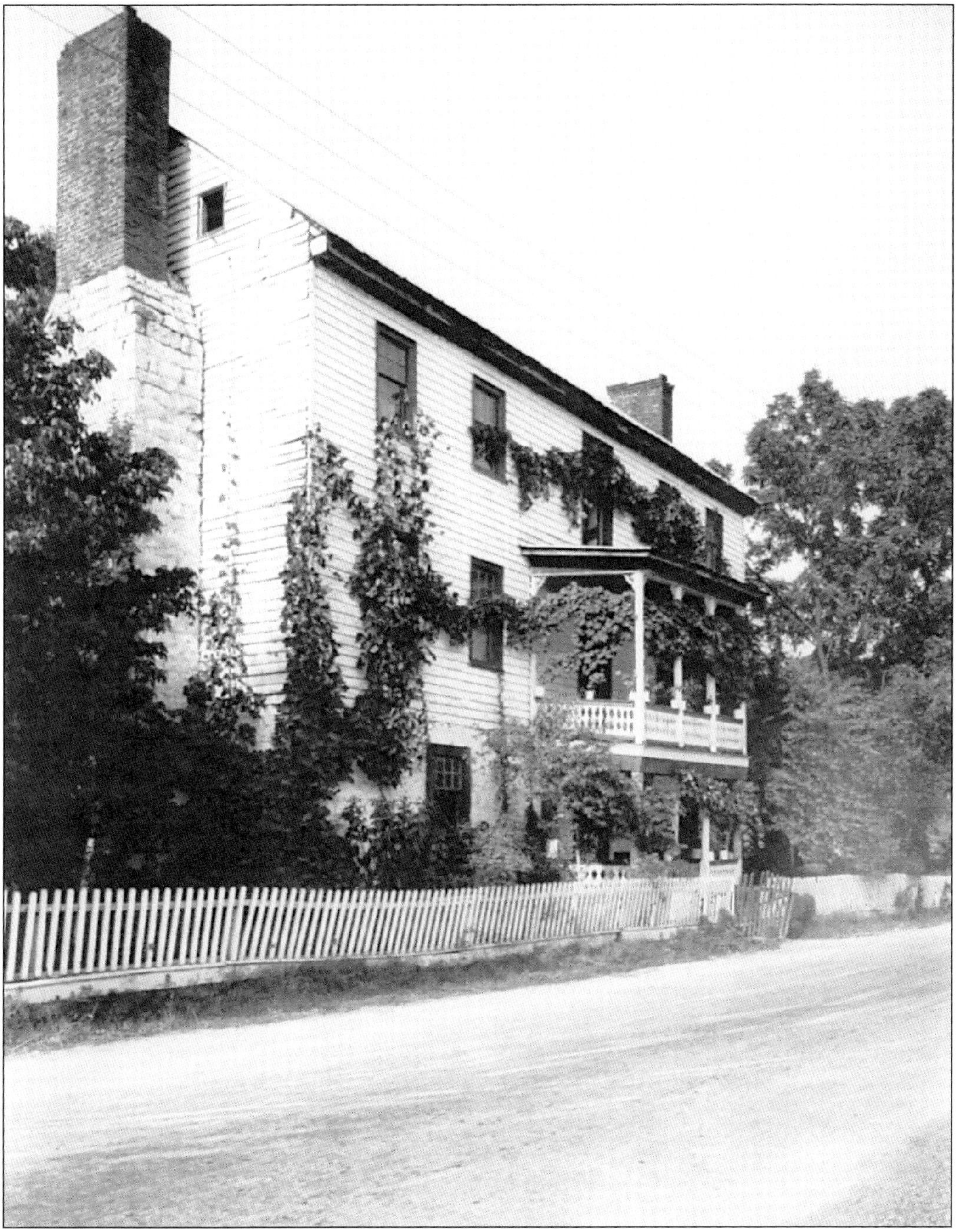

On the Great Stage Road, the primary route to western Kentucky and eastern Tennessee, Netherland Inn founder Richard Netherland (1764–1832) obtained a stage contract and in 1818 began operating the distinguished three-story building as an inn and tavern. Prominent friends of the Netherland family visited the inn, including Presidents Andrew Jackson and Andrew Johnson. Along with the Boat Yard Complex, Netherland Inn, located on Netherland Inn Road, is a National Registered Historic Site. Open to the public, the historical complex is fully preserved.

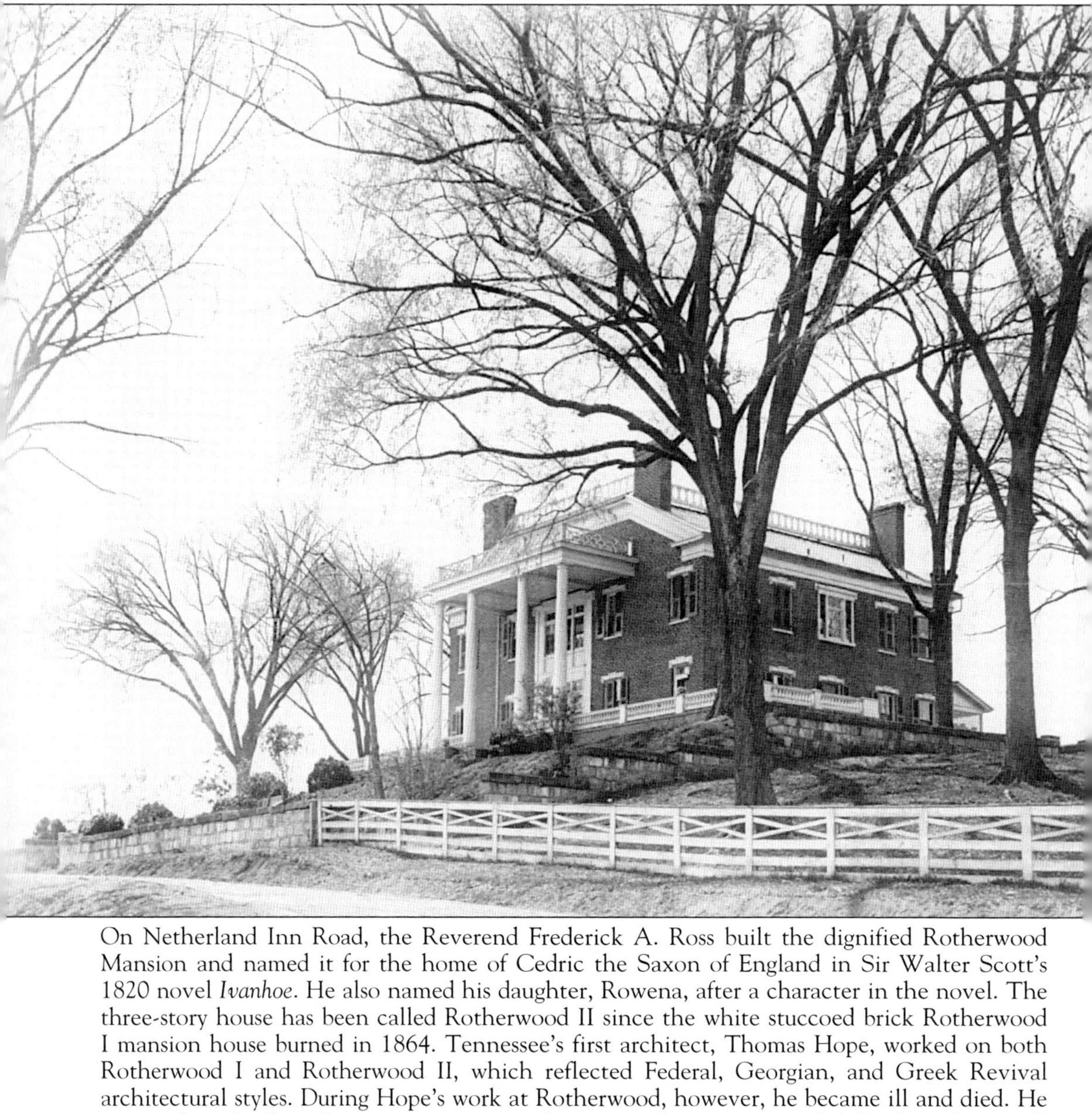

On Netherland Inn Road, the Reverend Frederick A. Ross built the dignified Rotherwood Mansion and named it for the home of Cedric the Saxon of England in Sir Walter Scott's 1820 novel *Ivanhoe*. He also named his daughter, Rowena, after a character in the novel. The three-story house has been called Rotherwood II since the white stuccoed brick Rotherwood I mansion house burned in 1864. Tennessee's first architect, Thomas Hope, worked on both Rotherwood I and Rotherwood II, which reflected Federal, Georgian, and Greek Revival architectural styles. During Hope's work at Rotherwood, however, he became ill and died. He is buried in the Ross Cemetery in an unmarked grave. Due to financial difficulties, Ross sold 1,900 acres of his plantation to his overseer, Joshua Phipps, in 1847. This acreage included all of the land bounded by the south fork of the Holston and the Great Stage Road, the property on which the present mansion now sits.

Reverend Frederick A. Ross laid out the town of Rossville (Kingsport) to the west near the earlier town of Christianville. Building the first bridge (1818) over the north fork of the Holston River, he rerouted the Great Stage Road over this easily traveled section. Ordained as a Presbyterian minister in 1825, he served the Boatyard Presbyterian Church as its minister for 25 years. Ross accepted no salary for his time as minister for his church.

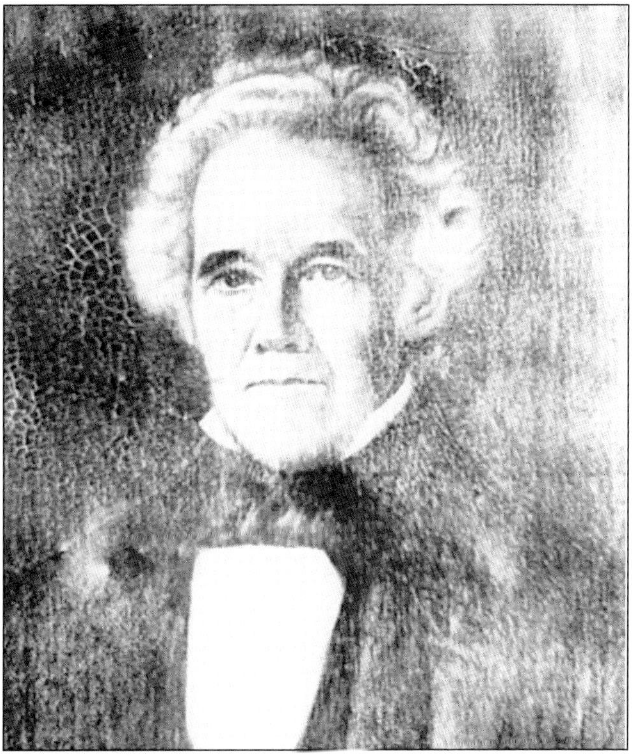

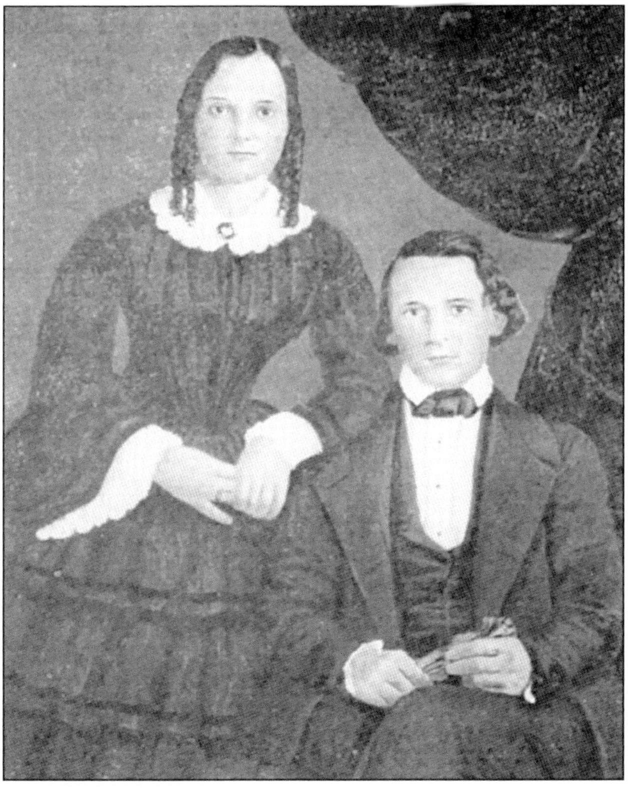

Shown here are Rowena and David Ross, the children of Reverend Frederick A. Ross and Theodocia Vance Ross. Rowena was educated at Mrs. Willard's school in Troy, New York, and in Philadelphia. During the 1840s, as she made her wedding plans, Rotherwood was enlarged and refined for her. Tragically, on the night before the wedding, the groom-to-be drowned in the Holston River. Rowena later married Edward Temple of Knoxville, who died of yellow fever in New Orleans. Her second marriage was to Wescom Hudgins. She died in Huntsville, AL, and was survived by one child, Theodocia Ross Temple. The painting dates from 1848, the year before David Ross left for the California gold fields.

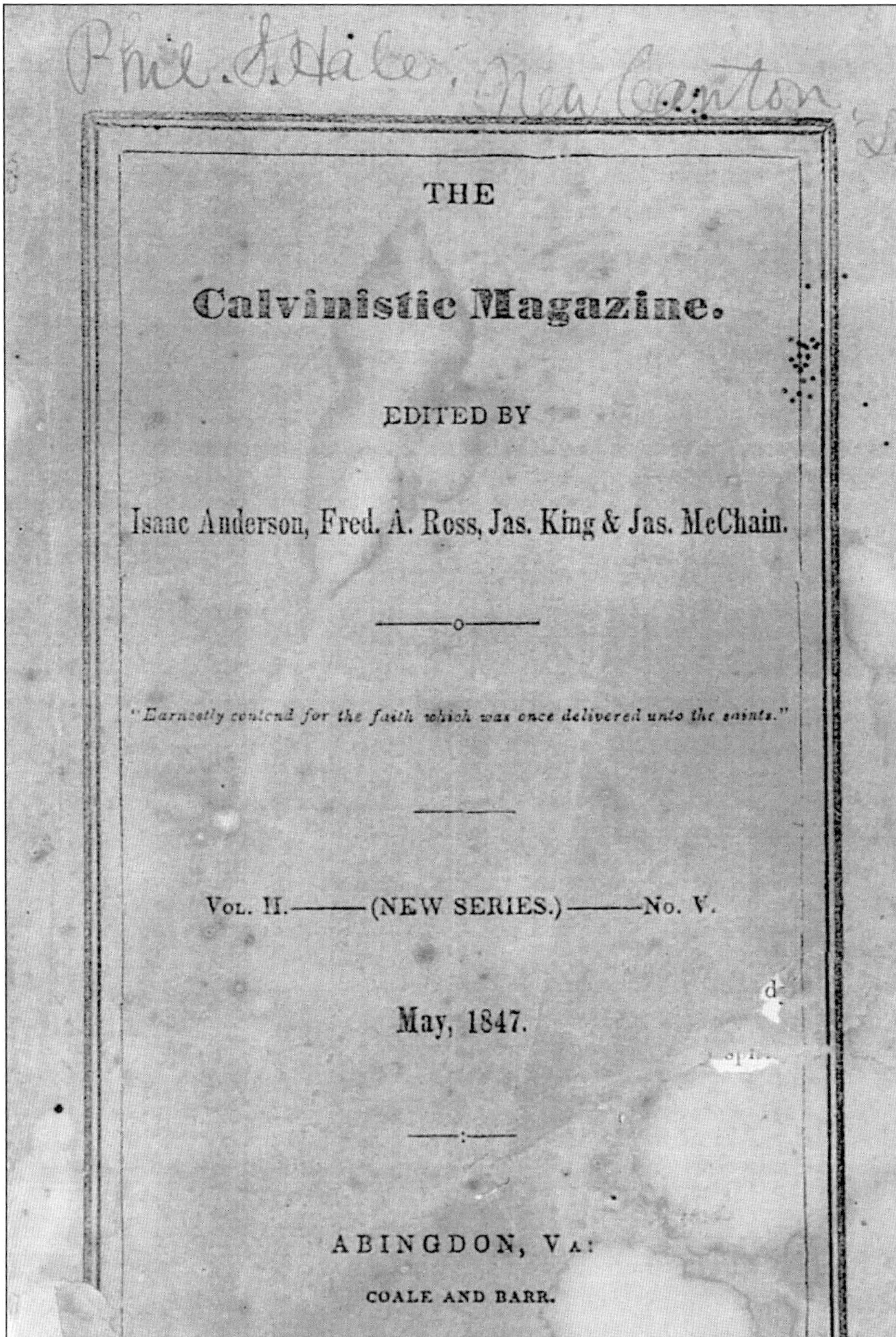
THE

Calvinistic Magazine.

EDITED BY

Isaac Anderson, Fred. A. Ross, Jas. King & Jas. McChain.

"Earnestly contend for the faith which was once delivered unto the saints."

Vol. II.——(NEW SERIES.)——No. V.

May, 1847.

ABINGDON, VA:

COALE AND BARR.

Along with Isaac Anderson, James King, and James McChain, Frederick Ross edited the *Calvinistic Magazine*. This edition from the second series, dated May 1847, contains articles addressing "Mode of Baptism," "Reminiscences of our Church," and "Raising up our own Ministers." Subscriptions were $1 per year, and all subscribers were listed in each publication.

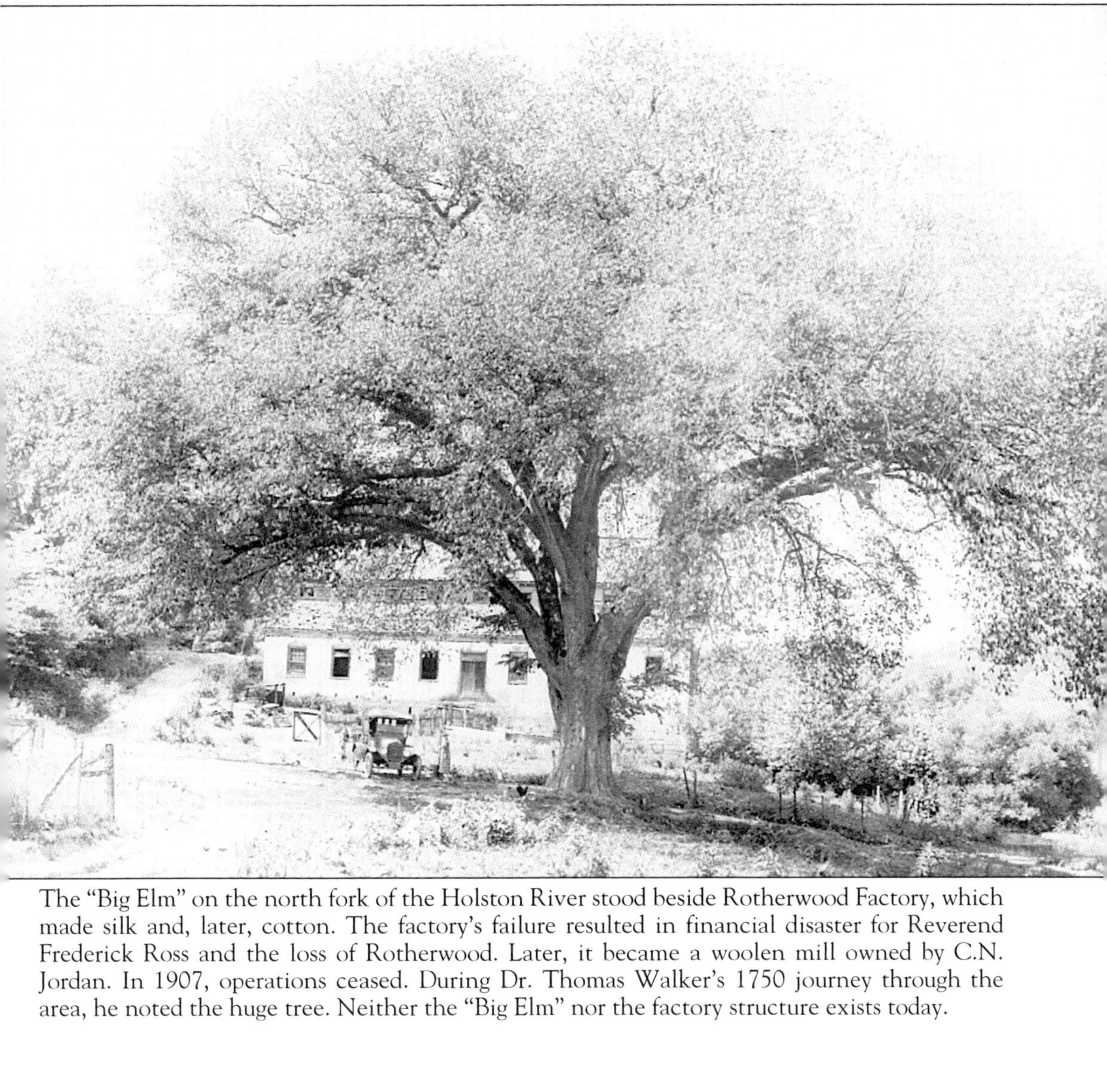

The "Big Elm" on the north fork of the Holston River stood beside Rotherwood Factory, which made silk and, later, cotton. The factory's failure resulted in financial disaster for Reverend Frederick Ross and the loss of Rotherwood. Later, it became a woolen mill owned by C.N. Jordan. In 1907, operations ceased. During Dr. Thomas Walker's 1750 journey through the area, he noted the huge tree. Neither the "Big Elm" nor the factory structure exists today.

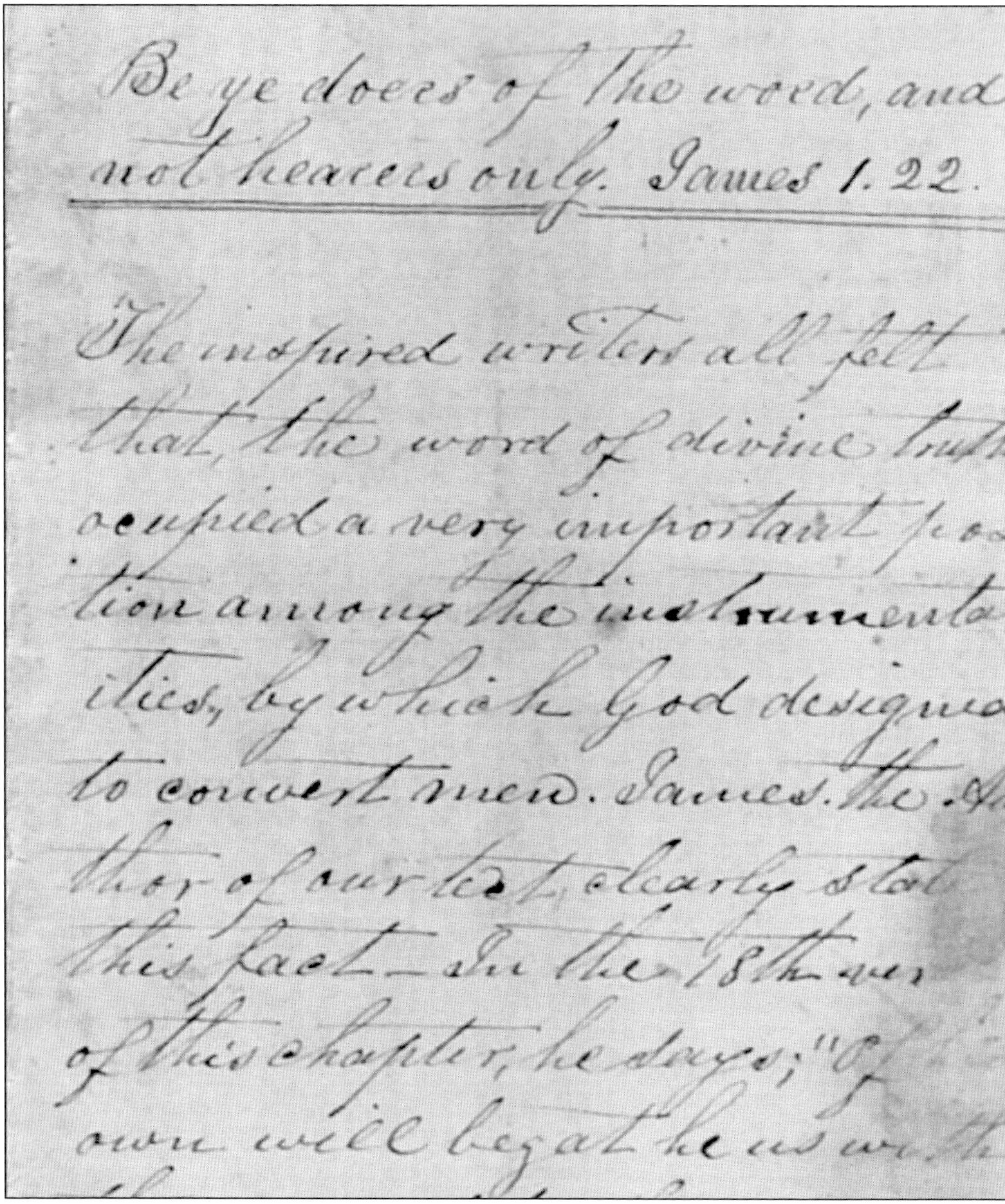

Be ye doers of the word, and not hearers only. James 1.22.

The inspired writers all felt that, the word of divine truth occupied a very important position among the instrumentalities, by which God designed to convert men. James the Author of our text, clearly states this fact—In the 18th verse of this chapter, he says; "Of his own will begat he us with

For more than 50 years in the Kingsport area, the Reverend Daniel Rogan Jr. (1806–1881) was a prominent Presbyterian minister. The son of an Irish immigrant who became one of Kingsport's most successful merchants, Daniel Jr. began his career as a clerk in his father's store. He served as the pastor of several churches including the Pleasant Grove Church near Bluff City and in 1836 the New Bethel Presbyterian Church in Piney Flats. Later, he lived in the Anderson log townhouse next to the Blountville Presbyterian Church. During Sunday services on July 27, 1836, while Rogan was preaching at this church, General Andrew Jackson, A.J. Donelson, Colonel McClellan, and about 15 others rode up to the church on horseback and in carriages. Reverend Rogan stopped preaching and announced Jackson's arrival and then proceeded to preach a sermon entitled "Remember the Sabbath day to keep it Holy." He was also pastor at the Kingsport Presbyterian Church for several years.

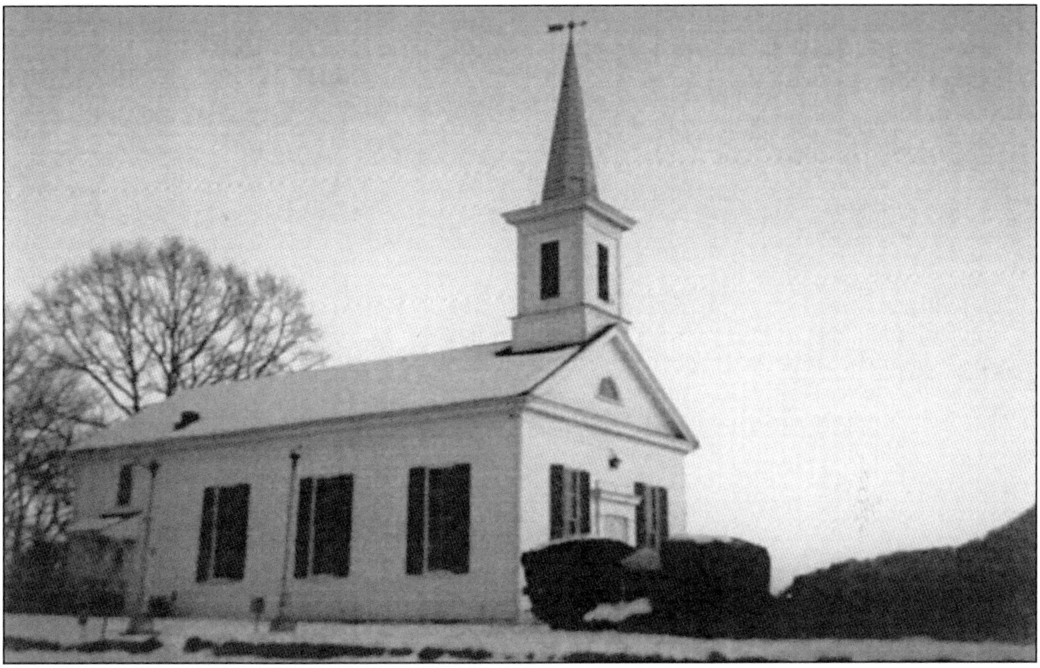

Boatyard Presbyterian Church, organized on May 20, 1820, by the Presbytery of Abingdon, VA, was first under the direction of James Gallaher, who later became the chaplain of the U.S. House of Representatives. When Frederick A. Ross had laid out the town of Rossville in 1818, he had reserved lots for the church. This beautiful 19th-century rural church is listed on the National Register of Historic Places and has an active congregation.

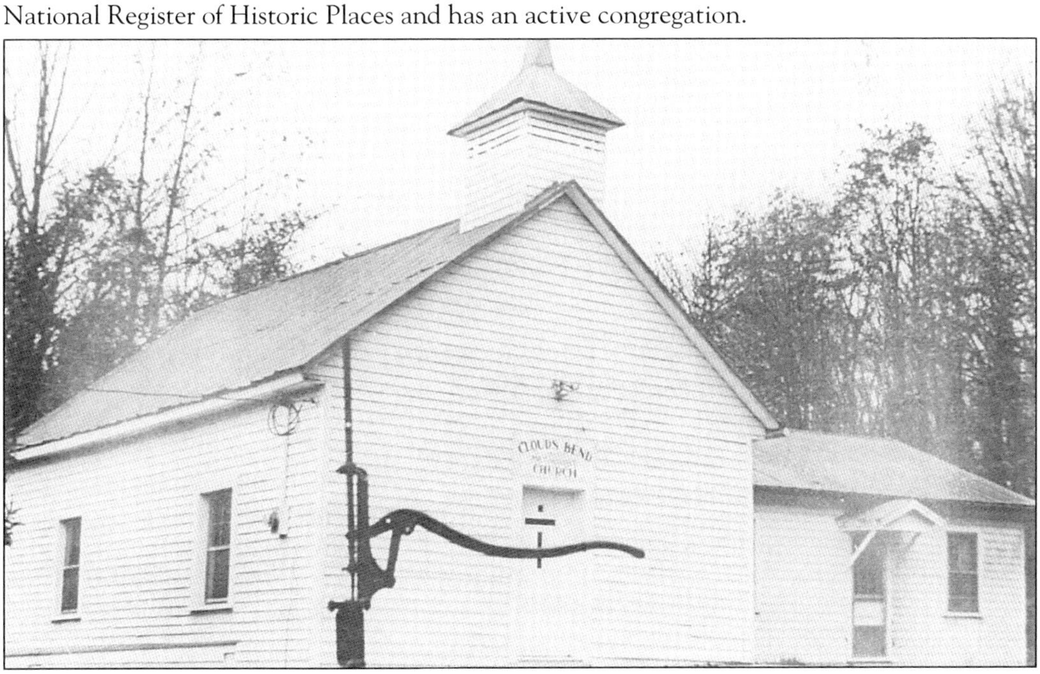

Cloud's Bend Methodist Church served the residents who lived near Bays Mountain, the present site of Ridgefields subdivision. This photograph shows the church as it was in 1910. It still has an active congregation.

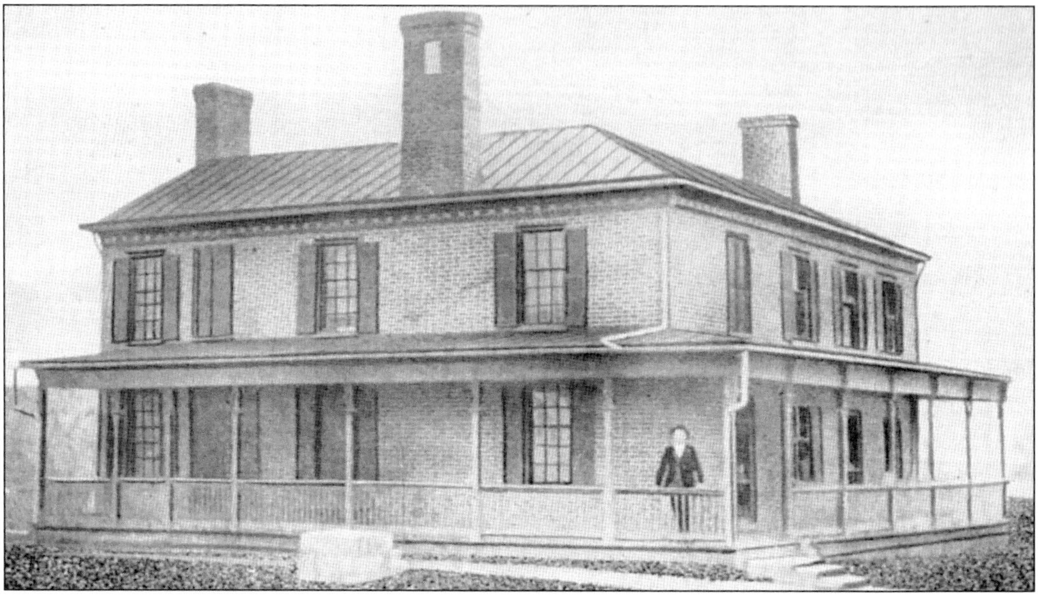

Kingsport First Bank is pictured above in May 1909. David Roller served as the president of the financial institution, and J.B. Nall was the cashier. Capital and stocks totaled $15,000.

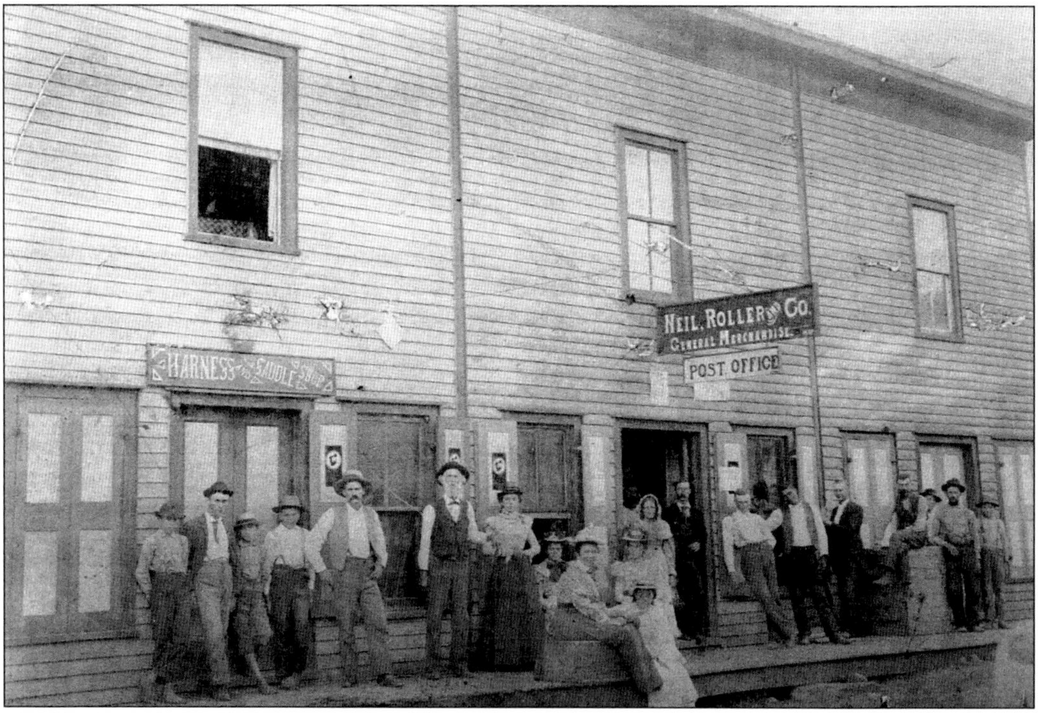

The Neil, Roller and Co. General Merchandise Store housed the Kingsport Post Office in the late 1800s. It was located in the Lovedale section of Kingsport with a harness and saddle shop next door to it. The group seen here, photographed in August 1890, includes Noia Smallwood, Bill Perry, Bert Nelms, George Bolton, Sam Kyle, Uncle Jimmy Neil, Bert Pyle, Nan Rose Patton, Nancy Cloud, Pink Pyle, James Neil, McBeth McIntosh, Dr. Alvin Roller, Pryor Moffit, Uncle Billy Bolton, and Ethel Moffit.

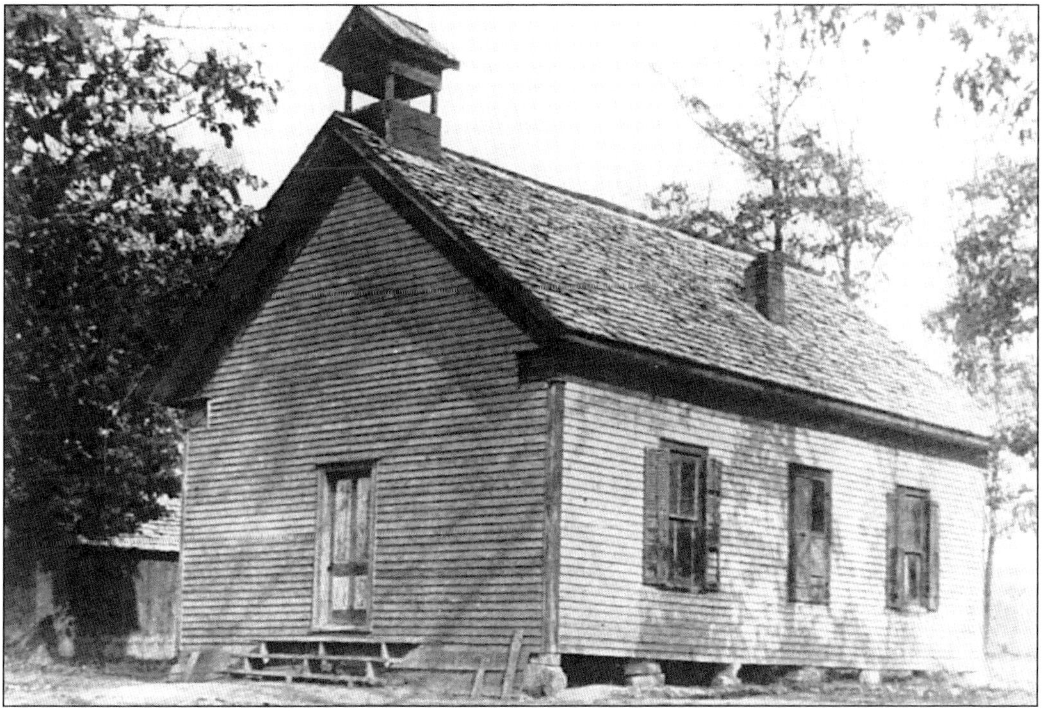

Built around 1890, the one-room Oklahoma School was located at the present Robert E. Lee School site.

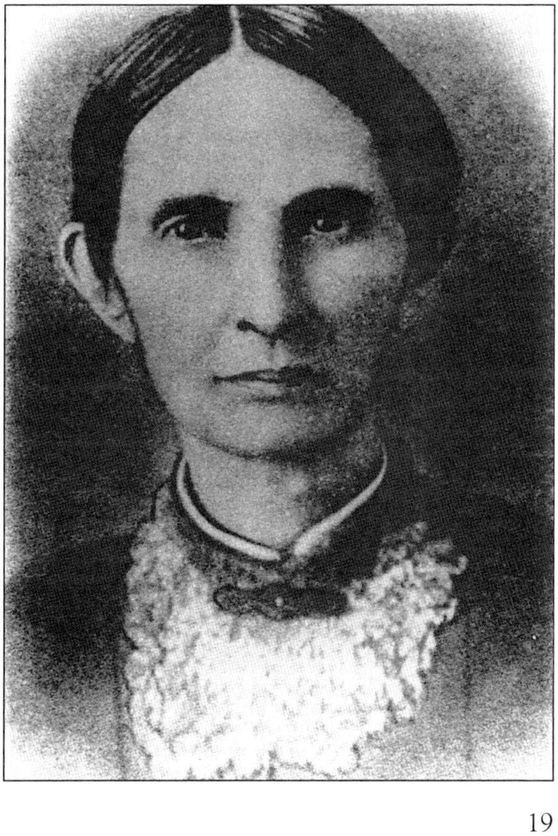

Lydia Childress Waterman was one of the first teachers in the Kingsport area. Her husband, David, was also an educator.

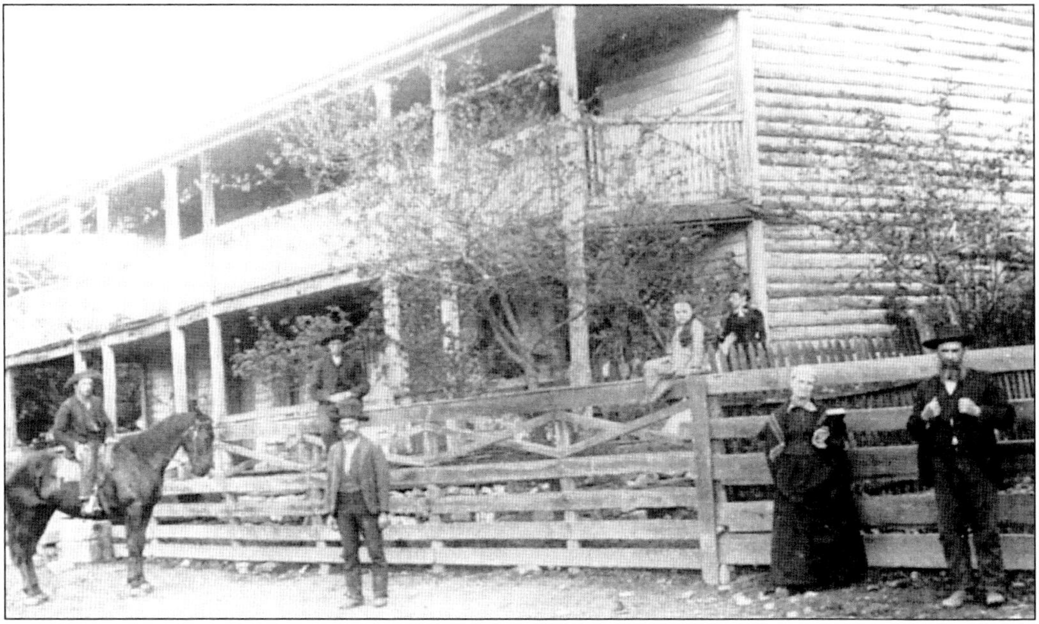

Built in the early 1800s, the DeVault Home was located in Old Kingsport on Netherland Inn Road. Pictured on the far right in this 1908 photograph is James Miller DeVault, who was born in 1828.

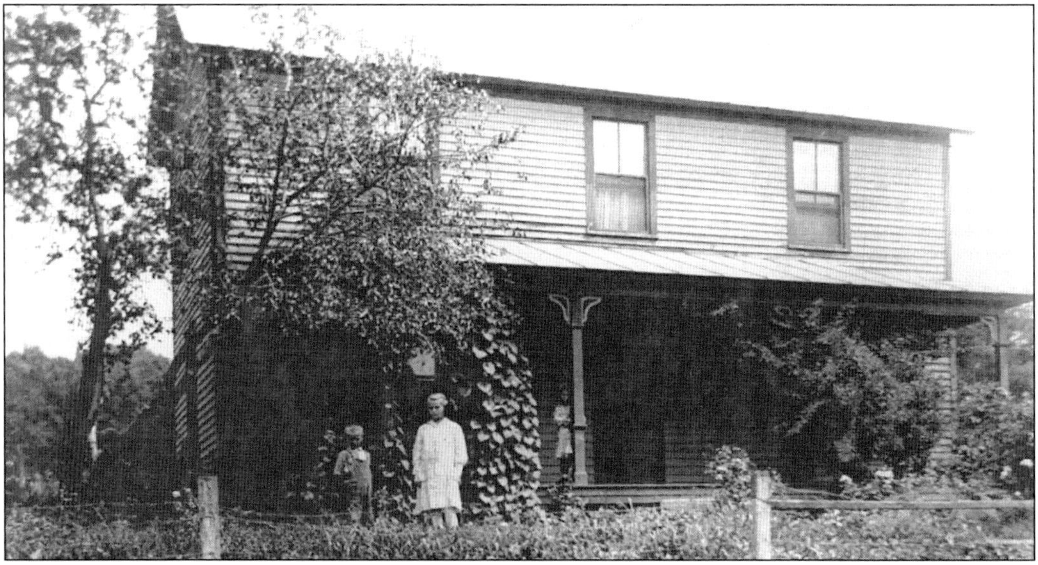

In 1820, Daniel and Catherine Rogan purchased Hale's store, located on the Great Stage Road in front of Sink Hole lot. Additionally, Rogan purchased a home and warehouse. Entering into the flatboat and wagon-freighting business, he eventually brought all of his sons into his business. His family of ten children included the well-known Presbyterian minister Daniel Rogan Jr.; Catherine (1803–1841), who married Richard Netherland Jr.; and Rebecca, who married George Thomas. The Thomas families, as well as Daniel, Griffith, and Perry Rogan, were partners with Frederick A. Ross in the Rotherwood Cotton manufacturing business. Some of the Rogans moved to Hawkins County, where many of their descendants reside today. Pictured here is the Rogan residence in 1912.

Two

The New South Comes to Northeast Tennessee

Kingsport, TN, provides "the unusual example of an entire town built by industrial promotion, combined for once with community planning," writes historian George B. Tindall. What happened in Kingsport during the first quarter of the 20th century was indeed unusual. In less than a decade, a town of slightly over a thousand was transformed into an industrialized, planned community of nearly 18,000. Combining a New South program of progress through economic growth with a Progressive-era emphasis on professional expertise and efficiency, Kingsport was created to generate business for the Carolina, Clinchfield and Ohio Railway. The city's founding entrepreneurs believed that to achieve their economic plans, a well-constructed social plan would need rapid implementation.

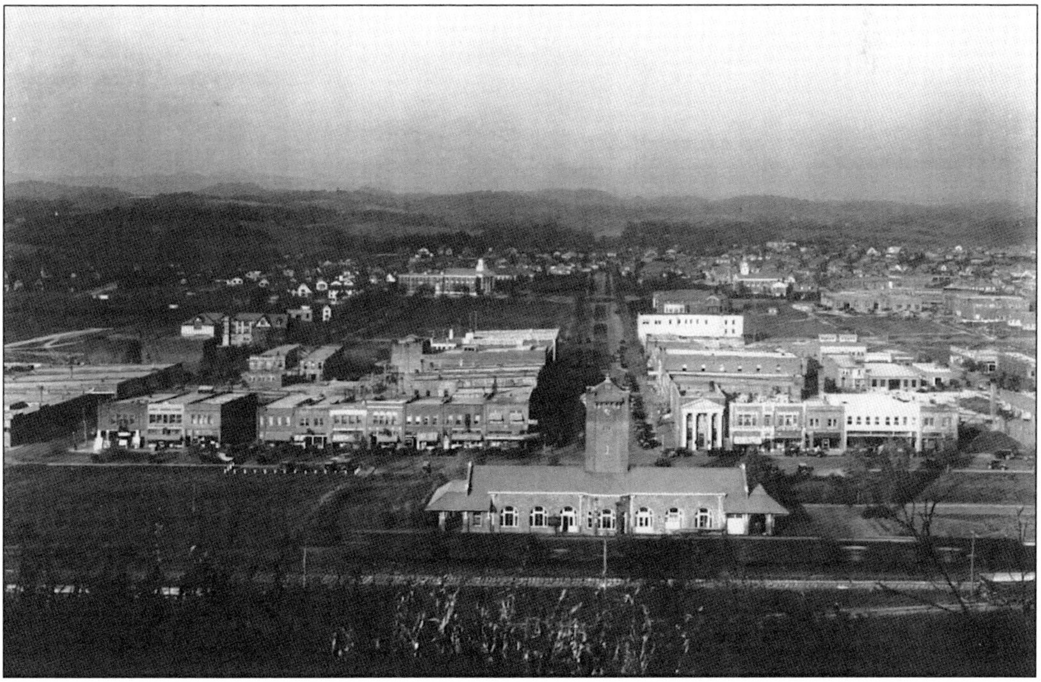

This 1928 view of Broad Street from a hill behind the train station was captured by photographer Mattie McDowell. Her photographic studio was housed at 126 Broad Street.

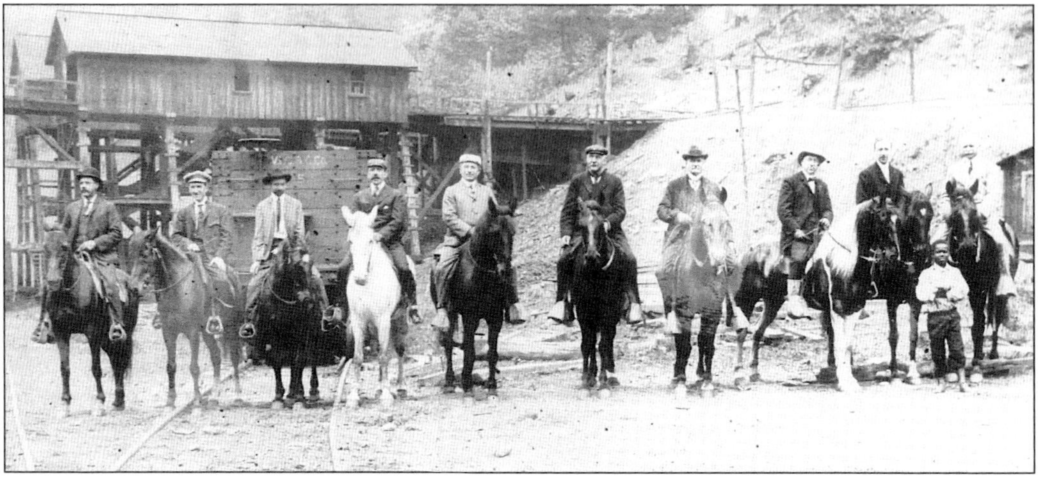

In 1902, Appalachian industrialist George L. Carter purchased existing tracts from Johnson City, TN, to Boonford, NC, and named the route the Southern and Western Railway. Rechartered in 1908 as the Carolina, Clinchfield and Ohio Railway, the route eventually operated in five states covering 277 miles. In order to complete the CC&O, Carter obtained the financial backing of powerful New York capitalist Thomas Fortune Ryan, who invested a reported $30 million in the project. John B. Dennis of Blair and Co., NY, also provided financial backing for the railroad and supported the development of Kingsport. The Northern investors who backed the construction of the South and Western Railway and, subsequently, the CC&O, met in 1905. Pictured from left to right are George L. Carter (S&W and CC&O head), Issac T. Mann, George A. Kent (chief engineer), John B. Dennis, W.M. Ritter, Norman B. Ream, Thomas F. Ryan, James A. Blair, Henry R. Dennis, unknown, and James Hammill.

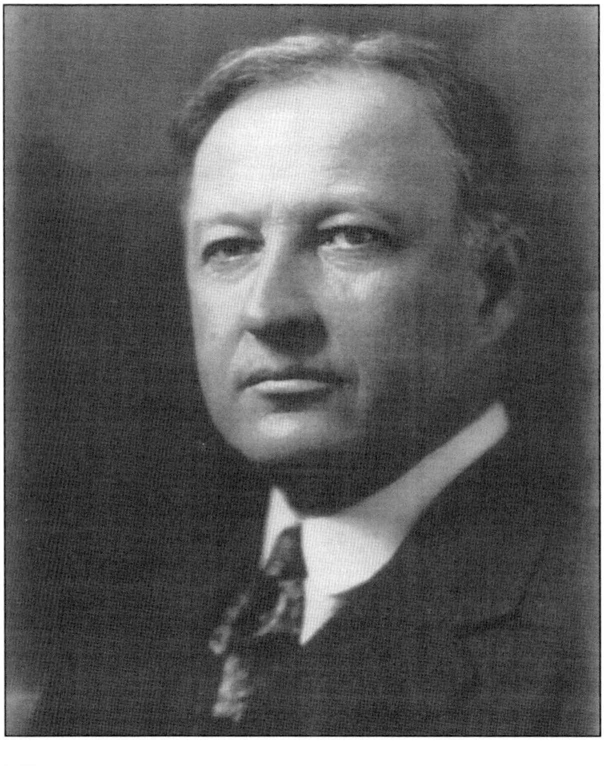

Mark W. Potter served as counsel, director, and president of the Carolina, Clinchfield and Ohio Railway. In 1911, he succeeded George L. Carter as president and chairman of the board of the CC&O. Carter remained on the Clinchfield Board of Directors. John B. Dennis, in 1916, assumed the position of board chairman while Potter remained as Clinchfield president until 1920; he then accepted a position on the Interstate Commerce Commission.

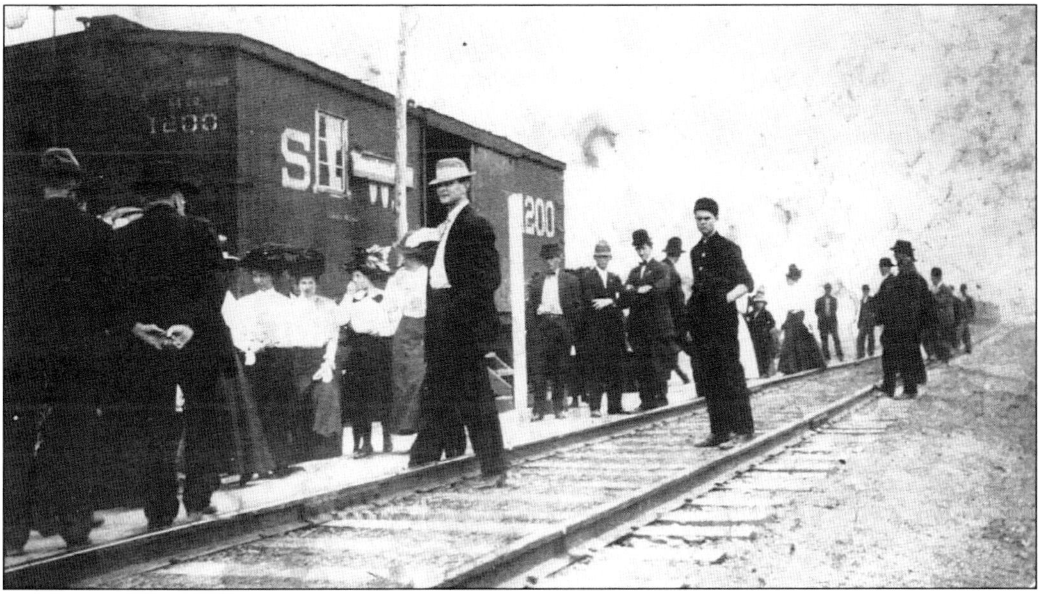

Kingsport's location on the route of the Clinchfield Railway played a vital role in the transformation of the city. Crossing the Blue Ridge Mountains from Elkhorn, KY, to Spartanburg, SC, and joining with other lines, the Clinchfield connected Charleston, SC, with Cincinnati, OH. This photograph shows Kingsport's first railroad station in 1910.

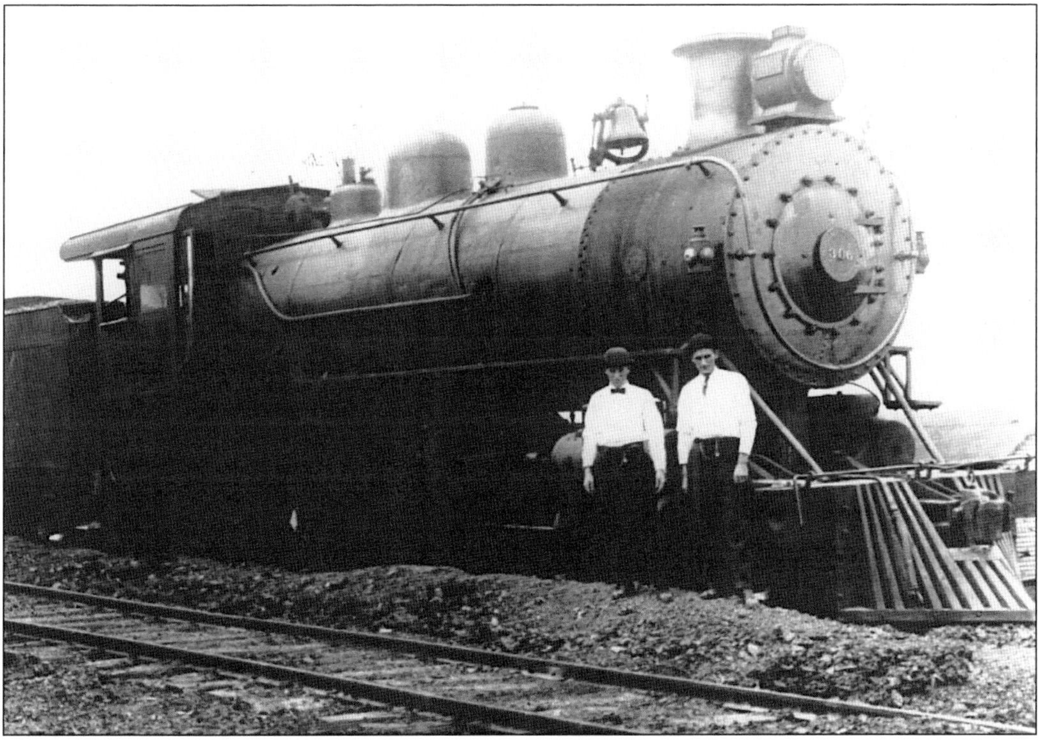

In 1912, engineer J.W. Ingrim and fireman C.R. Lowe are pictured next to Clinchfield Railroad steam locomotive #306 on the south end of the number three track in the Kingsport railroad yard.

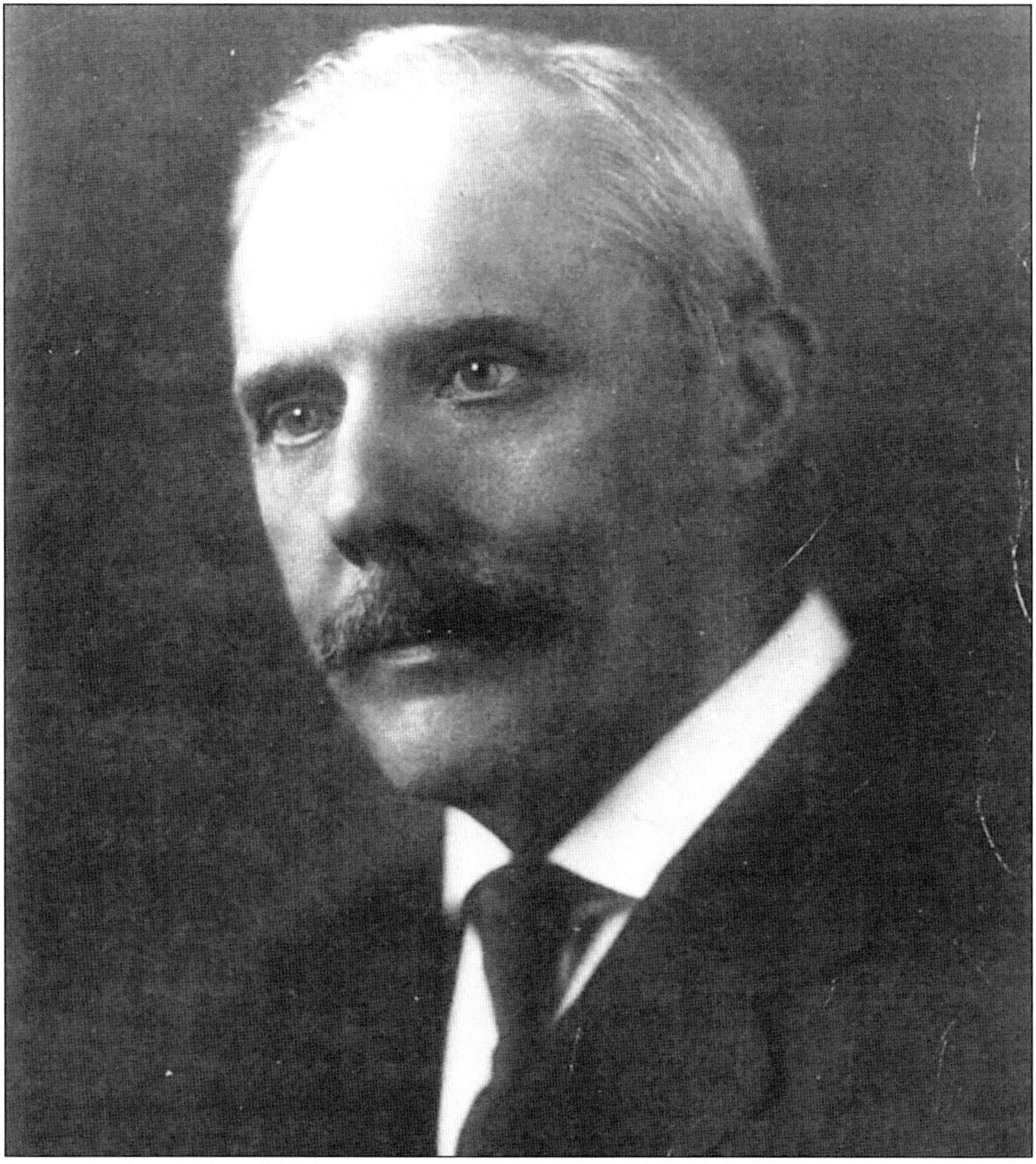

During the late 19th and 20th centuries, George L. Carter shaped the economic transformation of northeast Tennessee and southwest Virginia in a modernizing Appalachian South. Known as the "empire builder of Southwest Virginia," Carter was a coal magnate who sought to establish railroads and add to his vast holdings. A native of Hillsville, VA, Carter built the Carolina, Clinchfield and Ohio Railway and as early as 1905 envisioned a new industrial city located at Kingsport. The *Johnson City Comet* reported that Carter's Unaka Corporation planned "to boom a town at Kingsport." In 1906, Carter hired an engineer from Philadelphia to inspect the area and draft a street arrangement. A few years later he sold 6,355 acres of land to Kingsport Farms, Inc., controlled by Blair and Company of New York. The Kingsport Improvement Company (KIC), with J. Fred Johnson as president, was soon chartered, and the KIC purchased land for the proposed town from Kingsport Farms. New York investor John B. Dennis had controlling interest in both companies and provided the financial backing.

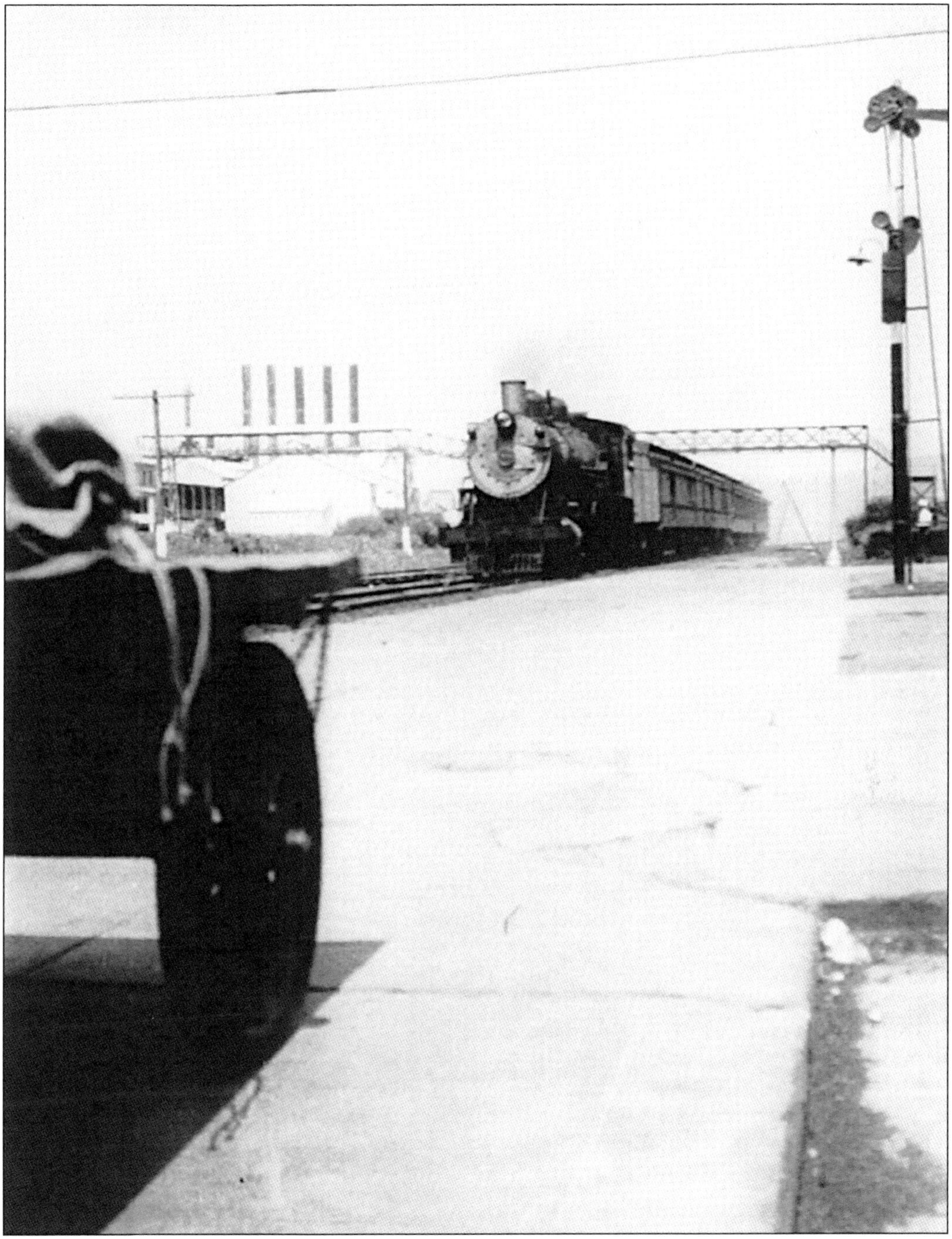

The completion of the Clinchfield Railroad in 1915 made industrial development a possibility along a route which, because of inadequate transportation, had long lain dormant. The Clinchfield Railroad came to Kingsport in 1909 and, when finally completed in 1915, encouraged closer business and social relations between the Midwest and the East Coast.

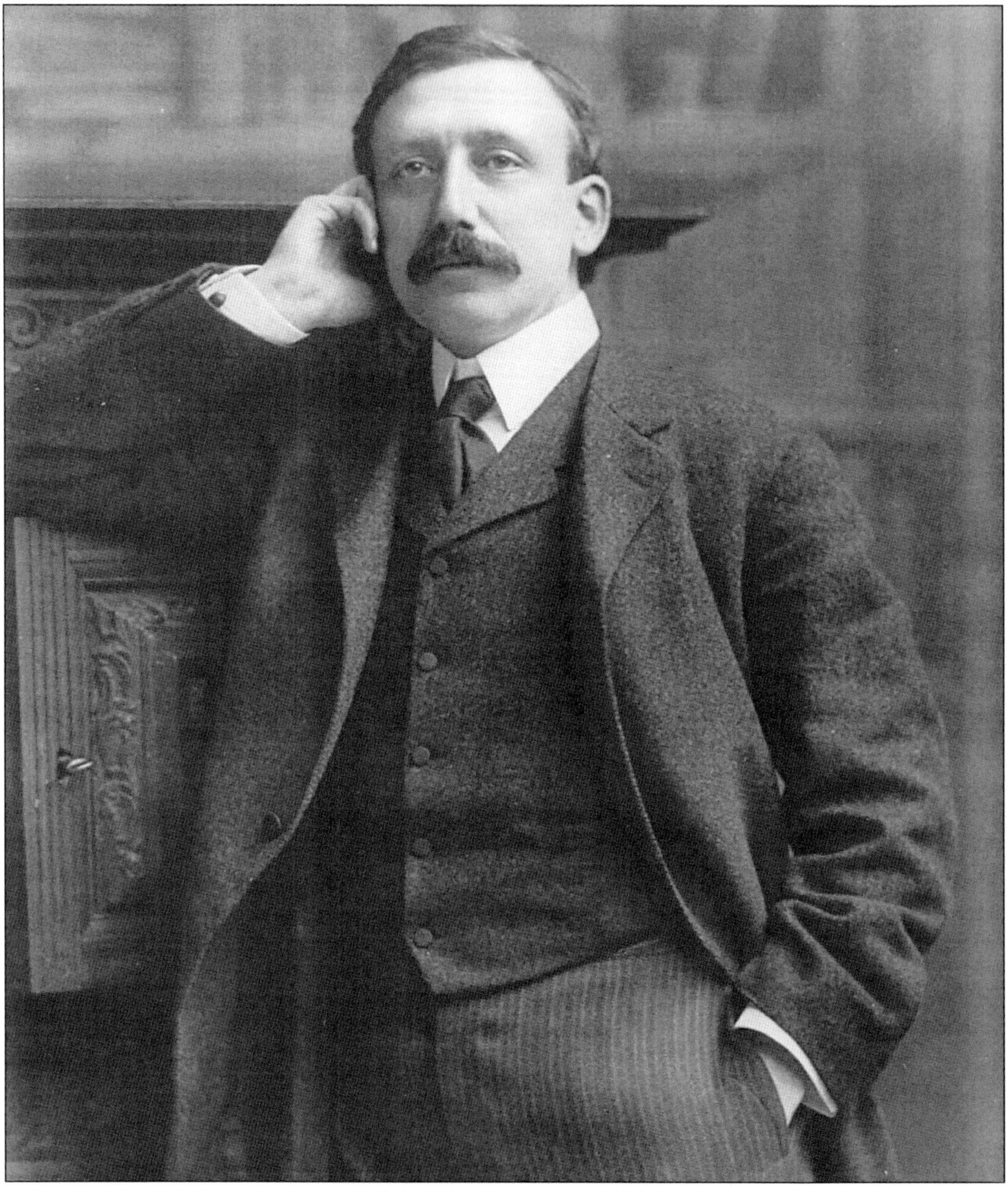

Remembered as the financier and creator of modern Kingsport, John B. Dennis directed the establishment and development of the model industrial city for more than a generation. When George L. Carter encountered financial difficulties, he turned to John B. Dennis of Blair and Company, New York City. Under the direction of Dennis, the Clinchfield Railroad was completed. Along with J. Fred Johnson, Dennis had envisioned an industrial city at Kingsport to generate business for the railroad. Born in Gardiner, MN, Dennis was educated at Cornell and Columbia Colleges. An investment banker and Blair Company representative, Dennis, along with Carter and Johnson, successfully managed the creation of a professionally planned industrial city. He held controlling interest in both Kingsport Farms Inc. and the Kingsport Improvement Company. For many years he resided at Rotherwood Mansion. Dennis is buried in Kingsport.

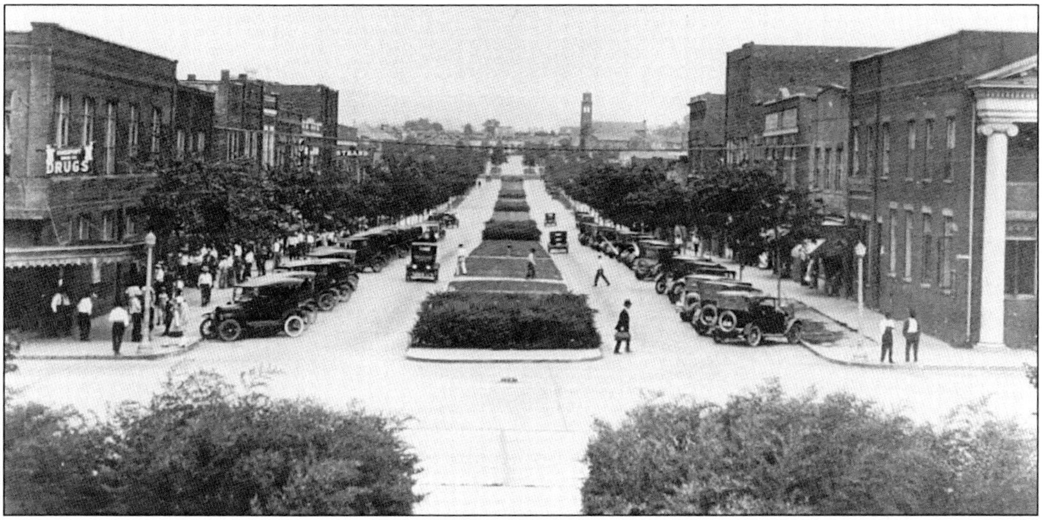

Kingsport founders engaged the Cambridge, MA firm of internationally known planner John Nolen to design the physical plan for Kingsport. From the beginning, the "Model City" was zoned for industrial, residential, and commercial development.

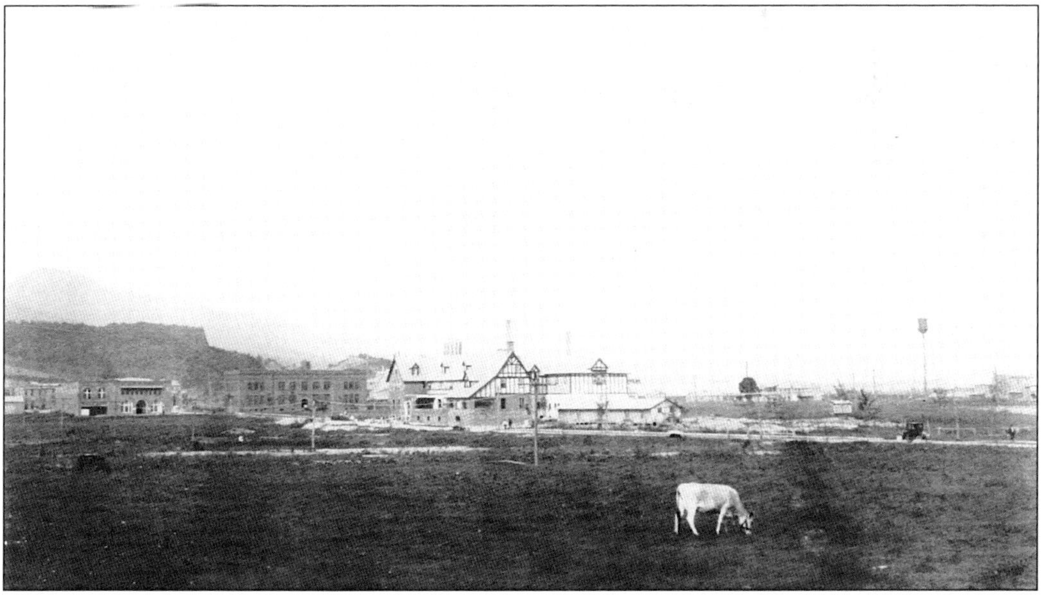

The Municipal Building of Kingsport, located at the present city hall site, housed city offices, a public library, the police department, the city jail, and the courthouse. The Kingsport Improvement Company building is visible behind the Municipal Building. The Kingsport Improvement Company, headed by J. Fred Johnson, led the effort to establish a town in Kingsport. It was in the KIC building on March 15, 1917, that the Kingsport Board of Mayor and Aldermen held its first meeting.

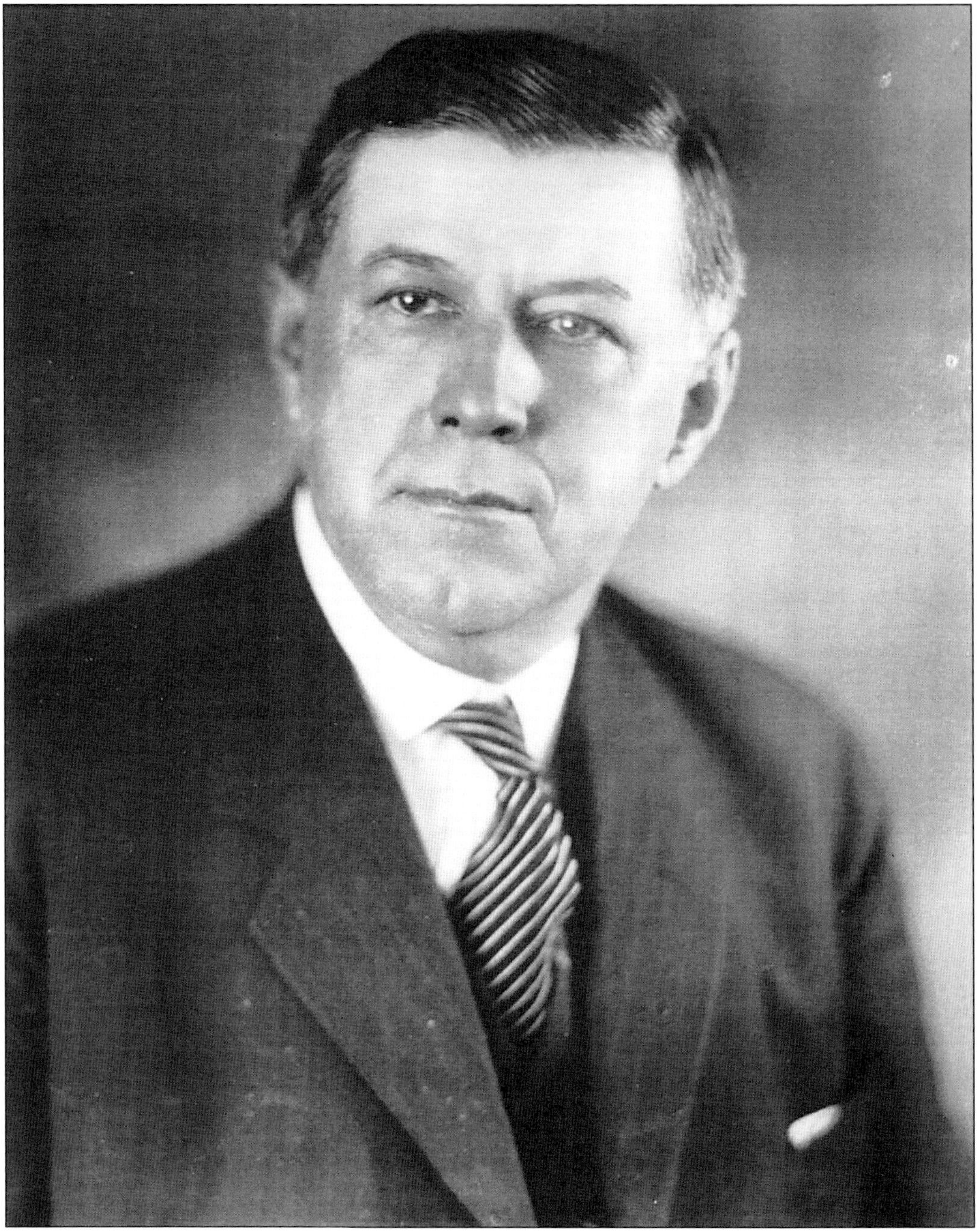

J. Fred Johnson was known as the "Father of Kingsport." As the primary promoter of the new town of Kingsport, Johnson dedicated his life to seeing that the city became a success. Hillsville native and brother-in-law to George L. Carter, Johnson began his career as an agent for the Clinchfield Railroad, purchasing land options along the proposed railroad route. As president of the Kingsport Improvement Company, Johnson and financier John B. Dennis created and planned a city that would attract diversified and integrated industries. A merchant, Johnson owned the Big Store and the J. Fred Johnson Store. His death in October 1944 marked the end of an era in Kingsport history.

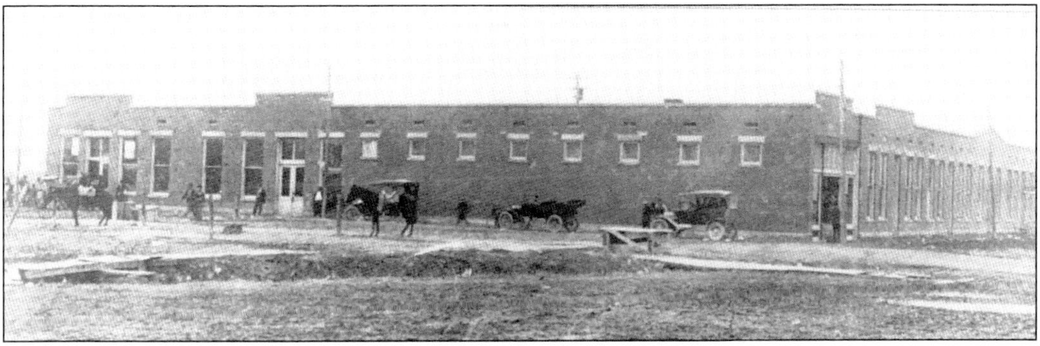

Along with establishing the town of Kingsport, J. Fred Johnson became a store merchant. Johnson's first store began in 1906 on the Holston River, with a branch store on Hammond Avenue and Compton Terrace. By 1910, the "Big Store" combined these two enterprises and was located on Shelby Street.

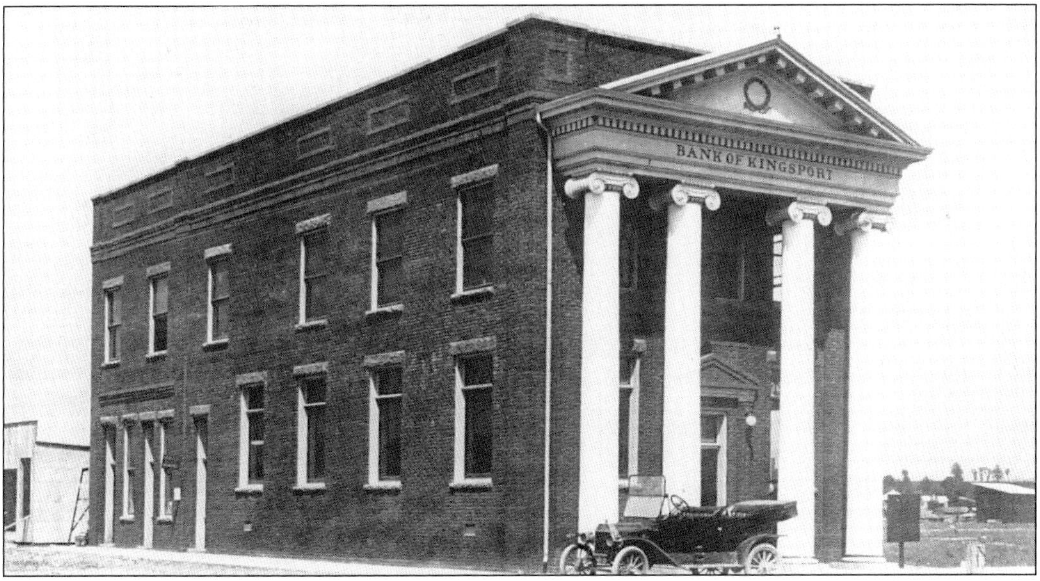

The Bank of Kingsport's board of directors included J. Fred Johnson, William Roller, Dr. E.W. Tipton, and W.R. Jennings. In 1931 the First National Bank absorbed this financial institution.

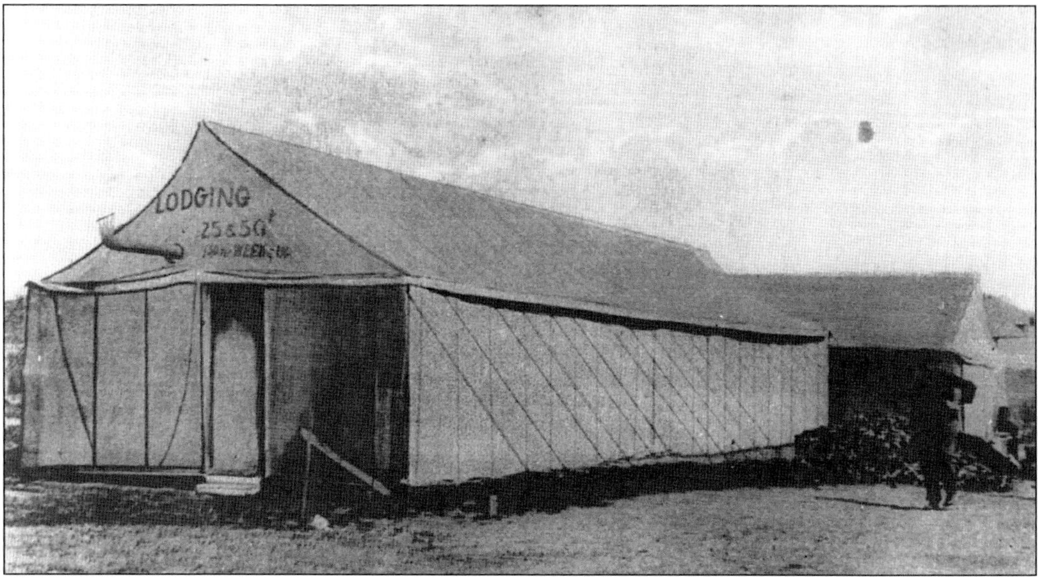

At certain times during its early years, the appearance of Kingsport had more in common with frontier towns than with model cities. Prior to the 1917 incorporation of Kingsport, a severe housing shortage resulted from the influx of workers. Hundreds of tents were then used to accommodate the growing workforce of the town.

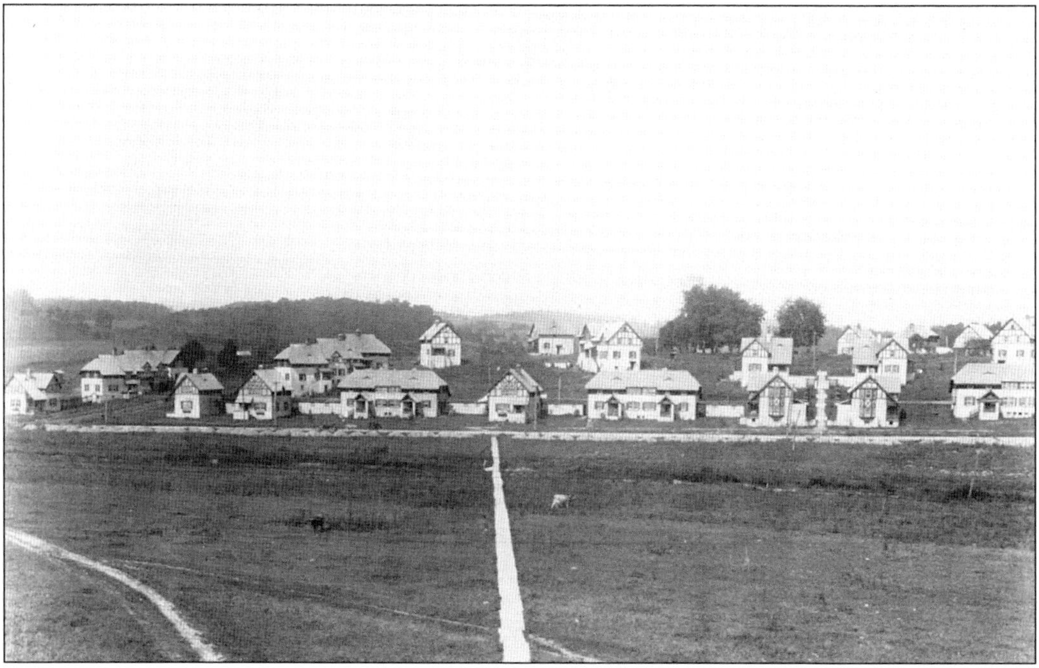

New York architect Clinton Mackenzie implemented many of the earliest professional designs for the planned city. Before his involvement with the Kingsport project, Mackenzie served as New Jersey tenement-house commissioner and director of the National Housing Association. The "Fifties," so called because of the number of houses, represented the first major housing project of the Kingsport Improvement Company. These Tudor-style row houses are located in the area of Shelby and Sullivan Streets.

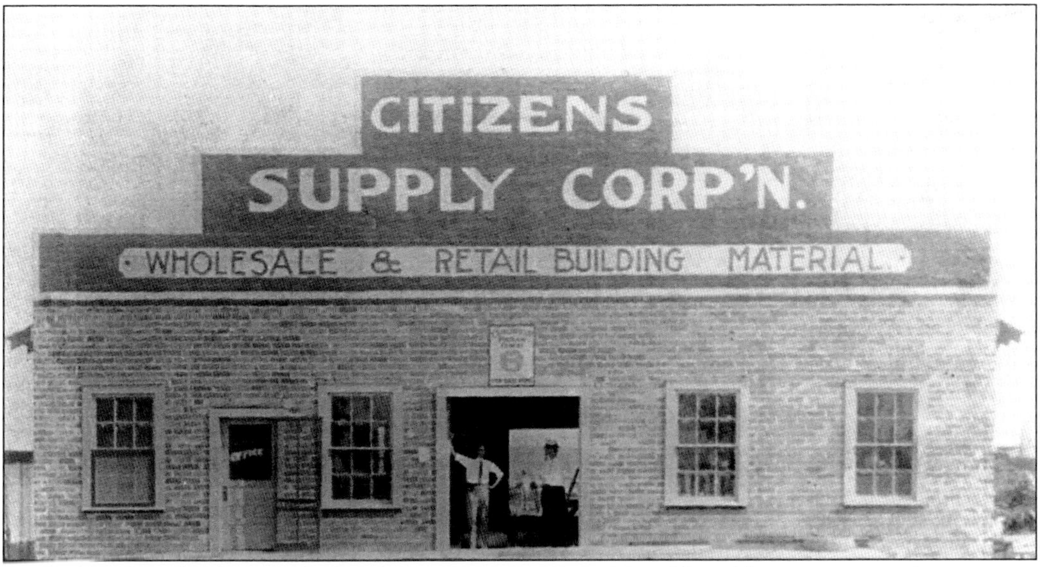

Owned by the Charles Brooks family, Citizens Supply is one of the oldest continuously operating businesses in Kingsport. Opened in 1915, it has supplied much of the material for the building of the town. Located on the Clinchfield rail line, the store was once a center for shipping and for sending building materials by rail to southwest Virginia and southeast Kentucky.

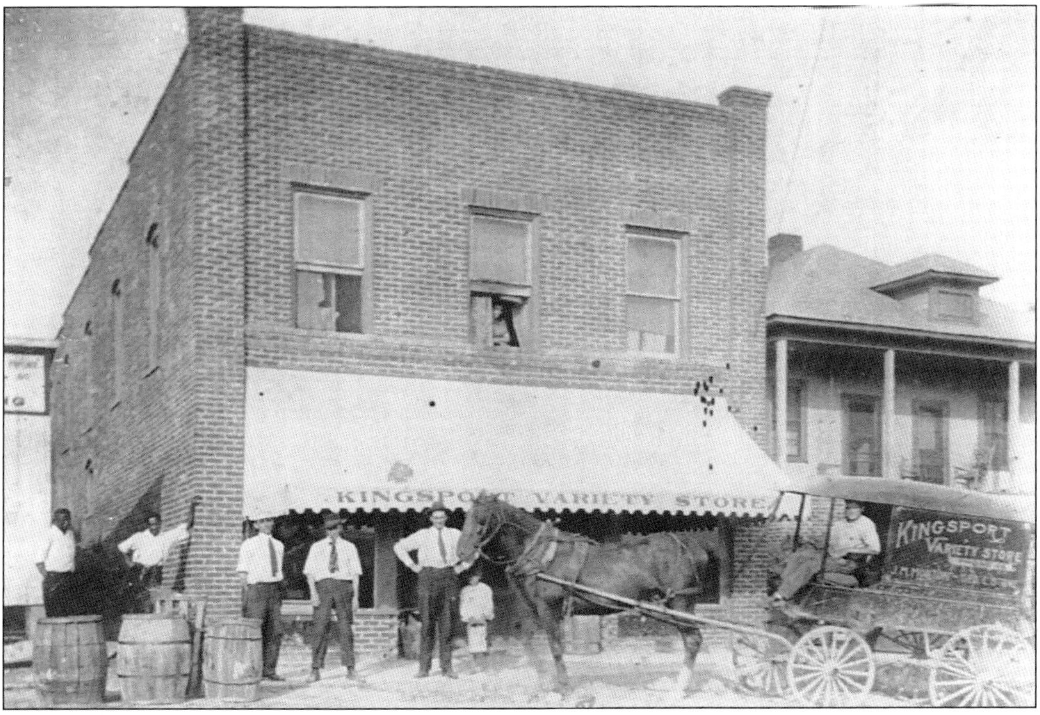

Located in the 700 block of Sullivan Street, the Kingsport Variety Store supplied the grocery and general merchandise needs of town residents in the 1920s. In 1927, Kingsport listed 25 grocers, which were generally small, locally owned enterprises.

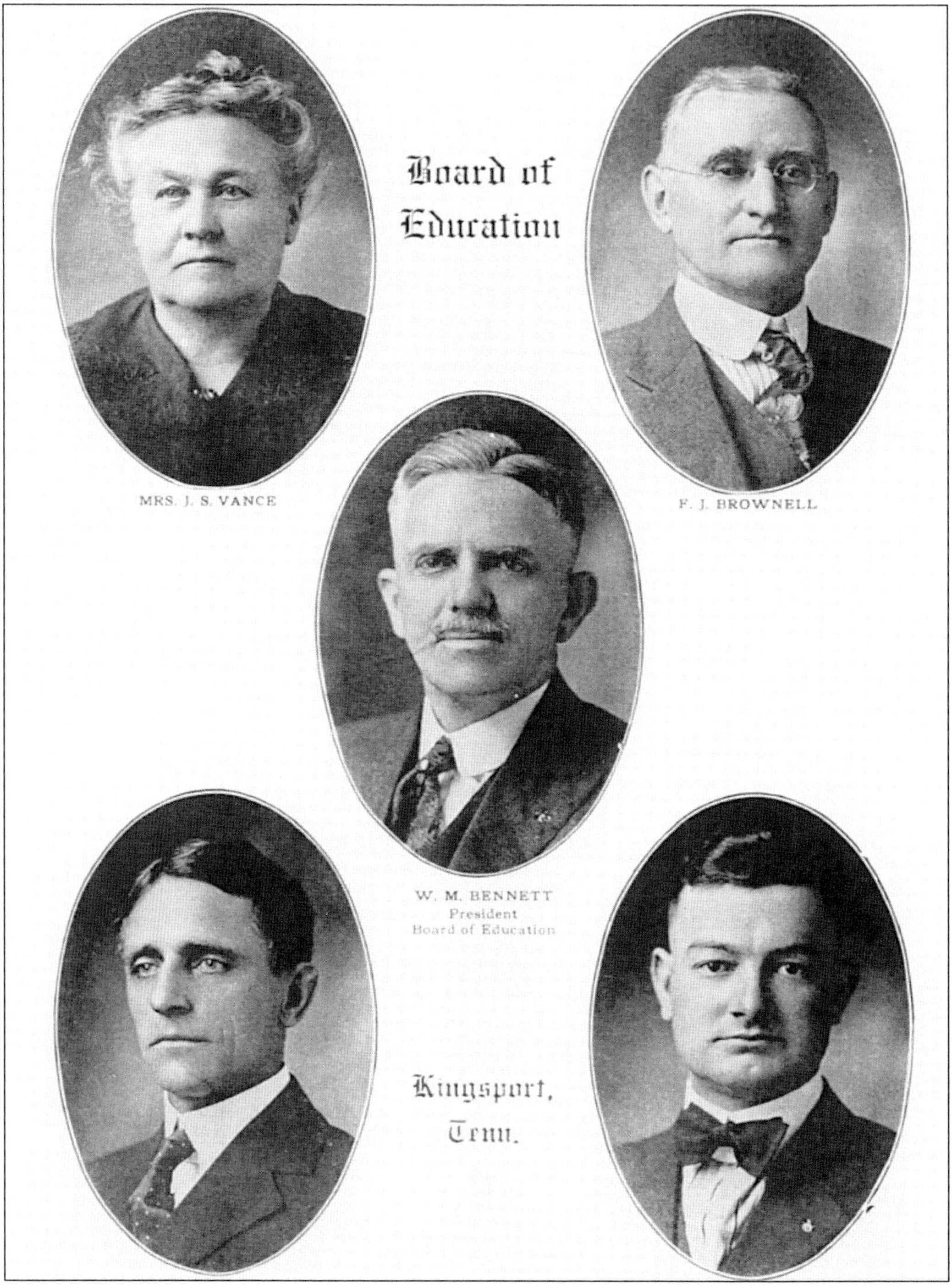

The Kingsport Improvement Company consulted Columbia University and developed an educational system comparable to the system in Gary, Indiana. On May 19, 1917, the Kingsport Board of Education was appointed, and in July of that year plans for a city high school were approved. The 1920 board is pictured here and includes Mr. W.M. Bennett, Mrs. Joe S. Vance, F.J. Brownell, S.C. Minnick, and Guy D. Pitts.

Frank Cloud (1884–1946), one of Kingsport's first city managers, served the city in this post from 1923 to 1946. Cloud is remembered with respect as a leader who guided the city through the problems of its formative years.

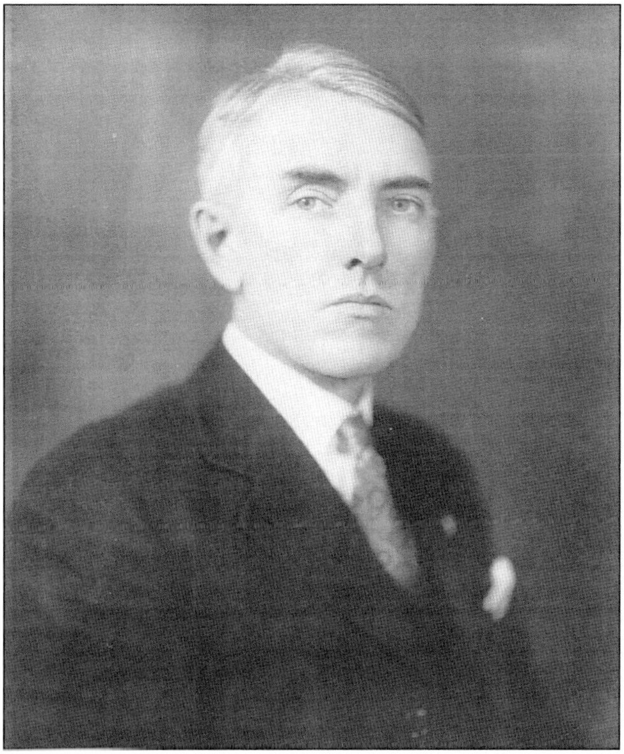

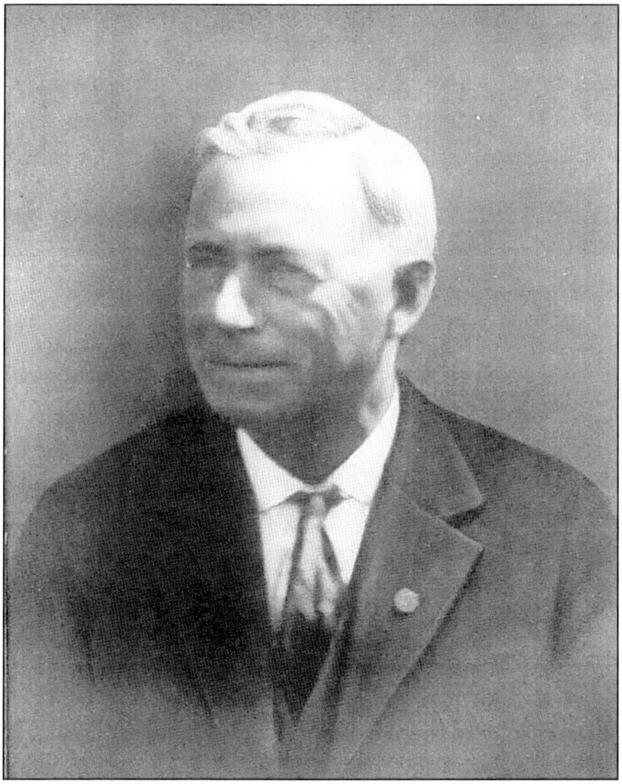

Kingsport's proposed charter was evaluated by the Bureau of Municipal Research of the Rockefeller Foundation, whose suggestions resulted in the city's adoption of a city manager form of municipal government. The city was officially incorporated on March 2, 1917. Kingsport's first mayor, James W. Dobyns, led the new city until December 12, 1923. Dobyns, a store manager, owned the tract of land that eventually became Fairacres subdivision.

THE BOOK CLUB

1921

Officers elected at the first meeting in January 1921.

President----------------------	Mrs. S. P. Platt
Vice President------------------	Mrs. Stuart Maher
Secretary----------------------	Mrs. H. J. Shivell
Treasurer----------------------	Mrs. Keefer Lindsay

MEMBERSHIP

Charter

Mrs. S. P. Platt	Mrs. Katherine Spotswood
Mrs. L. A. DaShiell	Mrs. R. Y. Grant
Mrs. K. W. Koeniger	Mrs. J. H. Thickens
Mrs. G. C. MacNaughton	Mrs. J. F. Johnson
Mrs. H. J. Shivell	Mrs. Floyd Smith*
Mrs. Stuart Maher*	Mrs. Keefer Lindsay
Mrs. J. A. Maher	Mrs. Harry Angle

Mrs. F. M. Kelley --------------	February 2
Mrs. Wilcox -------------------	" "
Mrs. Herbert Williamson ---------	March 16
Mrs. Hufford -------------------	" "
Mrs. Felix Gunther--------------	" "

The Kingsport Book Club sponsored projects, including a theater production, to aid in the establishment of a public library. To benefit the library, the Kingsport Community Players staged *Everybody's Husband* in the high school auditorium. The cast of this production included J. Fred Johnson, Mrs. Herbert Williamson, Mrs. W.R. Gilmer, Allen Dryden Sr., Mrs. S.P. Platt, Mrs. H.J. Shivell, and others. Minutes from the March 1921 meeting of the Kingsport Book Club report that proceeds from the play totaled $1,005 and "various and necessary steps in starting a library were discussed and considered."

The

KINGSPORT MUSIC CLUB

and

ASSISTING ARTISTS

Present

AN ORATORIO

"THE LAST JUDGMENT"

By

LOUIS SPHOR

at the

FIRST BAPTIST CHURCH

SUNDAY, MAY 7th, 1933, at 3:30 P.M.

KINGSPORT, TENNESSEE

NATIONAL MUSIC WEEK, MAY 7th TO 14th

To encourage the development of cultural life, the Kingsport Music Club was formed in 1927. Throughout the 1920s and 1930s, the organization sponsored musical presentations and developed musical programs for civic groups and the community.

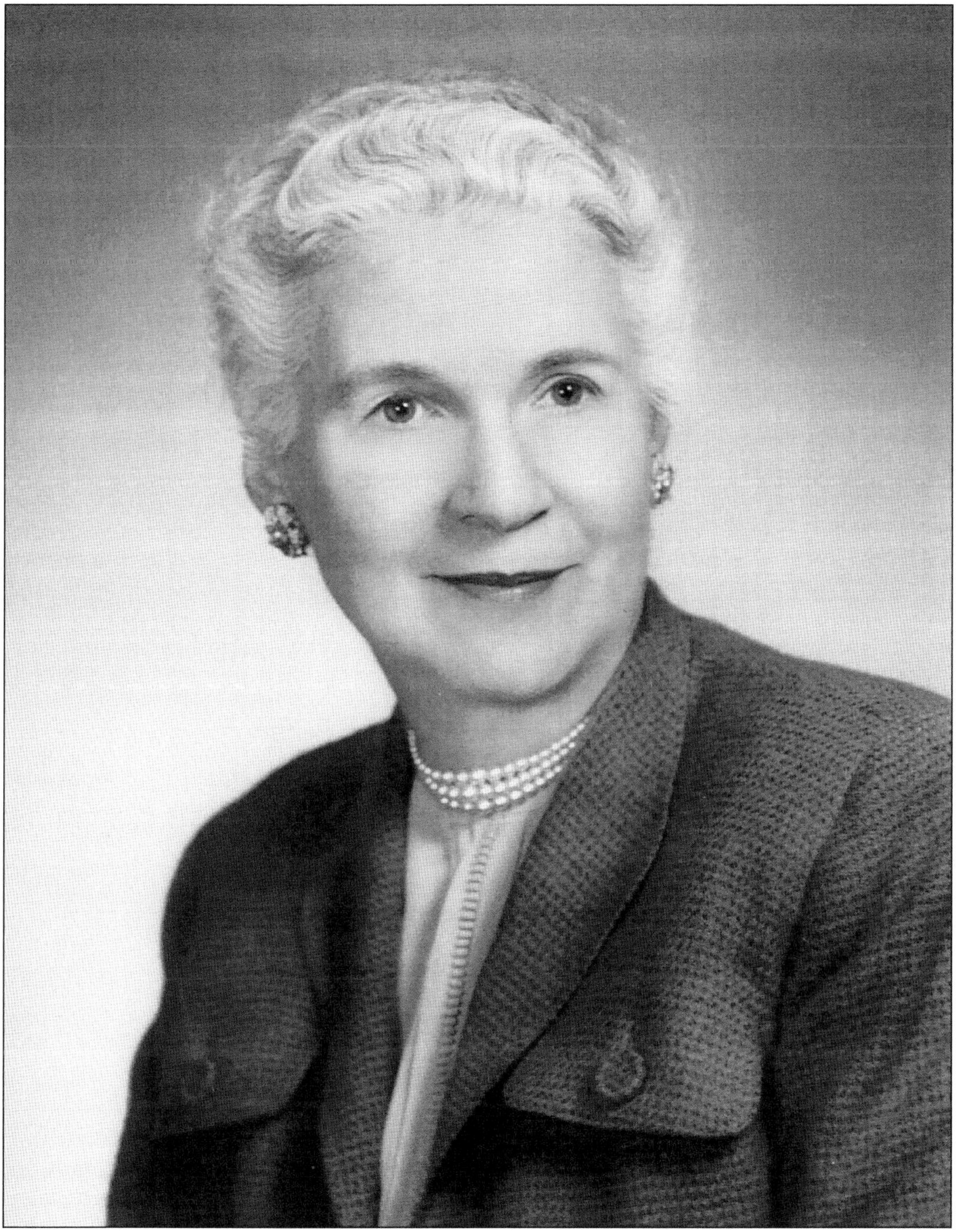

The founder of the Kingsport Public Library, Genevieve Shivell (d. 1994), was an early settler of modern Kingsport and spearheaded efforts to improve the quality of life in her new hometown. Shivell was a founding member of the Kingsport Book Club and led the effort to establish a public library for Kingsport. After the creation of the city library, Mrs. Shivell continued to play a central role as a member of the Kingsport Library Board of Trustees and, later, of the Kingsport Library Commission. She was instrumental in organizing the Women's Auxiliary of the Holston Valley Community Hospital.

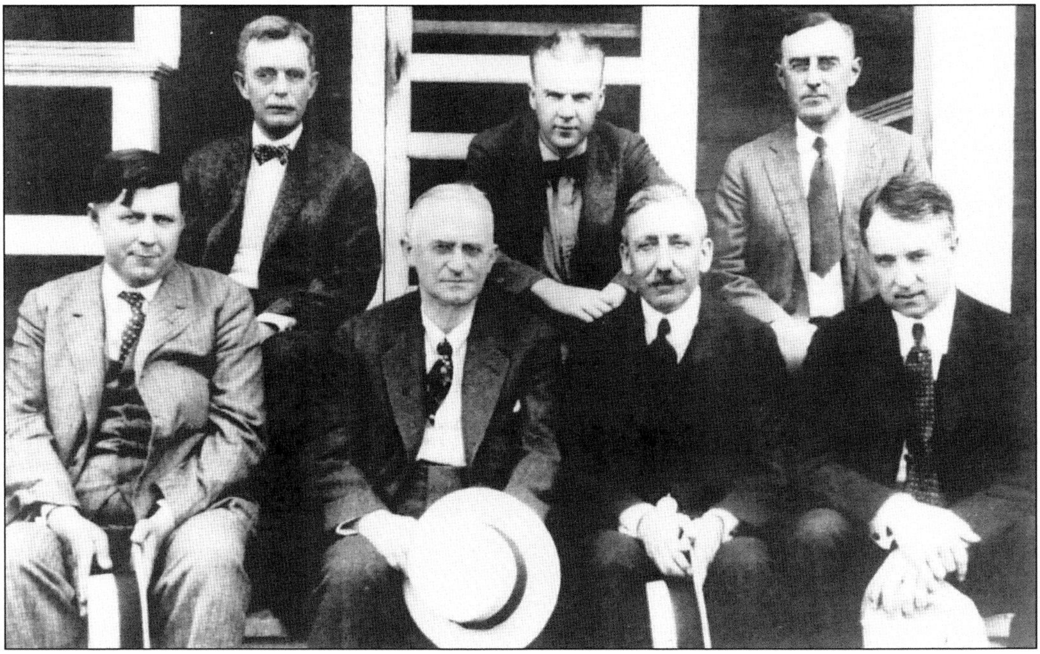

Town booster J. Fred Johnson and New York financier John B. Dennis launched a vigorous recruiting campaign to persuade George Eastman to locate a subsidiary of the Eastman Kodak Company in Kingsport. When Eastman agreed in 1920, Kodak Park assistant superintendent Perley Wilcox became general manager of the newly formed Tennessee Eastman Company (TEC). Pictured in this photo is George Eastman during a visit to Kingsport to inspect his new plant. Pictured from left to right are the following: (front row) J. Fred Johnson, George Eastman, John B. Dennis, and Frank Lovejoy (Kodak official); (back row) James S. Havens (Kodak official), Herbert Williamson (Tennessee Eastman superintendent), and Perley Wilcox.

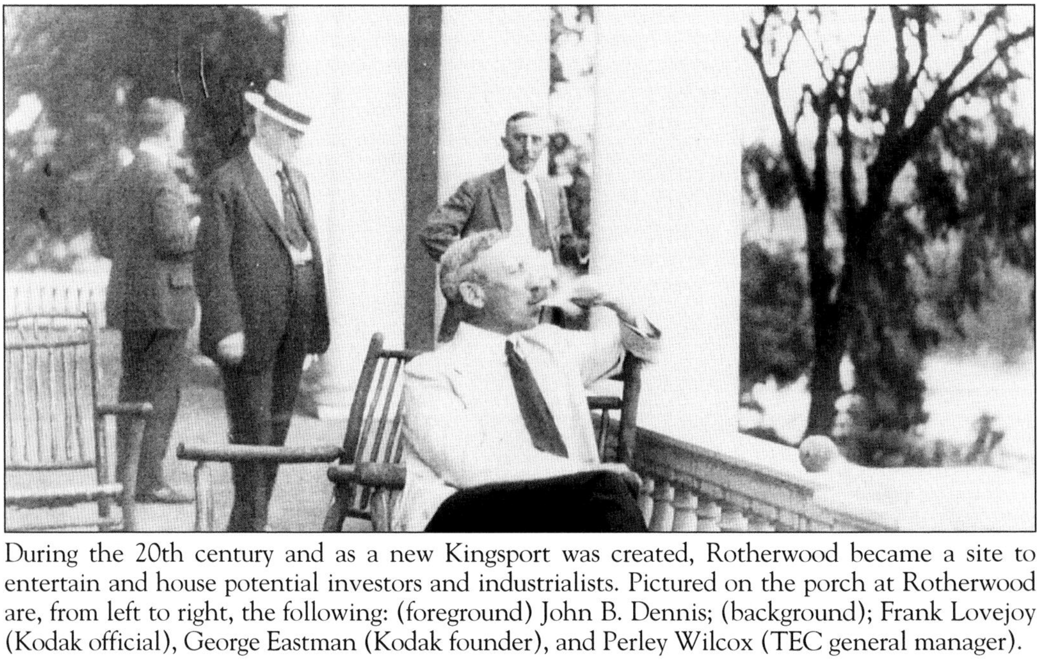

During the 20th century and as a new Kingsport was created, Rotherwood became a site to entertain and house potential investors and industrialists. Pictured on the porch at Rotherwood are, from left to right, the following: (foreground) John B. Dennis; (background); Frank Lovejoy (Kodak official), George Eastman (Kodak founder), and Perley Wilcox (TEC general manager).

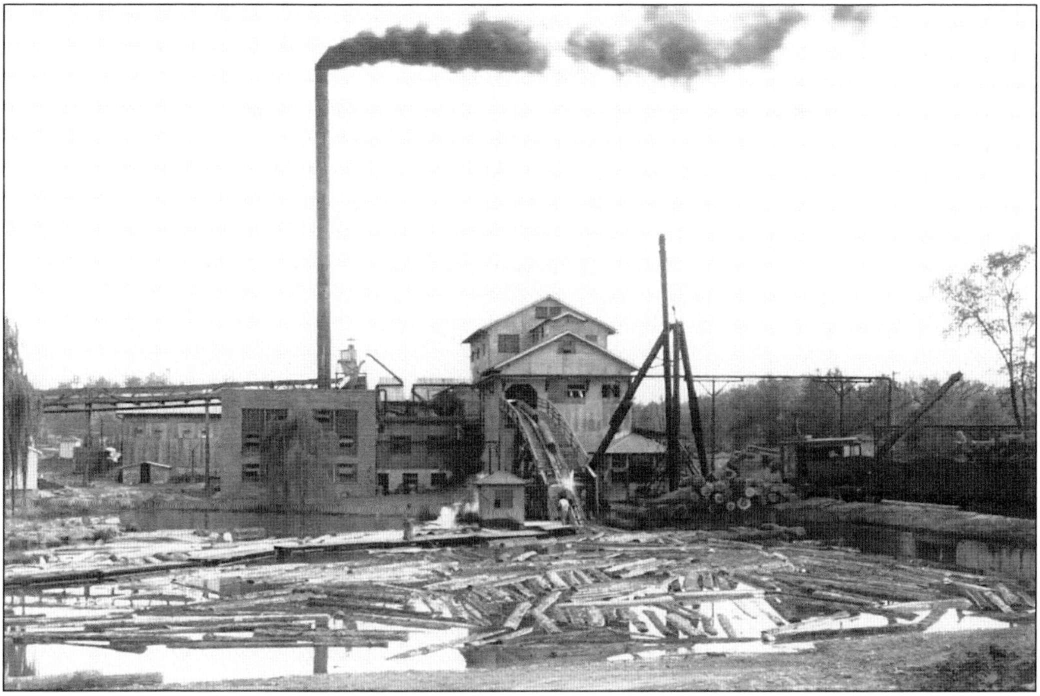

Tennessee Eastman's band sawmill operation was integral to the welfare of Eastman Kodak in the 1920s. When World War I disrupted the German supply of photographic paper, optical glass, gelatin, and an assortment of chemicals such as methanol, acetic acid, and acetone, Kodak faced a serious problem. The forests of the Appalachian South supplied raw materials for the manufacture of acetone and methanol, chemicals needed for photographic film. The sawmill at the Tennessee Eastman Company was in production into the 1940s.

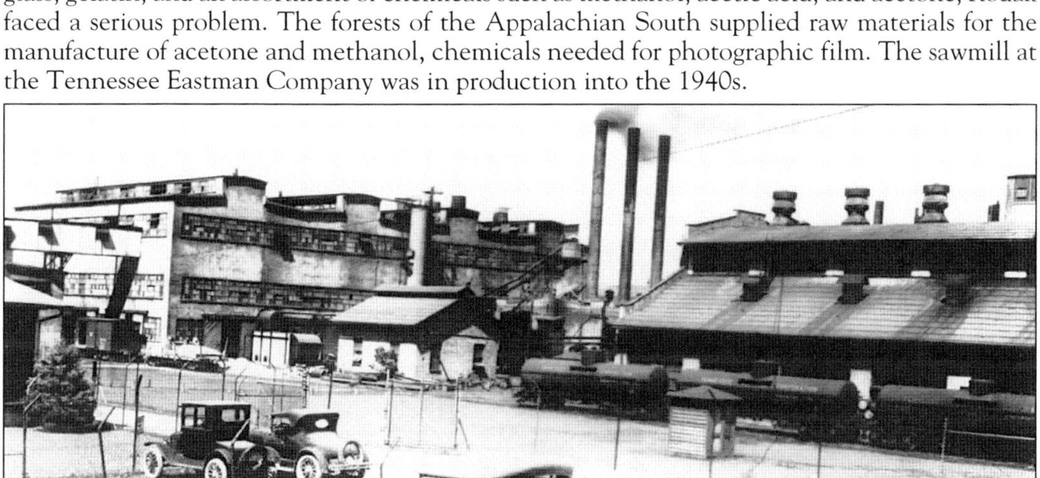

The Tennessee Eastman Company, a subsidiary of Eastman Kodak, Rochester, NY, acquired the property and plant buildings of the American Wood Reduction Company from the U.S. government in June 1920. In these early years, TEC manufactured methanol (wood alcohol) and various by-products through the dry distillation of wood. Some of these products included charcoal, acetic acid, hardwood pitch, and wood-preserving oil through the process. After eight years of operation, TEC employed 422 people. Today, the Eastman Chemical Company is organized separately from Kodak and is Tennessee's largest private employer with a workforce of 16,000 worldwide.

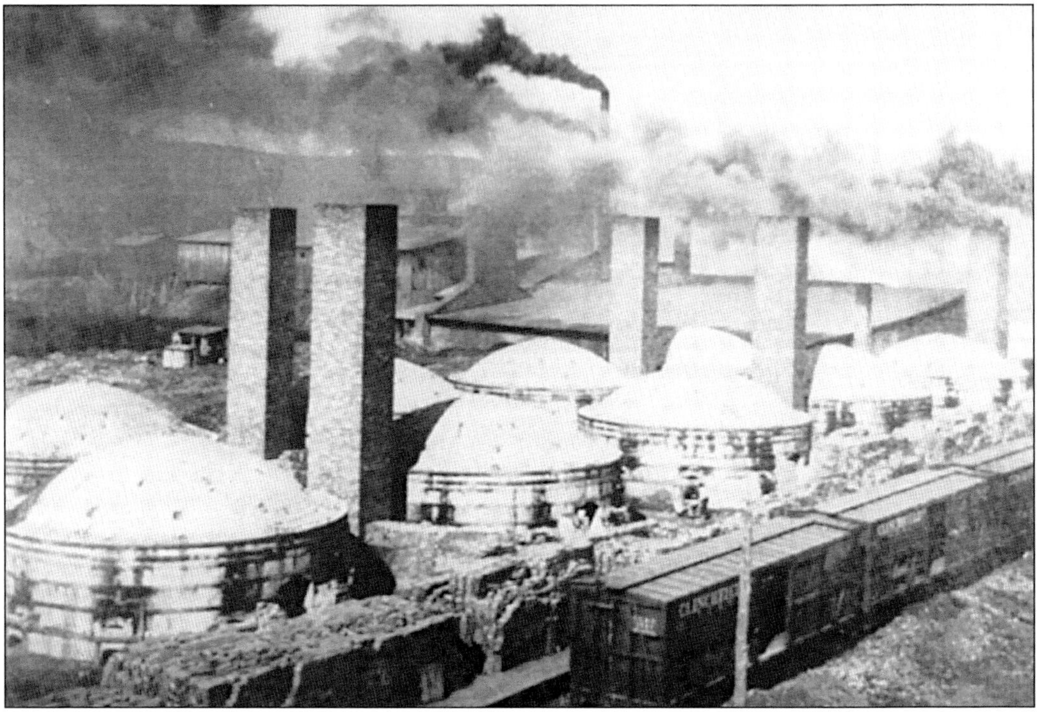

The Kingsport Brick Company, which began construction in July 1910, provided the crucial foundation for the Clinchfield officials' implementation of their concept of interlocking industries. Incorporated with $50,000 capital stock, J.D. Whitaker of Atlanta was the first president. In 1911, J. Fred Johnson assumed the top position in the firm, which agreed to a daily capacity of 50,000 bricks. Later becoming the General Shale Products Corporation, the plant produced 135,000 bricks per day by 1927.

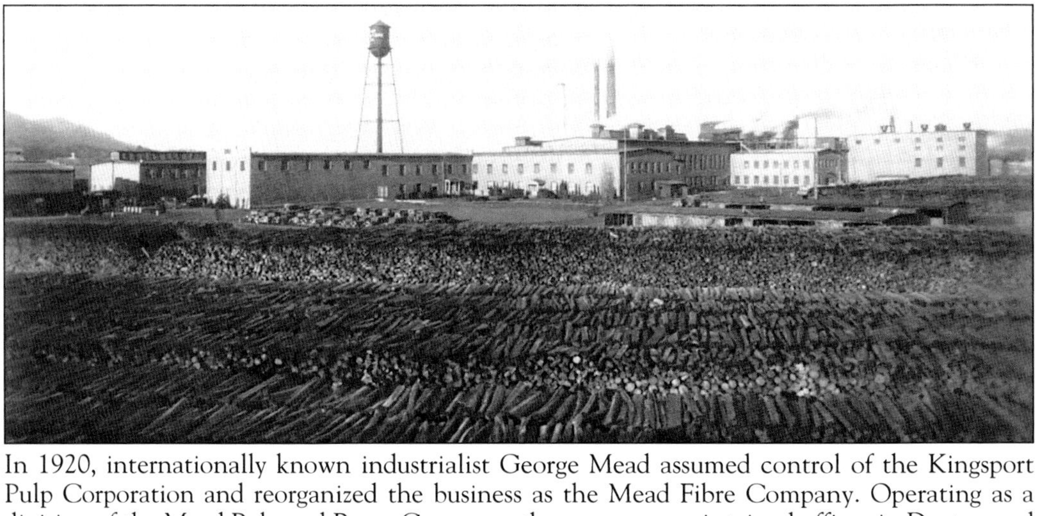

In 1920, internationally known industrialist George Mead assumed control of the Kingsport Pulp Corporation and reorganized the business as the Mead Fibre Company. Operating as a division of the Mead Pulp and Paper Company, the company maintained offices in Dayton and Chillicothe, OH, as well as in Kingsport.

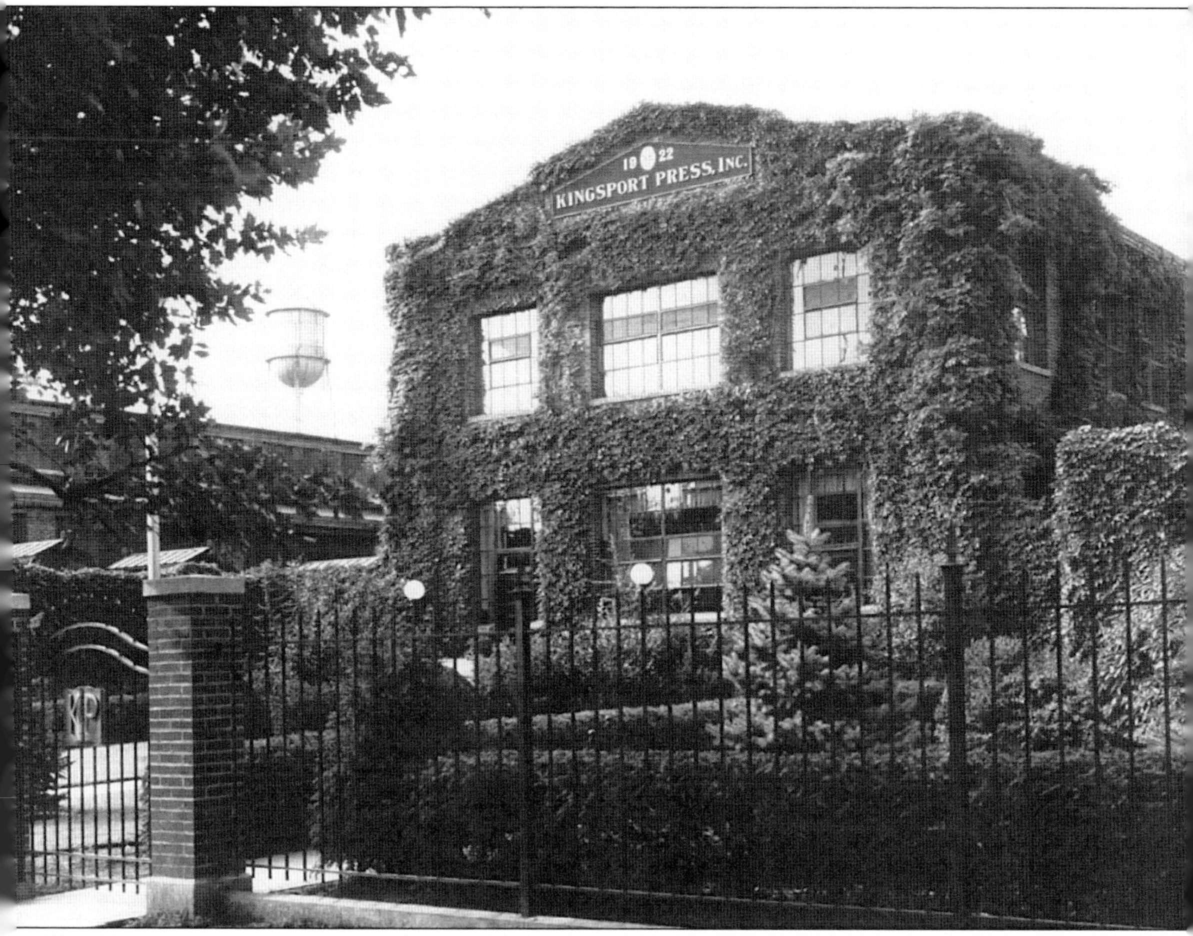

The Kingsport Press was established in 1922 by John B. Dennis and Blair and Company, the New York bankers who financed the Clinchfield Railway. The initial buildings of the press consisted of four unused concrete structures originally intended to serve as a harness and saddlery during World War I.

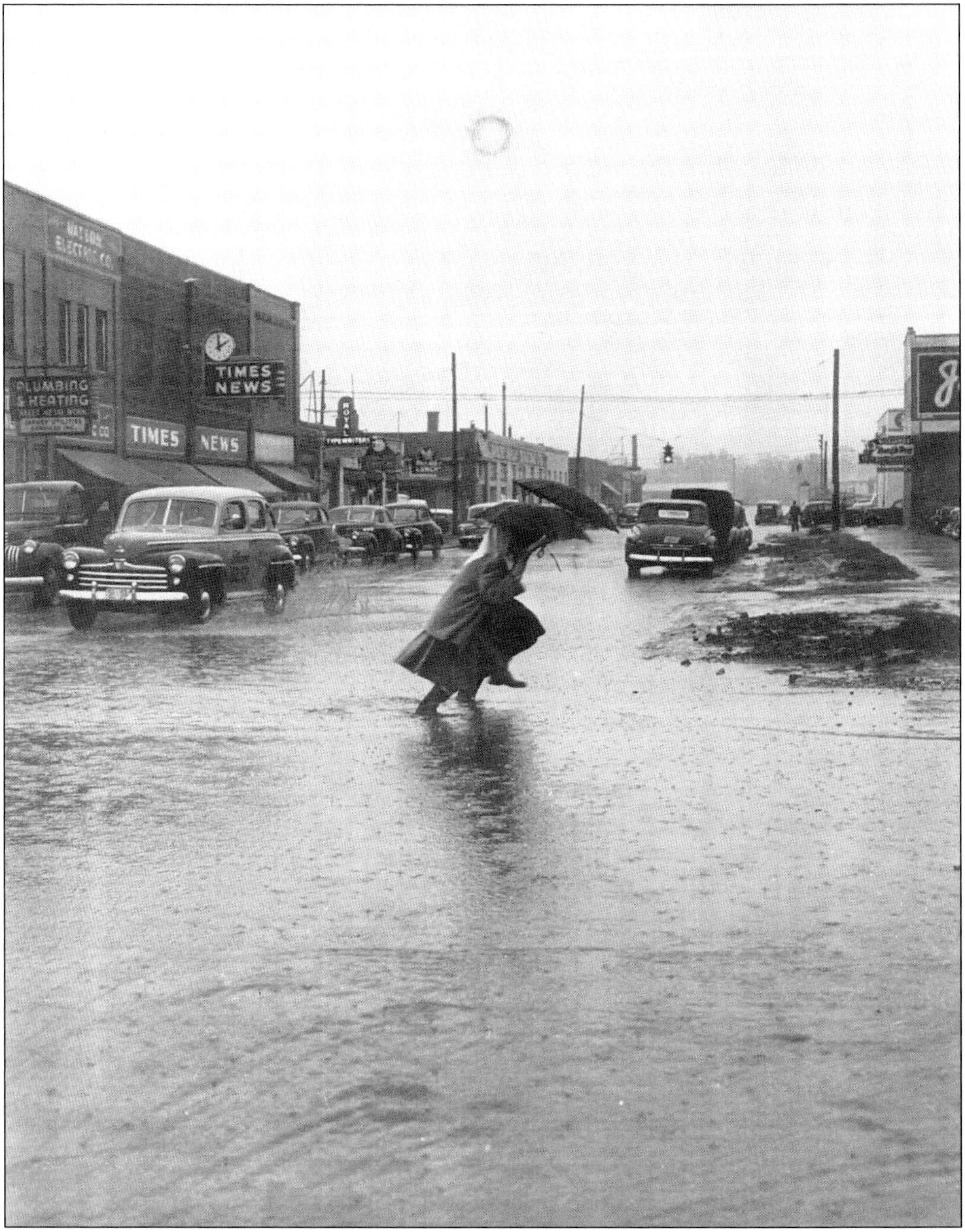

Beginning publication in 1916, Kingsport Publishing, Inc. first located its offices on Main Street in what later became the Gem Theatre. For many years, however, the *Kingsport Times*, which became a daily in 1921, occupied offices at 220 Market Street as portrayed in this scene by photographer Ellis Binkley.

Three

KINGSPORT IN A MODERNIZING AMERICA

The city of Kingsport, it has been said, may be viewed as a 20th-century prototype—a model of city planning in the 1910s and 1920s and a success story of economic development in the 1930s and 1940s. Kingsport illustrated that the advantages of modernization and economic growth far outweighed any disadvantages. Despite the worst depression in U.S. history, followed by a war that encompassed virtually the entire globe, Kingsport industry grew and adapted technologically during this extraordinary period. During World War II, its corporate leaders developed a new partnership with the government. Noted commentator Robert St. John, in an NBC radio broadcast in 1944, called Kingsport, "THE ideal community." The success of the interlocking concept of industry—that is the location of industries which complemented each other while developing non-local markets—along with the simultaneous attainment of a well-constructed social plan produced a model for other American towns to emulate. Articles about Kingsport, "The Model City," appeared in national publications, such as the Saturday Evening Post, because the new city set a standard for developing urban areas worthy of imitation.

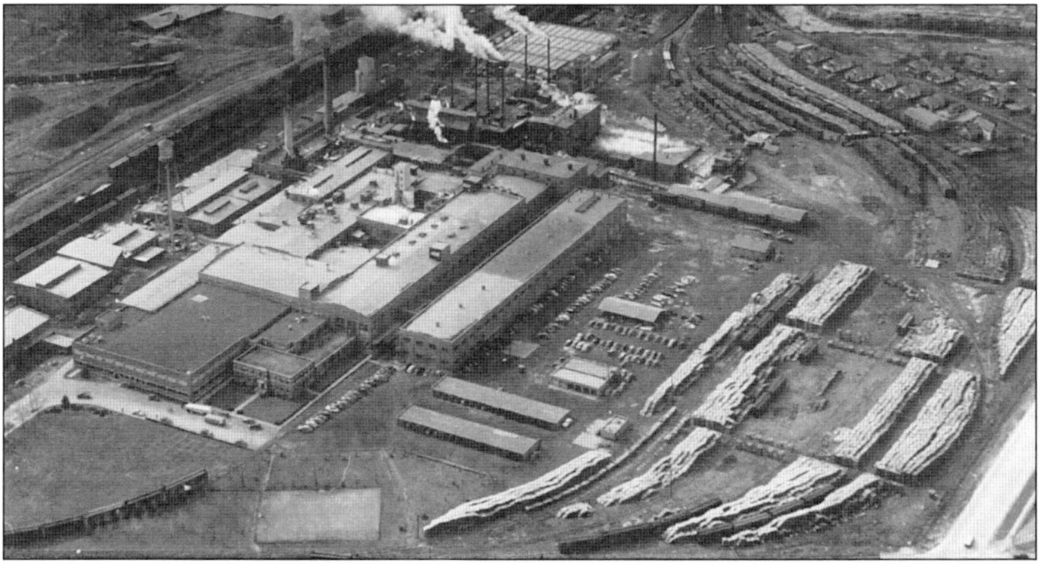

The Great Depression of the 1930s did not effect Kingsport at the crisis level experienced by most American communities. Between 1930 and 1945, Kingsport's population grew from 24,000 to nearly 51,000. In the ten years from 1935 to 1945, Kingsport's industrial employment increased from 3,824 to 19,672.

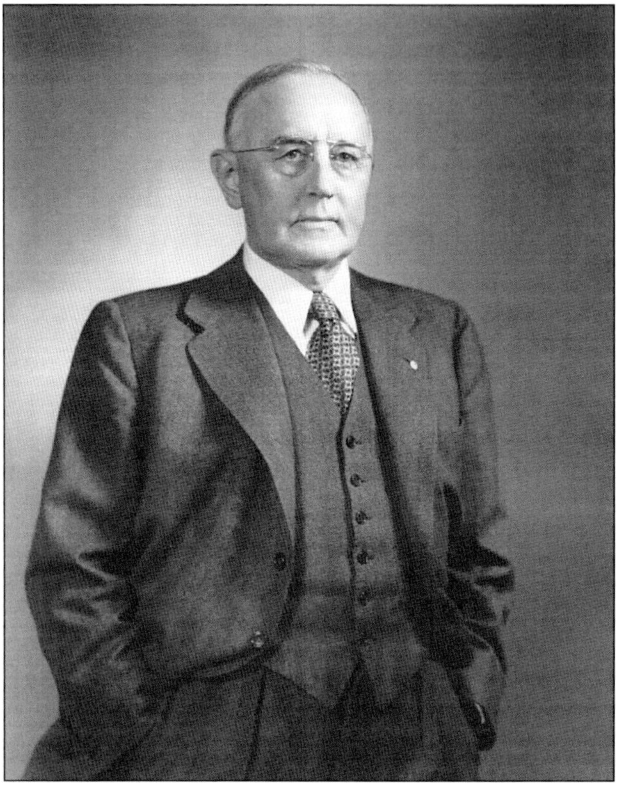

Perley Wilcox (1874–1953) was referred to as the "father" of the Tennessee Eastman Corporation or, more commonly, as "Uncle Perley" by many Kingsport residents. In 1921, Wilcox was elected a director and was appointed general manager of the newly formed TEC. A Cornell graduate, Wilcox served in various executive positions over the years. In 1945, he became chairman of the Kodak Board. Wilcox spearheaded the 1933 effort to obtain a charter for a nonprofit Kingsport hospital—Holston Valley Community Hospital.

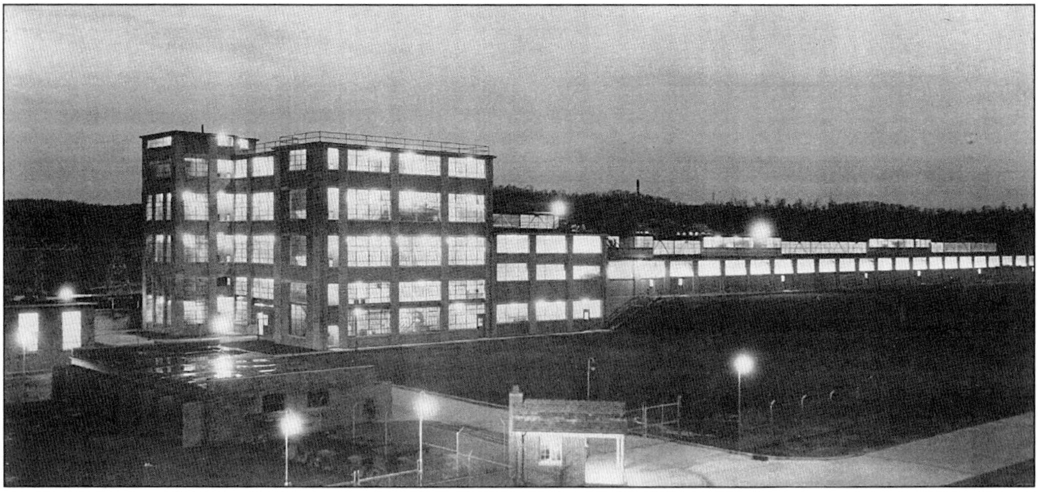

In 1929, Kodak Park transferred cellulose acetate production to the Tennessee Eastman Company. That same year, TEC began production of acetic anhydride. In 1930, efforts began to develop the production of cellulose acetate yarn, and by 1931 acetate yarn was produced on a large scale. In the early 1930s, TEC employed A.M. Tenney Associates to market cellulose acetate textiles. In conjunction with the acetate yarn production, TEC initiated production of Tenite cellulosic plastics and acetate dyestuffs, as well as Tenite II, a cellulose acetate butyrate molding composition. Used by the automobile and communications industry, these products had far-ranging ramifications for design and methods of production. By 1940, annual sales reached $29 million.

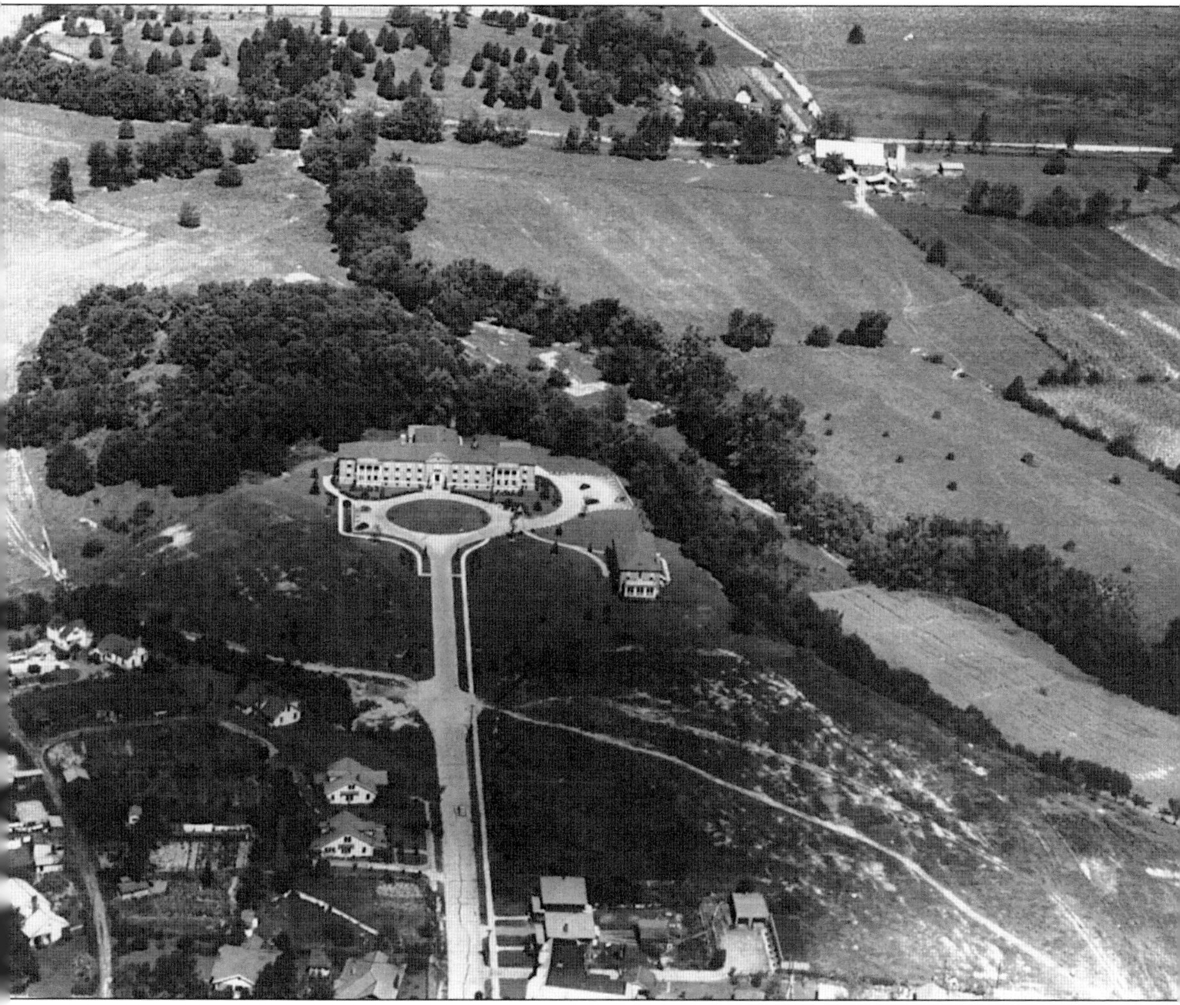

Holston Valley Community Hospital was completed in 1935 at a cost of $300,000. Modern hospital service became available within a 25-mile radius of Kingsport. In this 1938 scene by photographer Richard Alvey, the Nurses Home (dormitory) is located at the right of the health care facility.

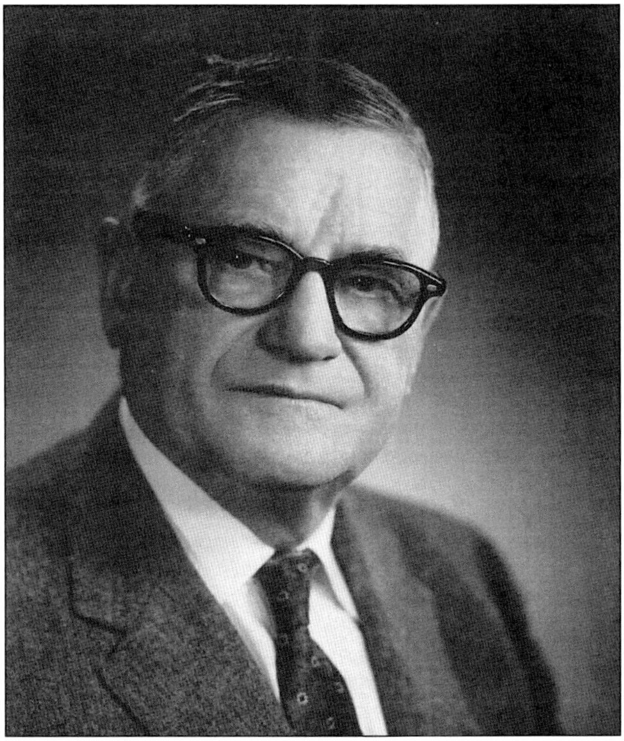

James C. White (1890–1973) joined Tennessee Eastman in 1920 as an expert on lumber and timber operations and rose to become one of Eastman's most widely respected and admired figures. In 1945, he became the president and general manager of TEC and was later named to the executive committee and board of directors of the Eastman Kodak Company. Among the many distinguished awards White received during his Eastman career was the Manhattan District Special Award, authorized by the War Department in recognition of his individual contribution to the atomic bomb program.

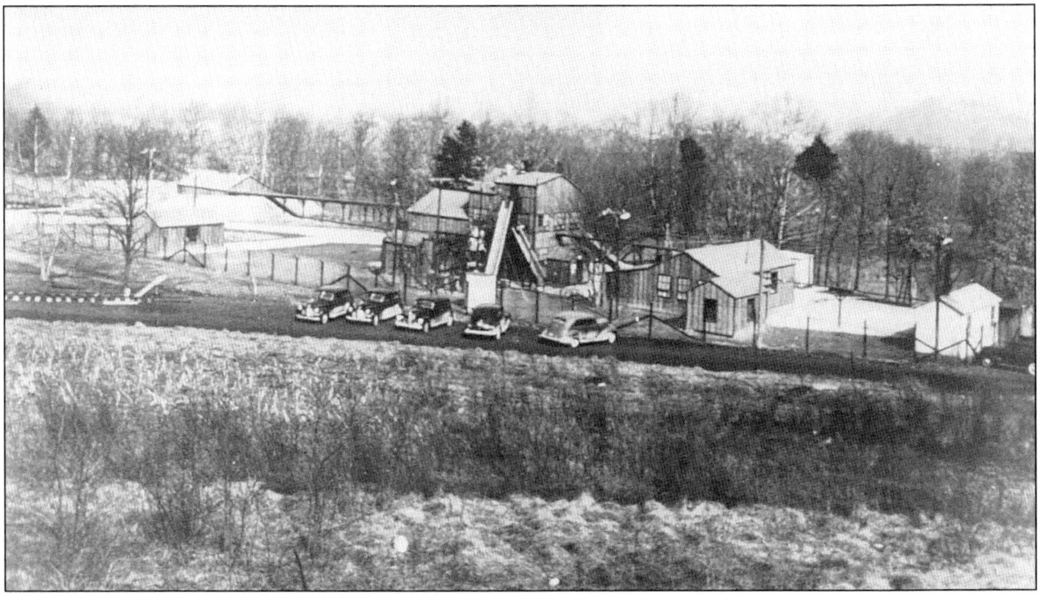

In 1942, Herbert G. Stone led Tennessee Eastman in an effort to develop a procedure for continuous production of the explosive RDX. The process was developed at the Wexler Bend Pilot Plant 26 days after the National Defense Research Committee asked TEC to initiate the project. Soon TEC was manufacturing RDX and Composition B in the large quantities needed to win the war in the European theater. In early June 1942, TEC received official authorization from the U.S. Army Ordnance Works to design and operate Holston Ordnance Works (HOW).

Herbert G. Stone (1897–1976), a native of Marion, VA,had attended the U.S. Naval Academy before locating in Kingsport to work with the Federal Dyestuffs and Chemical Corporation. He joined TEC in 1927. Stone served as the general superintendent of research, engineering, and manufacturing during the 1930s. In 1942 he led a team of Eastman scientists and engineers as they developed the process for making the powerful explosive RDX. Stone was appointed works manager for Holston Ordnance Works for the remainder of World War II. His distinguished career included appointments as the assistant vice-president and vice-president of TEC.

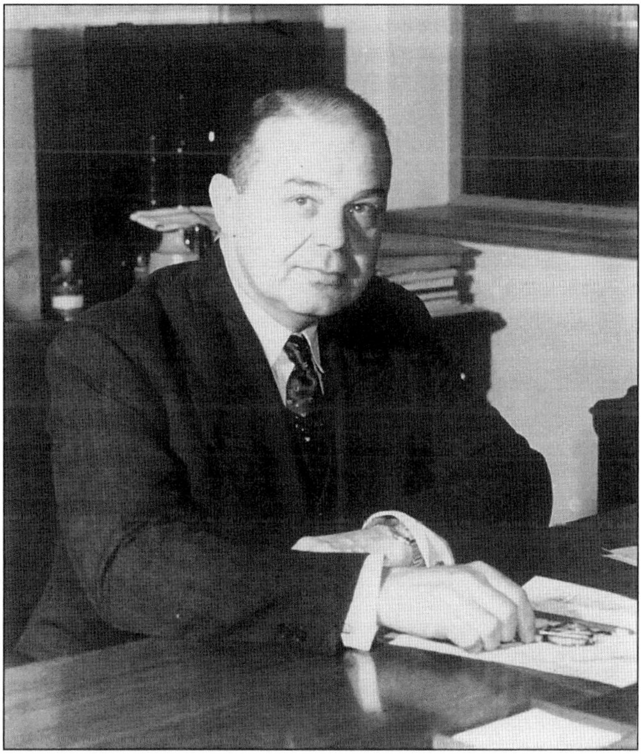

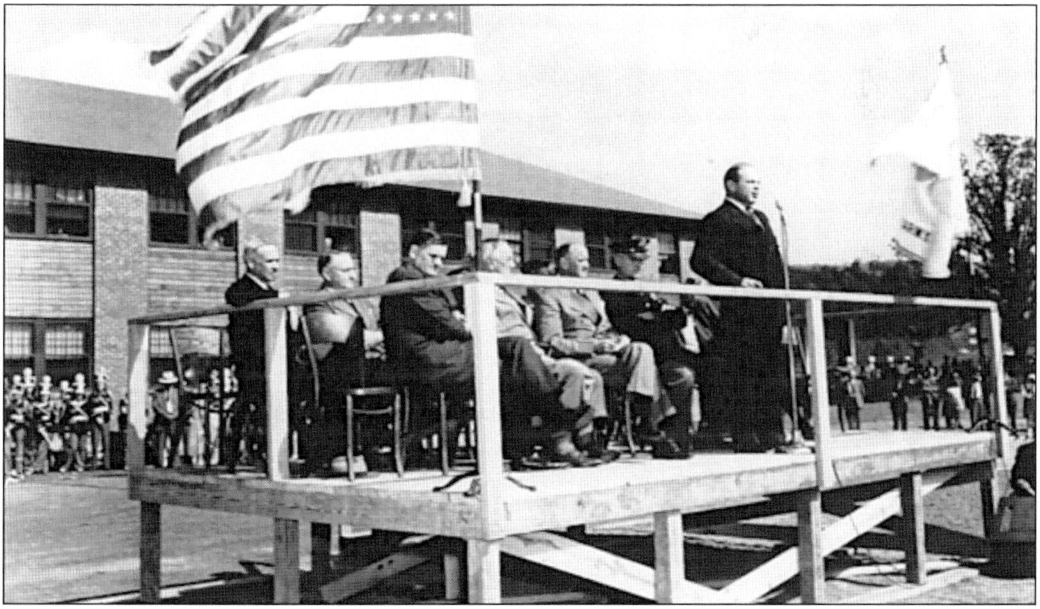

Holston Ordnance Works became the world's largest manufacturer of high explosives. Now known as Holston Defense and the Holston Army Ammunition Plant, the company continues to be one of the world's largest producers of explosives. In 1943, TEC and HOW received the prestigious Army-Navy "E" Award for "outstanding achievement in the production of materials of war." In this HDC photo, Herb Stone addresses the audience as James C. White listens (seated, far left).

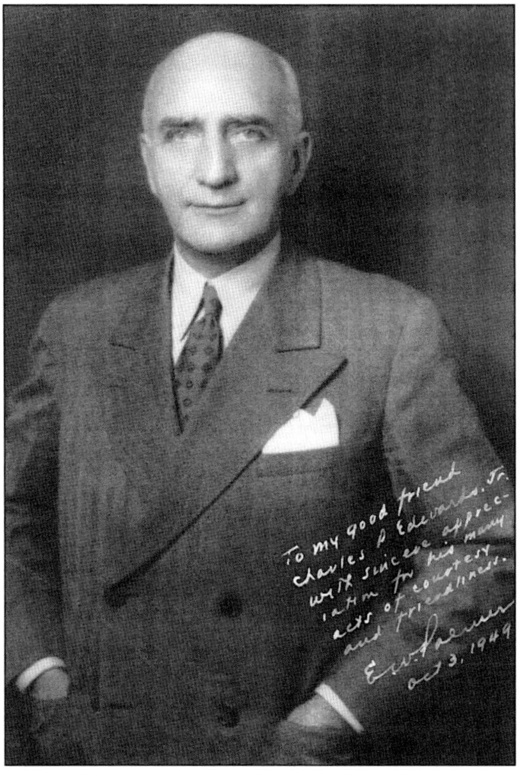

Colonel Elbridge W. Palmer (1886–1953) served as the president of Kingsport Press from 1925 until his death in 1953. He began his career in printing as a stenographer in 1905, advanced to an executive position at the Plimpton Press Company of Norwood, MA, and soon became the president of J.F. Tapley, a New York bookbinding company. During his 28 years at Kingsport Press, Palmer evolved into one of the country's leading industrialists and civic leaders. During World War II, he received the honorary rank of colonel for his work in the adjutant general's department. After the war, Palmer was awarded the Legion of Merit for his distinguished service during active duty. Serving as president of the Tennessee Society of Crippled Children and Adults for 18 years, he also was president, trustee, and treasurer of the national Society for Crippled Children and Adults. Locally, Palmer was founder of the Kingsport Building and Loans Association, an original incorporator of Holston Valley Community Hospital, and a supporter of the Kingsport Public Library.

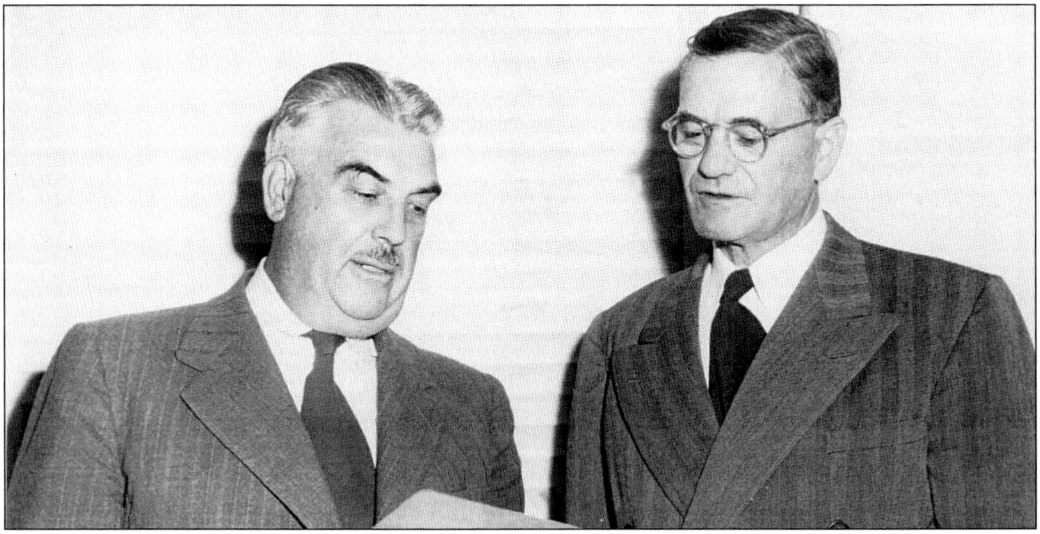

Slip-Not Belting Corporation founder H.J. Shivell, pictured here with TEC President James C. White, began his firm in 1926. During the 1940s, the company operated as a manufacturer and a jobbing distributor. The tanning of hides, the currying and processing of leather, and the making of leather belting and mechanical leather specialties are included in its manufacturing processes. During this time, Slip-Not developed a national reputation for the manufacture of transmission belts. In 1933, a complete line of power transmission equipment to supplement the belting services was added. Later, the company became actively identified with the distribution of stainless steel for industrial purposes.

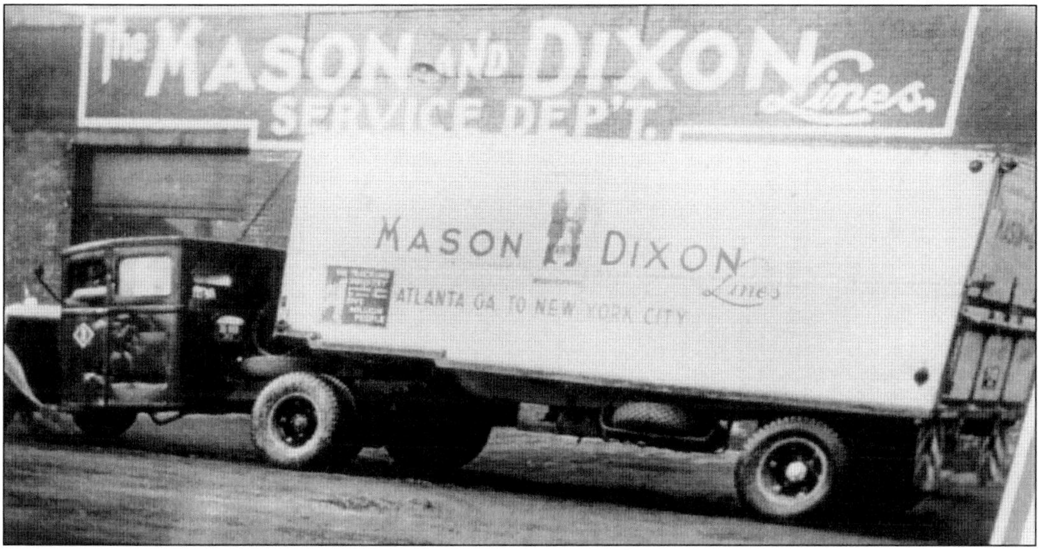

The famous trademark of Mason Dixon Lines showing Civil War Generals Lee and Grant shaking hands and featuring the slogan "Now joining the North and South" was a distinctive part of the fabric of Kingsport business and community life for over 50 years. The story of Mason Dixon Lines, Inc. is unique in transportation history. The largest privately owned carrier in the United States, the motor freight transportation company was created by E. Ward King in 1932. By 1982 Mason Dixon employed over 4,000 employees and grossed $121,000,000 in revenue. The company's history was one of consistent growth and expansion. In 1947, Mason Dixon had 21 terminals, a new general office, and revenues of over $4 million.

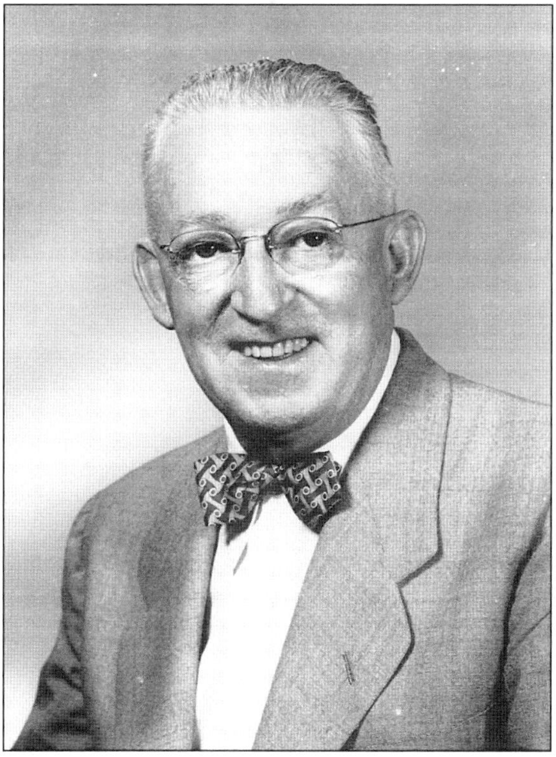

The son of a Methodist minister, E. Ward King served with the 414th Motor Supply Train in World War I, hauling ammunition to the front. For ten years, King worked in Kingsport in car sales before turning to trucking. A family enterprise, Mason Dixon skyrocketed under the leadership of King and his sons, E. William and John R. King. At one point, the motor carrier industry consisted of some 15,000 regulated companies, of which Mason Dixon ranked 15th in size. The leadership of King extended to many professional and community organizations. Most notably, his legacy continues in the area of education. King was a member of the delegation of business leaders who presented the need for a medical school at East Tennessee State University. His legacy extends to the University of Tennessee, King College (Bristol), Emory and Henry College, and Vanderbilt University.

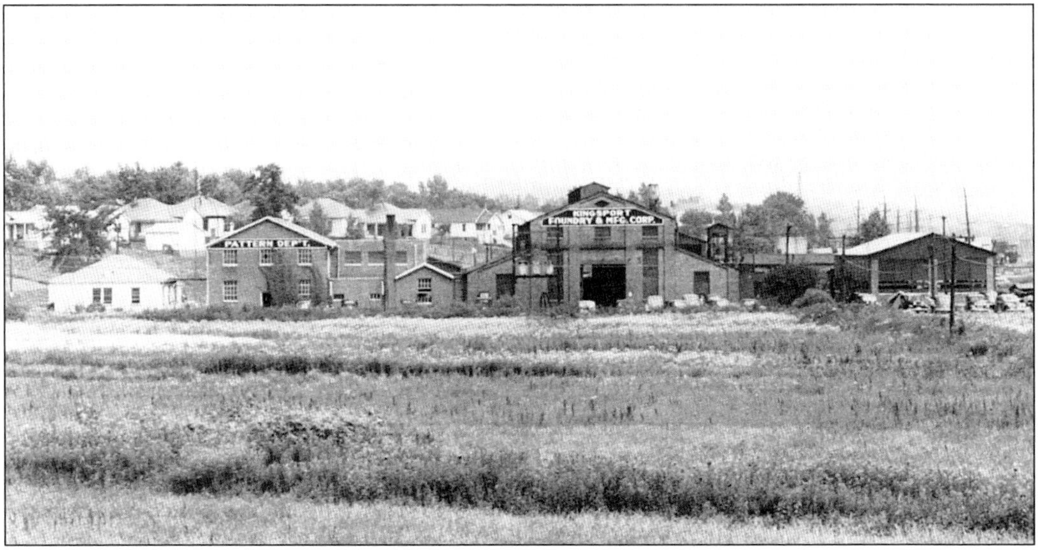

During the Depression and World War II, the Kingsport Foundry and Manufacturing Corporation pursued major expansions in 1929, 1941, and 1946. Built in 1927, the company was designed to produce heavy chemical processing castings of up to 15 tons per unit. Alloyed to meet the needs of the chemical industry, the castings had to meet specific requirements. Other regular productions during the war years included electric furnace machinery for the chemical industry and blast furnace equipment such as the gas-controlled apparatus utilized by the steel industry.

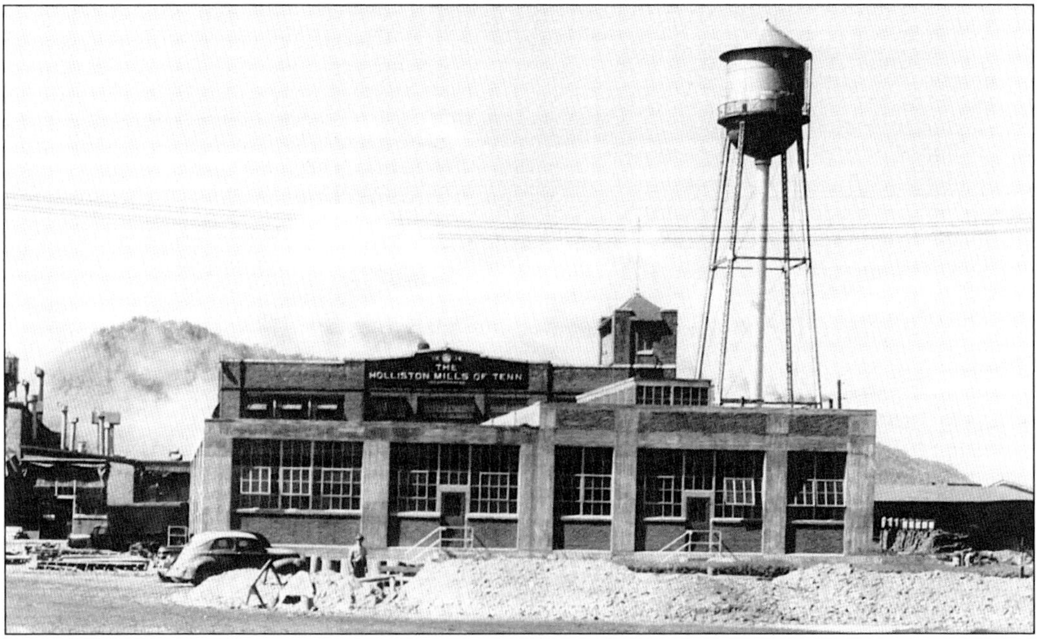

Holliston Mills, an integral component in fulfilling the interlocking concept of industry upon which Kingsport's founders created the planned industrial city, complements the activities of both Borden Mills, Inc. and Kingsport Press, Inc. as a manufacturer of bookcloth, shade cloth, and window shades. Established in 1926 in Kingsport, the parent company, located in Norwood, MA, was incorporated in 1893.

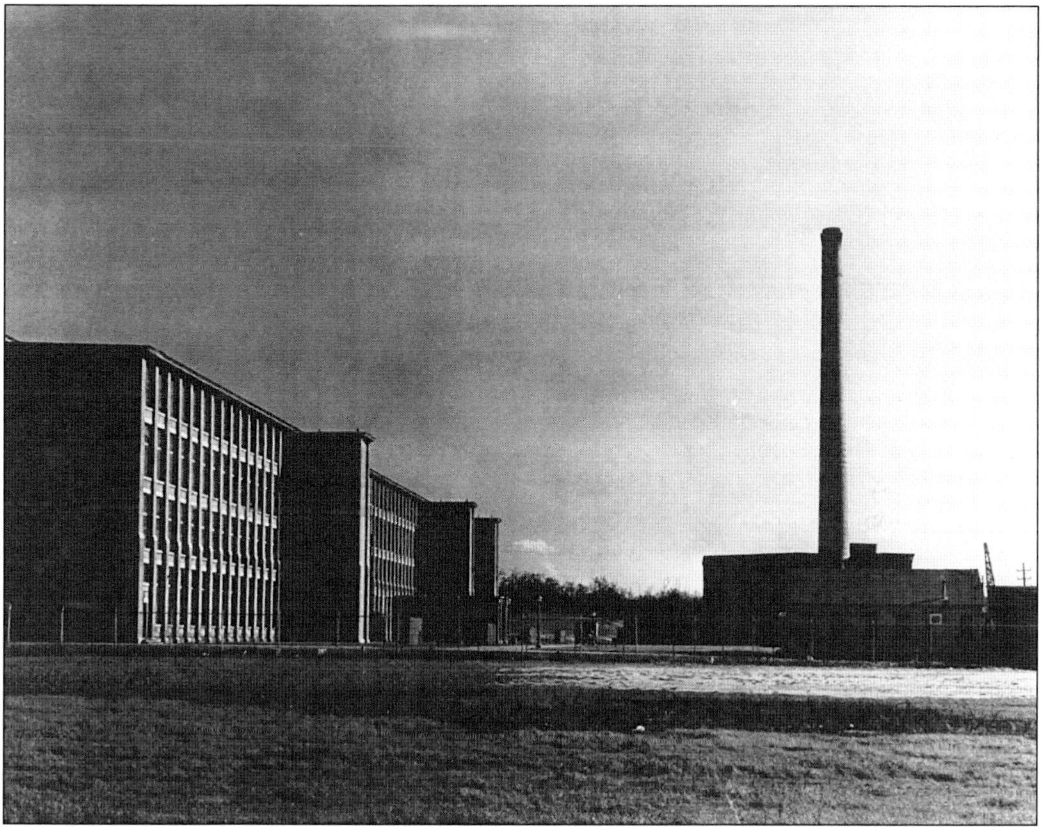

In 1946, Cotton cloth manufacturer Borden Mills, Inc. boasted weekly production of 1,125,000 yards of cloth. Because of the efforts of Borden Mills during World War II, the employees were presented the distinguished Army-Navy "E" Award and pennant for excellence. Located in Kingsport in 1924, Borden Mills, Inc. was headquartered in Fall River, MA. By 1928 this manufacturer of cotton cloth was Kingsport's largest employer with 1,227 workers.

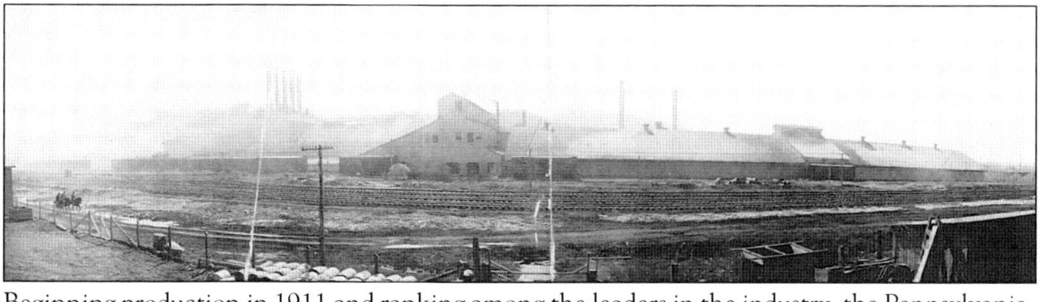

Beginning production in 1911 and ranking among the leaders in the industry, the Pennsylvania-Dixie Cement Corporation was one of modern Kingsport's foundation industries. By 1946, the output of the plant was such that it annually required 320,000 tons of limestone, 77,000 tons of shale, 75,000 tons of coal, and 10,000 tons of gypsum to make the cement.

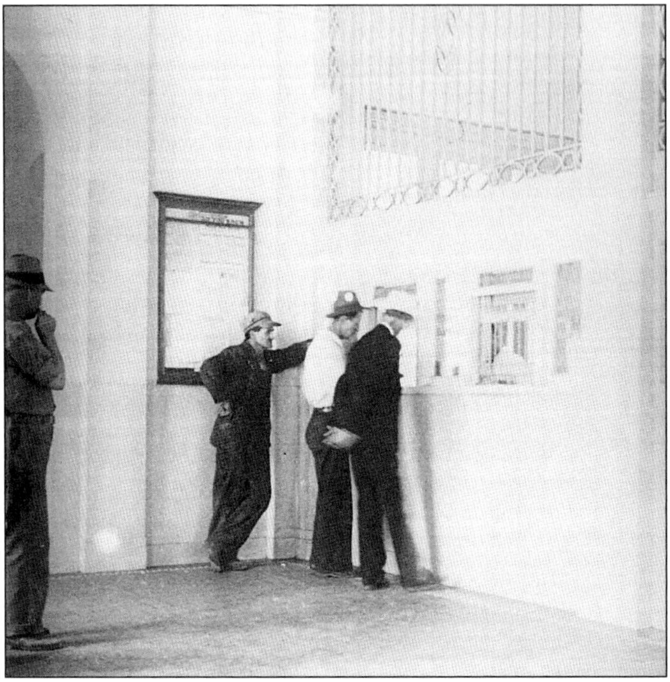

First National Bank, enjoying growth throughout the Depression and war years, published its statements as of December 31, 1945, showing deposits of more than $21,000,000, capital of $247,000, and surplus and undivided profits and reserves of $496,460.

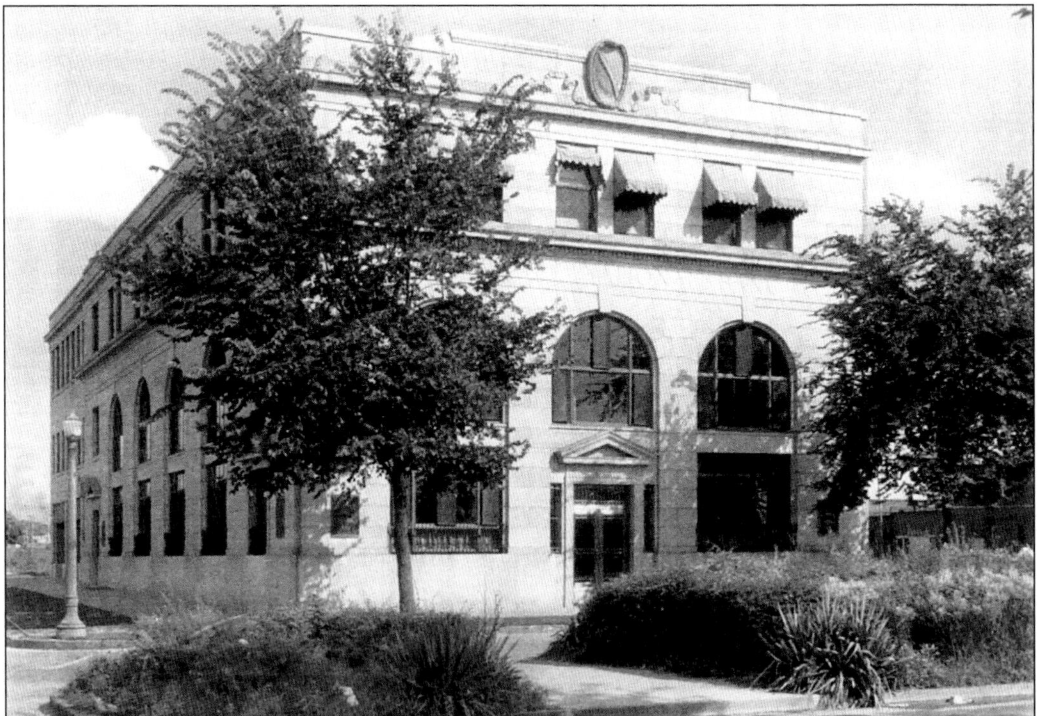

As seen in this photograph, First National Bank moved to the corner of Broad and Center Streets from the corner of Main and Commerce Streets in 1927. Between its beginning in 1916 and the end of World War II, the bank had three presidents: William Roller, J. Fred Johnson, and A.D. Brockman.

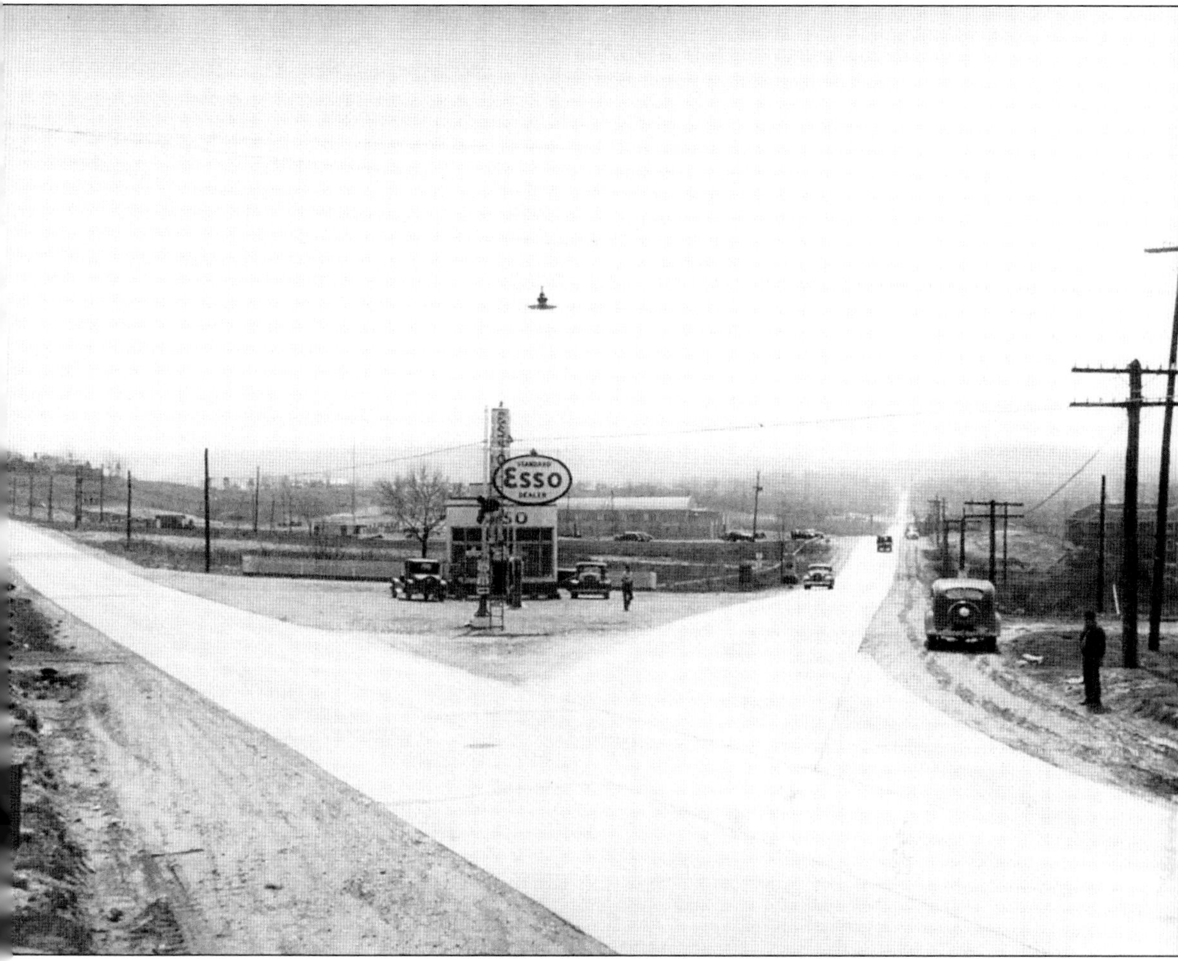

An important junction in the east section of Kingsport is shown here: left to Bristol via U.S. 11W and right to Johnson City via U.S. 23.

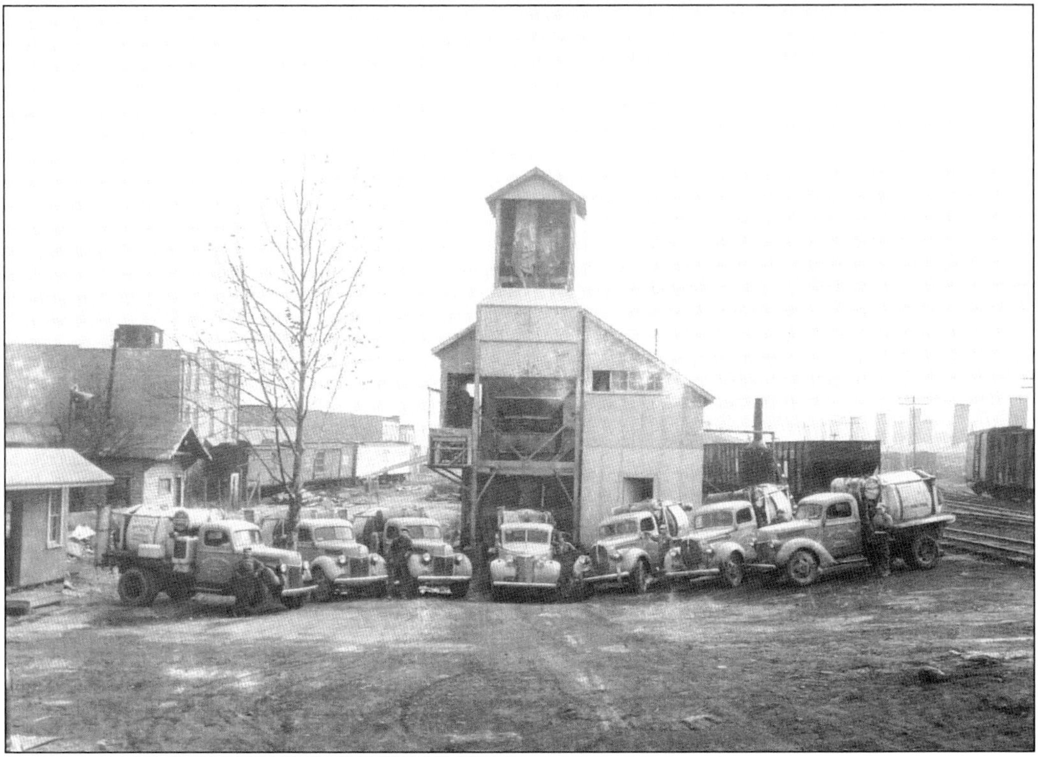

Providing sand, gravel, and ready-mixed concrete, the Brooks Sand and Gravel Company responded to the needs of the construction industry during this era of growth in Kingsport.

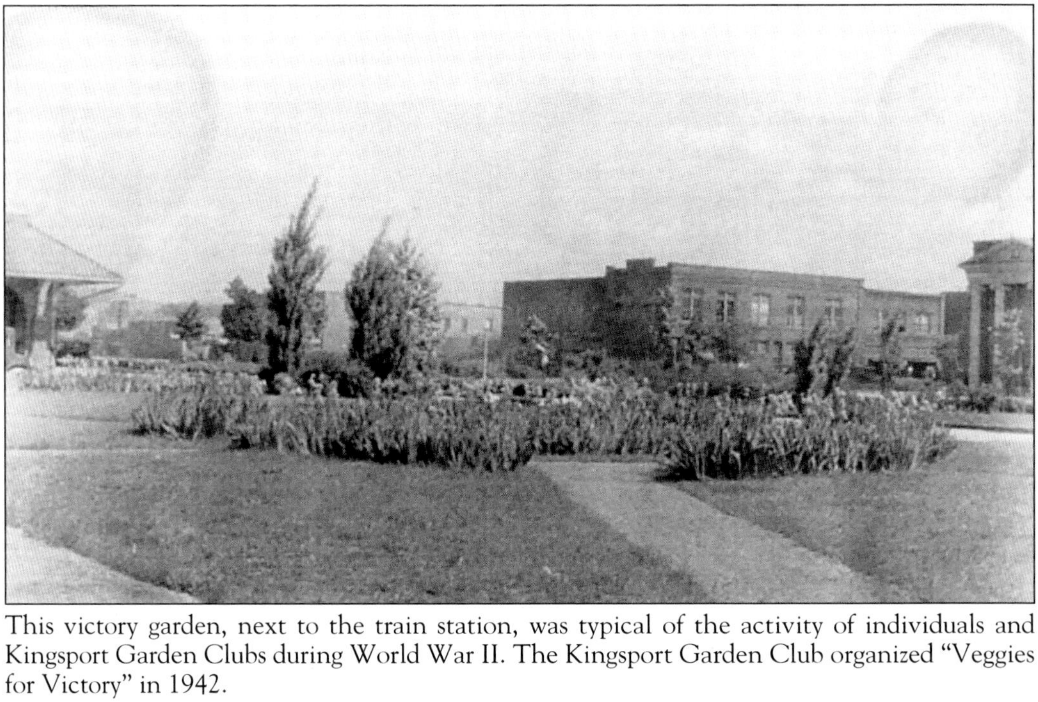

This victory garden, next to the train station, was typical of the activity of individuals and Kingsport Garden Clubs during World War II. The Kingsport Garden Club organized "Veggies for Victory" in 1942.

Beginning operation on July 15, 1940, WKPT radio station was the first and only radio station in Kingsport. It was a full-time NBC affiliate. By 1946, operating with a staff of 19 employees, WKPT proclaimed itself in its slogan, "The Nation's Model Station!"

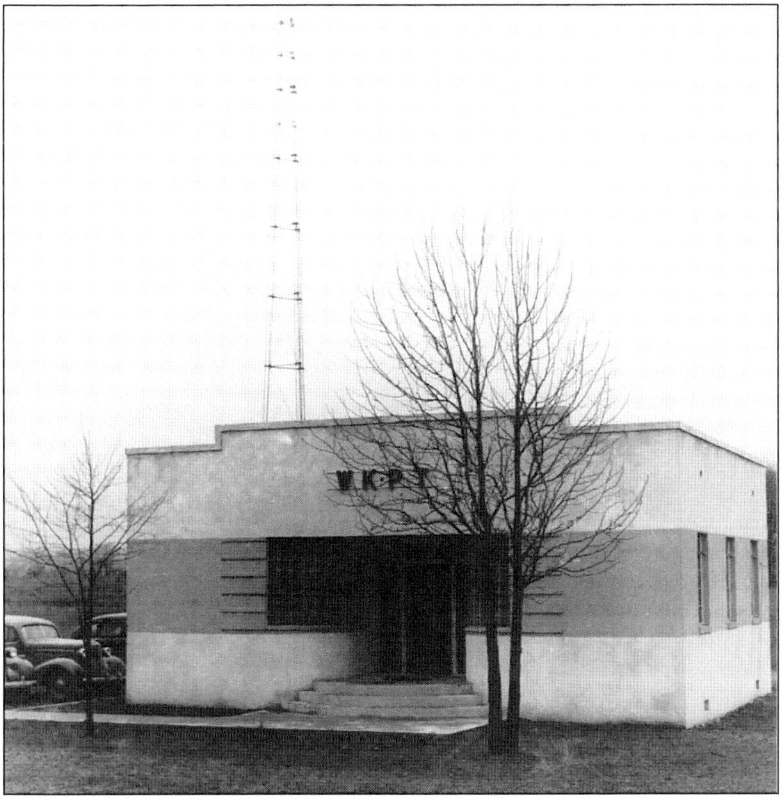

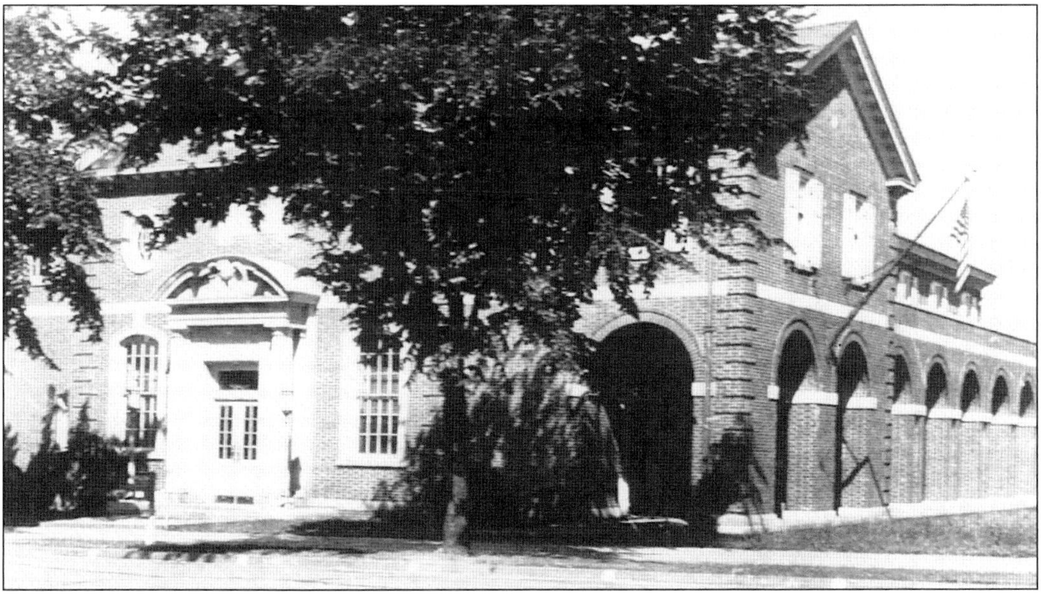

New York architect Thomas Hastings designed the post office. With work beginning on the structure in 1930, the public project alleviated unemployment. During 1931, construction was completed.

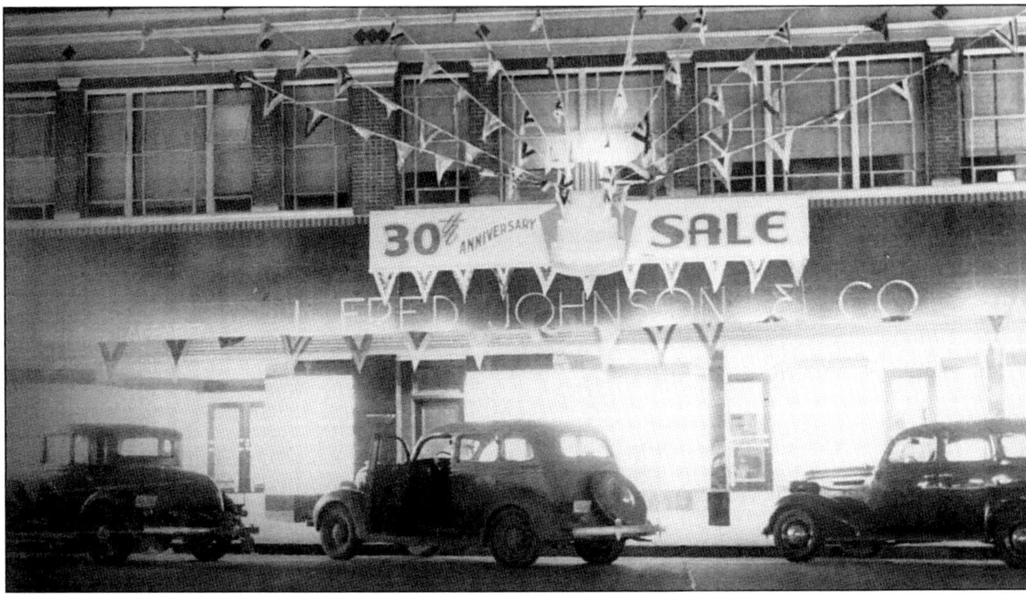

J. Fred Johnson and Co. evolved from the "Big Store" to a full-fledged department store, which was situated at 144–146 Broad Street, as pictured here in 1938. Johnson died in 1944; the store he founded was later moved to the corner of Broad and Center Streets and eventually was sold to Miller's of Knoxville.

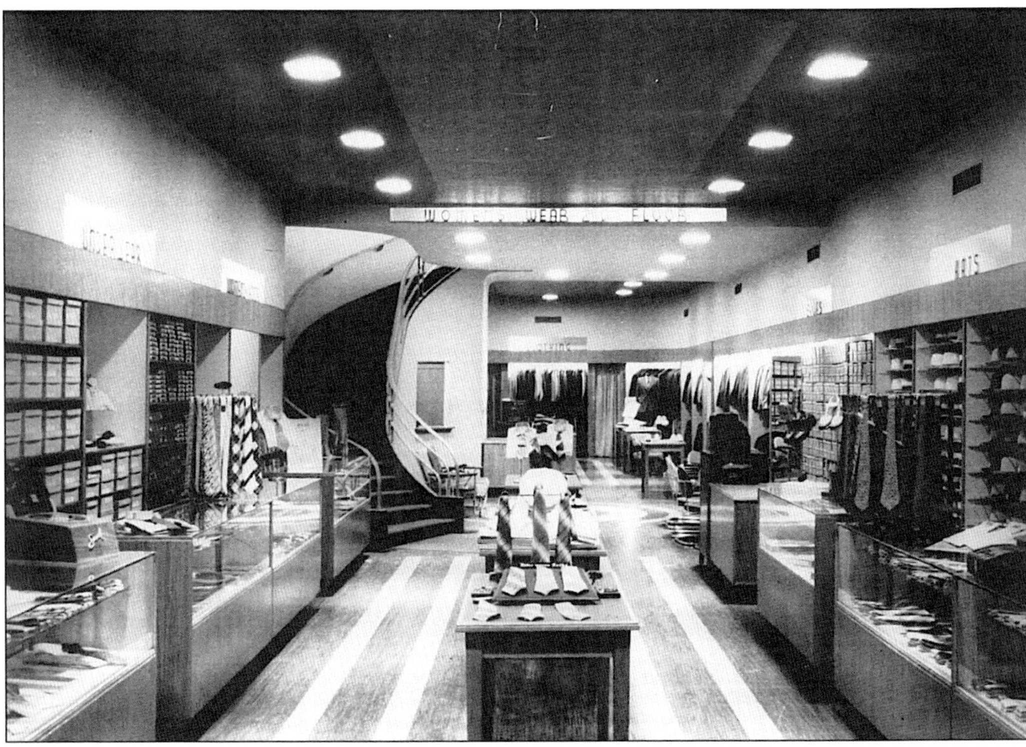

Fuller and Hillman, Inc. served as "Men's and Women's Quality Clothiers" in the 1940s at 240 Broad Street. For decades the store, owned by Irvin M. Fuller and W. Ray Hillman, was a Kingsport fixture.

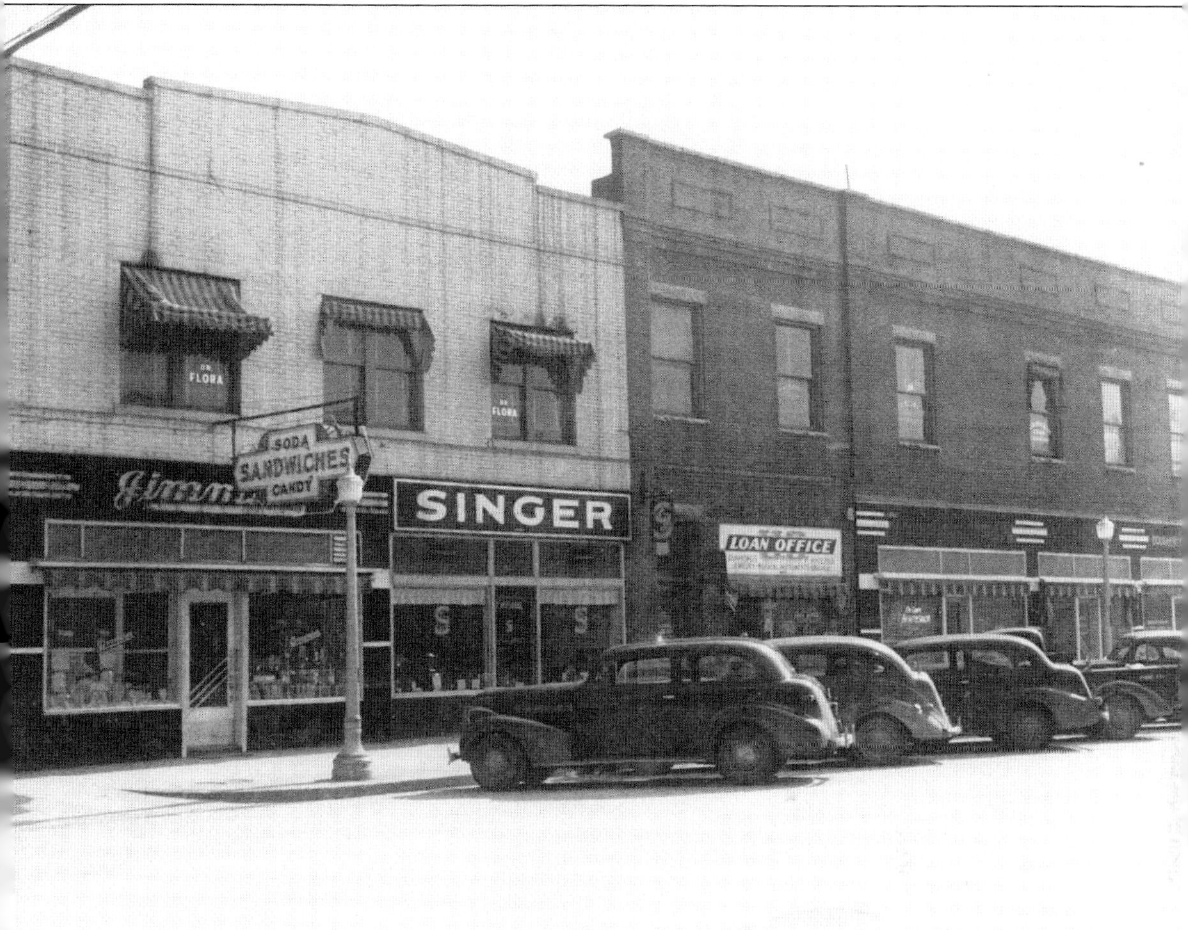

Jimmy's Candy Kitchen was a popular downtown eatery for many years. For 18 months during World War II, owner Jimmy Vallis kept the store's doors open 19 hours per day, from 7 a.m. to 2 a.m., to serve workers at the Holston Ordnance Works.

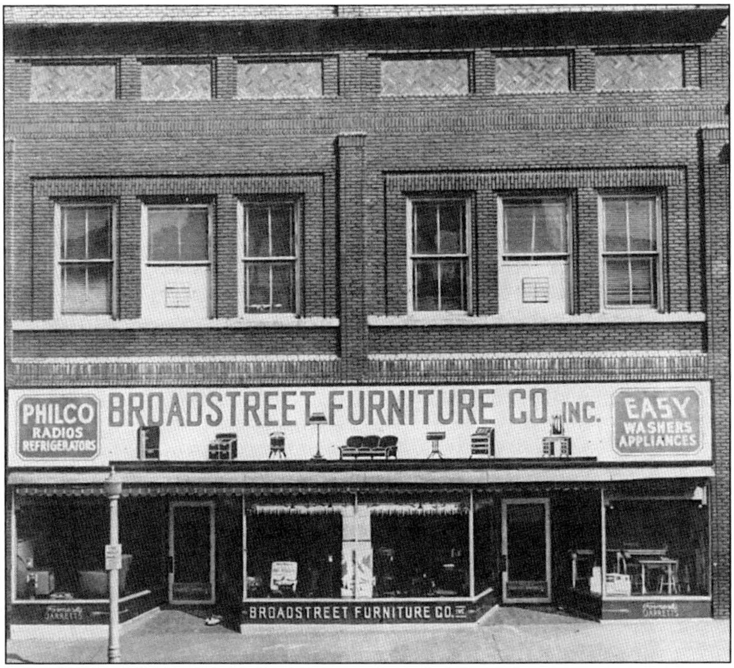

By the end of World War II, Kingsport residents had their choice of furniture stores from which to choose, including Broadstreet Furniture, Baylor-Nelms, Sterchi Brothers, Johnson-Gentry, Dobyns-Taylor, W.B. Green, Co., and Anderson's.

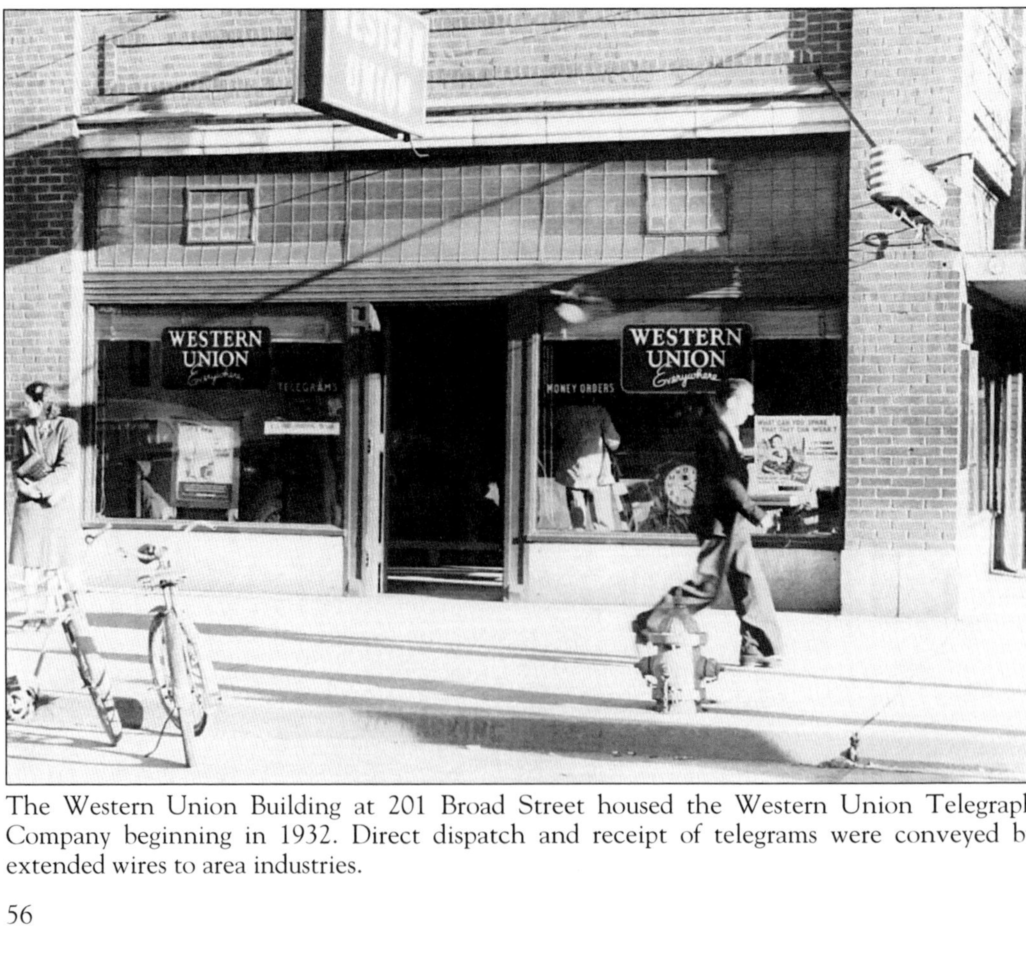

The Western Union Building at 201 Broad Street housed the Western Union Telegraph Company beginning in 1932. Direct dispatch and receipt of telegrams were conveyed by extended wires to area industries.

Four

Model City Streets and Scenes

The modern American city seemed to come into existence during the 1920s. The unique legacy of Kingsport as a planned and industrially diversified city owed much to planning consultant John Nolen. From 1916 to 1920, Nolen, a leader in the definition of land use planning as a distinct profession, contributed to the design and layout of what became known as the "model city."

Undoubtedly, city planning encouraged the fine domestic architecture of Kingsport, but in many other ways, Kingsport, between the years 1920 to 1950, seemed representative of other towns and cities that were to give form and substance to the society and culture we think of as American. Promoting a sense of community, the streets and neighborhoods of Kingsport portray the details of everyday living and enable later generations to follow the patterns of different community groups. By examining the housing created for distinct and diverse groups, the progress of Kingsport as a city may be documented.

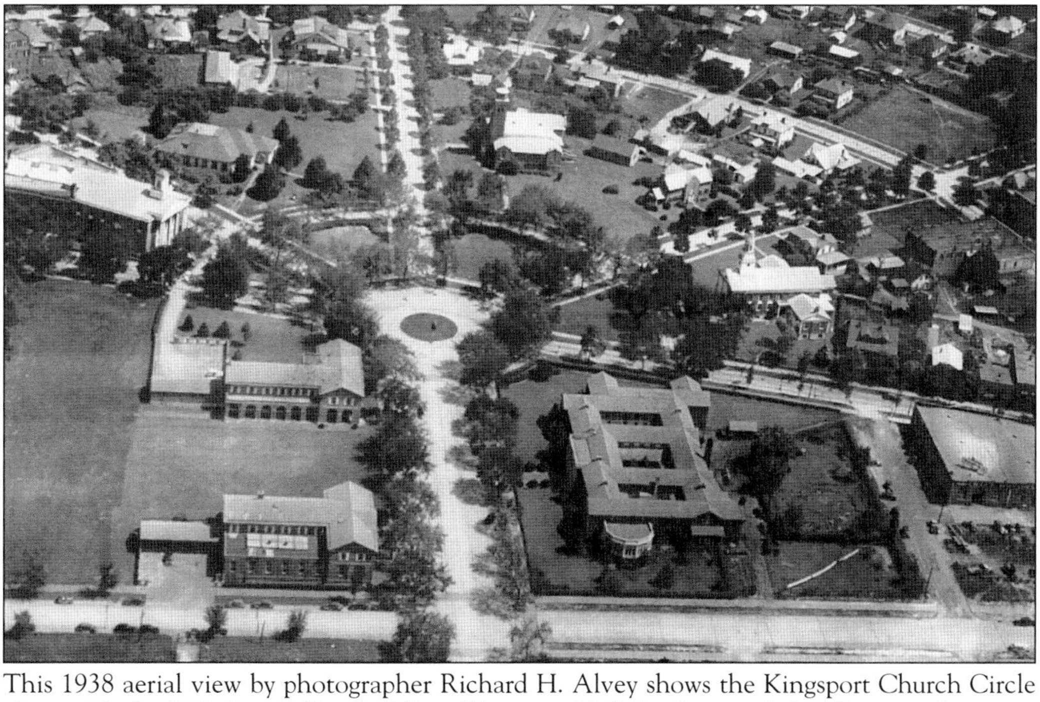

This 1938 aerial view by photographer Richard H. Alvey shows the Kingsport Church Circle along with the U.S. Post Office Building, Kingsport Utilities, Inc., and the Kingsport Inn.

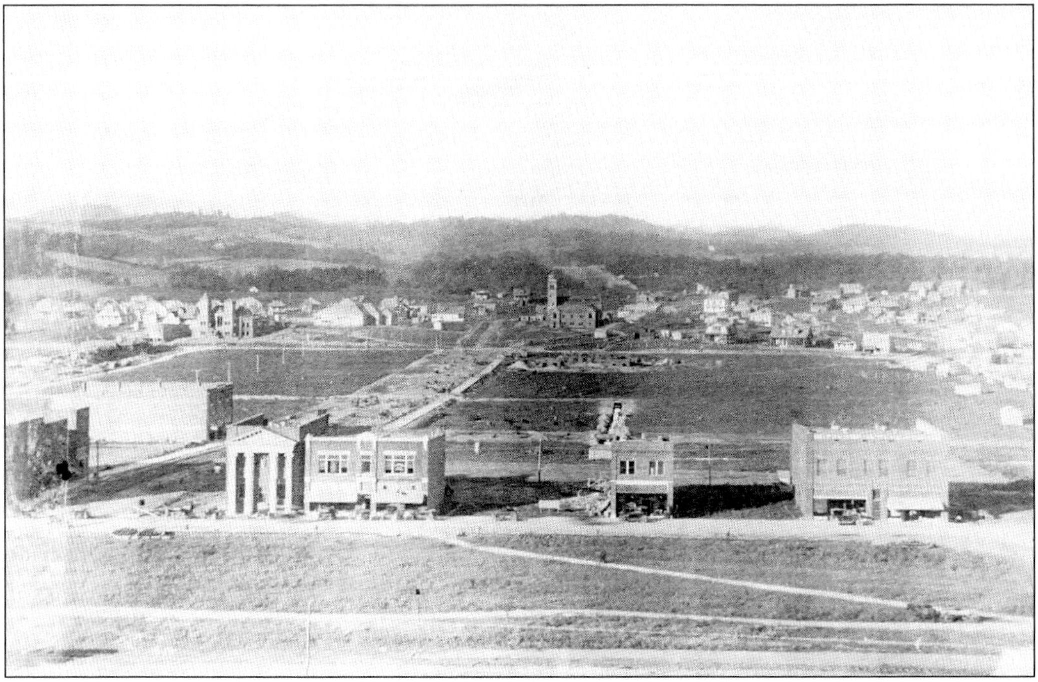

This picture, taken in the summer of 1916, shows the Nolen plan with Broad Street as the main thoroughfare between the train station and what will be Church Circle. The Bank of Kingsport is shown on Main Street, and in the distance the First Baptist Church (on far left) and the First Methodist Church (on far right) may be clearly seen.

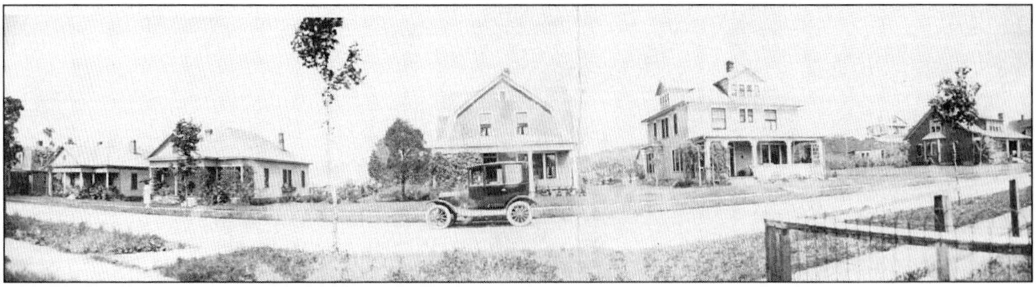

Houses on Wanola Street, although a part of "old" Kingsport, became a part of the new neighborhoods that were created after 1917.

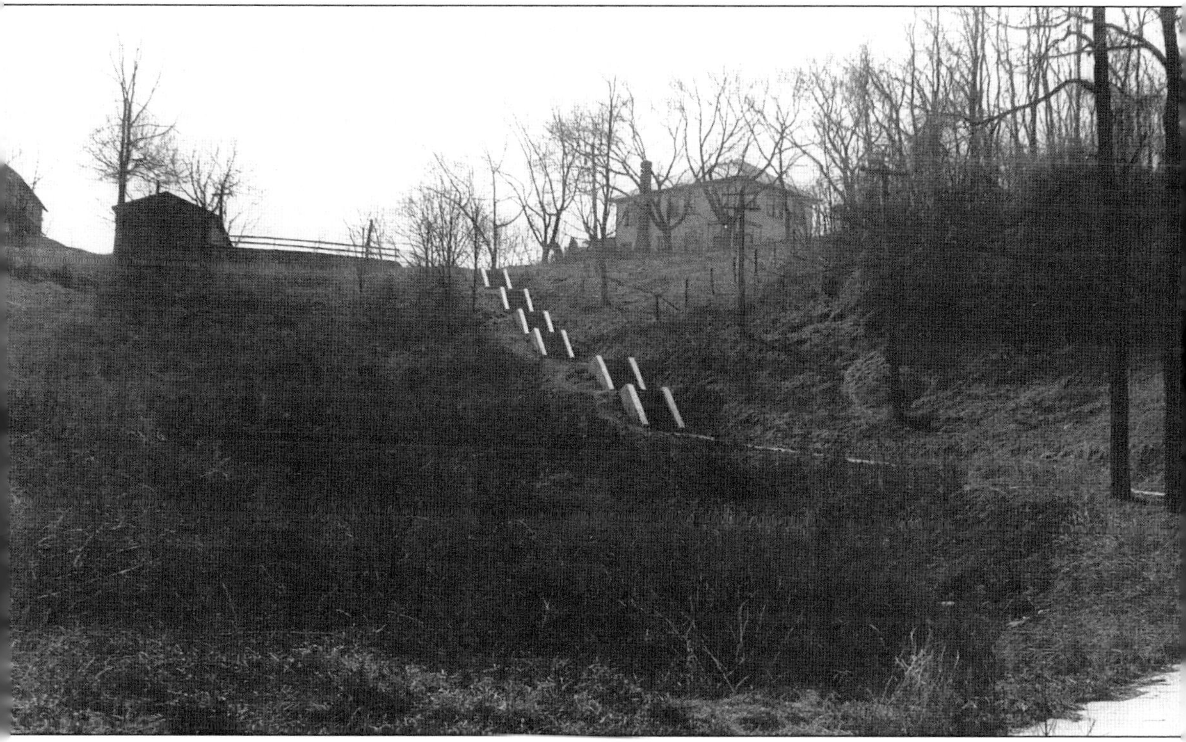

Behind the train station and the Penn-Dixie Cement plant is the stairway to "Cement Hill," a section of housing where company employees resided well into the 1950s.

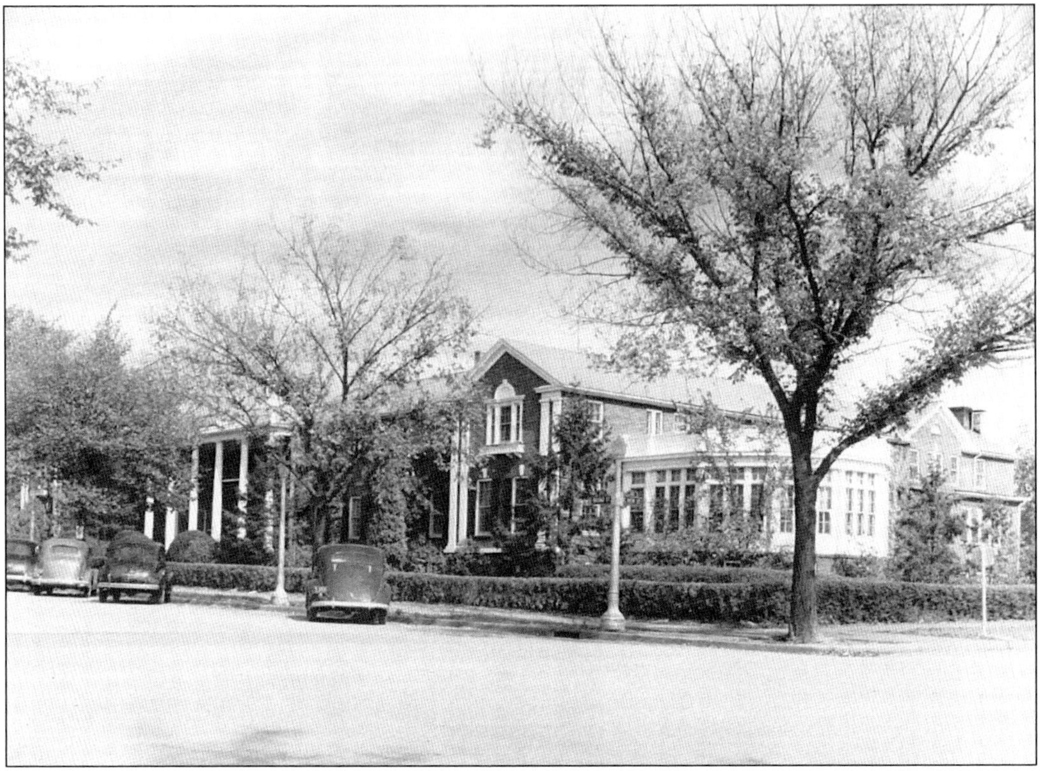

Designed by New York architect Clinton Mackenzie, the Kingsport Inn accommodated visiting industrialists in its early days and served as a site for numerous social events. With a wide portico and high, white columns in the Southern style, the Georgian architecture of the inn created an atmosphere of beauty and charm. A nationally known stopping place with over 100 rooms, the Kingsport Inn was the center of community activity for more than three decades.

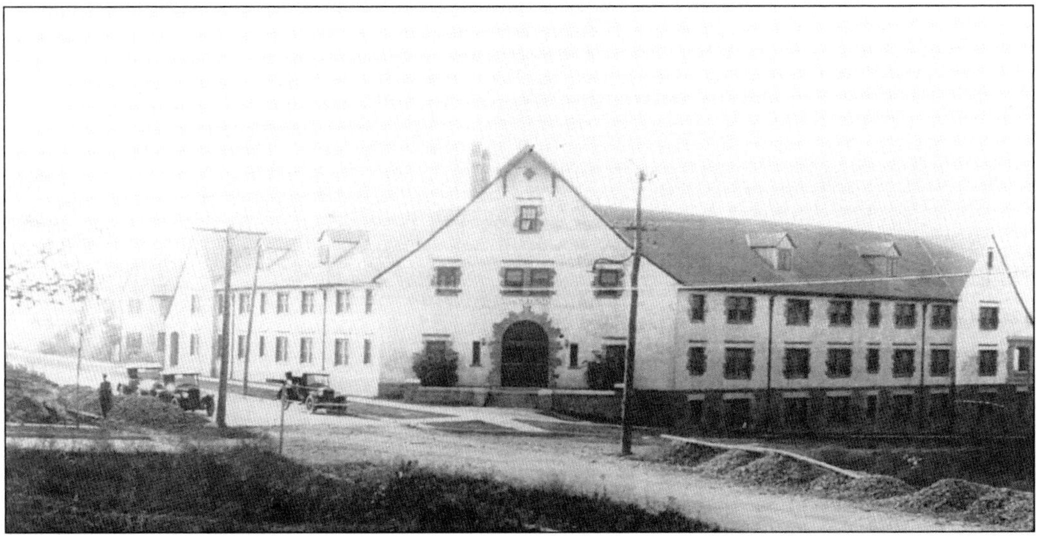

In 1918, the Grant Leather Company built the Homestead Hotel to use as a clubhouse. Soon it was remodeled and used as a hotel for many years. Located on the corner of Clay and Sullivan Streets, the "Homestead" provided accommodations for 110 guests during the 1920s and 1930s.

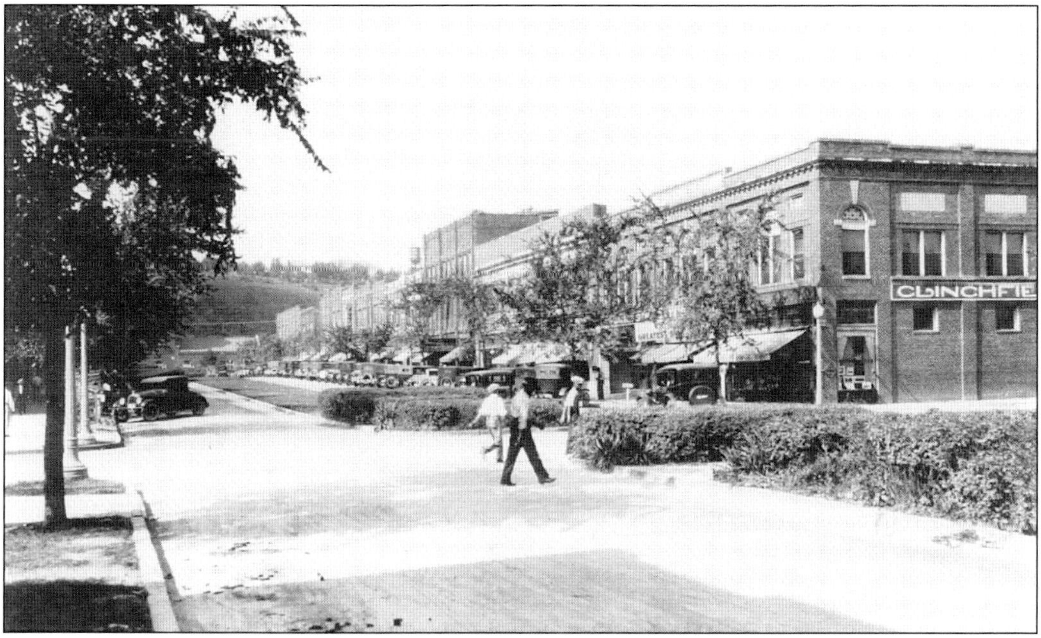

This picture of downtown Kingsport at the corner of Broad and Market Streets shows the original street plan for the commercial district, which featured a median down Broad Street.

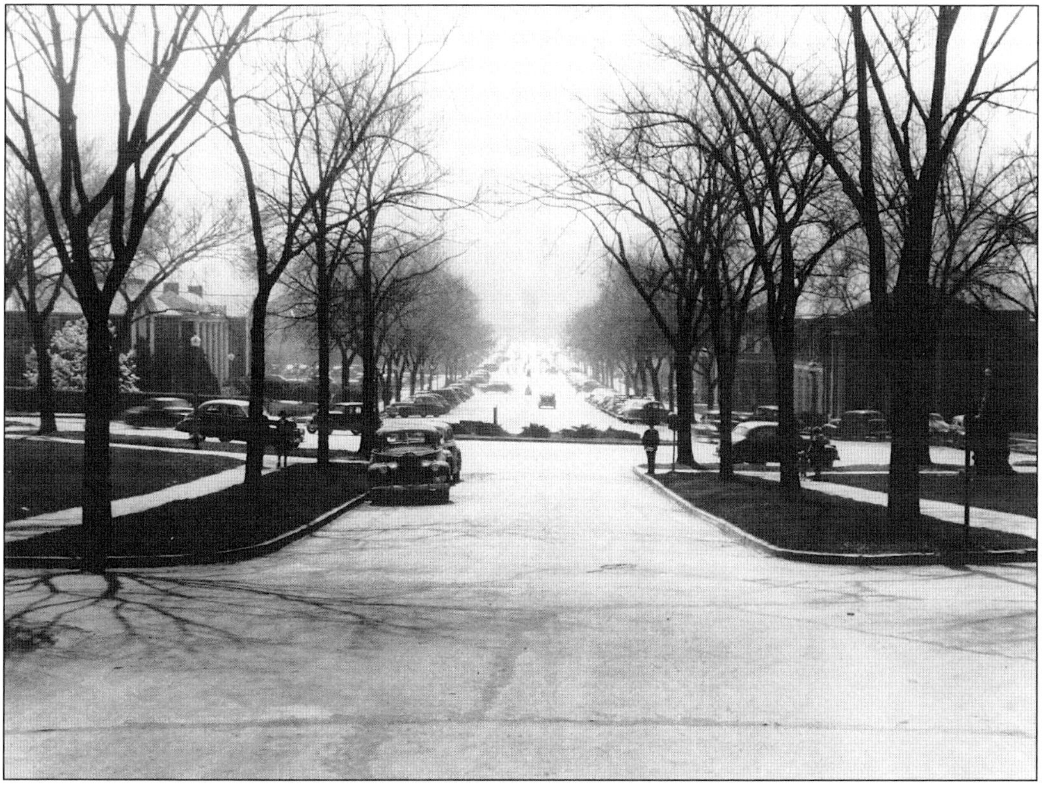

In the 1940s, the commercial district of Kingsport was still primarily contained within the traditional downtown area. In 1938, the median was removed.

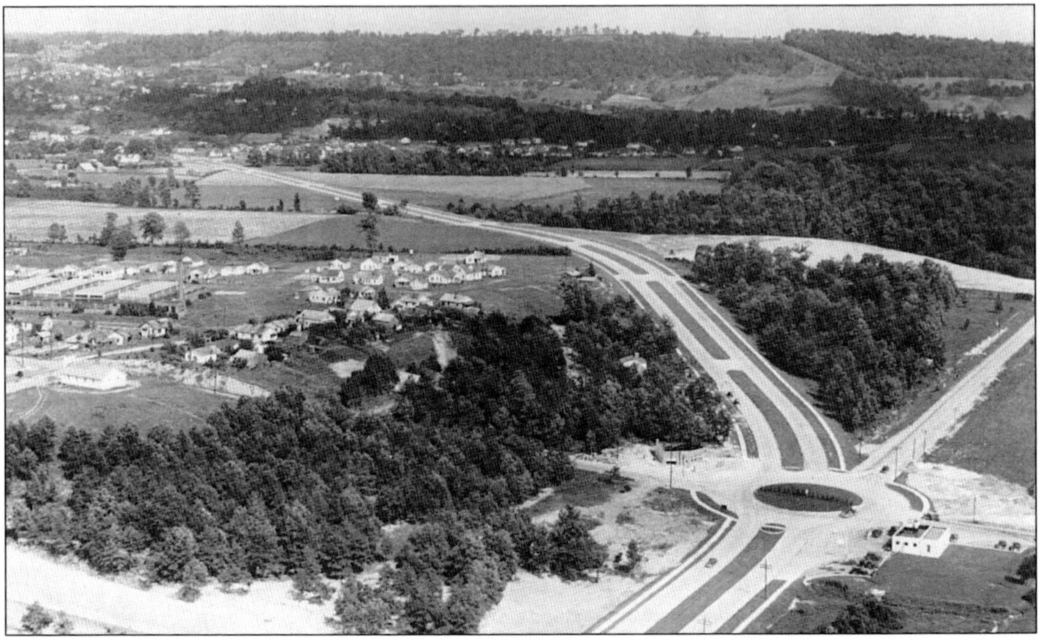

A 1940 aerial view of East Brooks Circle reflects the present intersection of Eastman Road and Ft. Henry Drive.

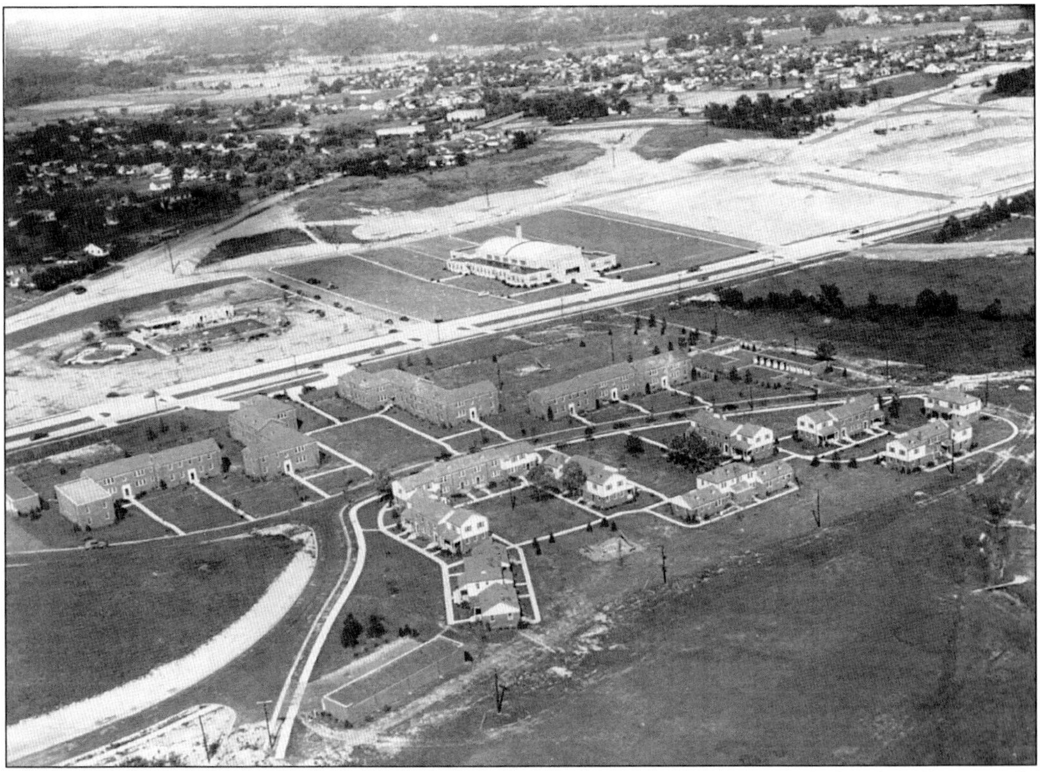

Located opposite the Civic Auditorium, Garden Apartments constituted the first large-scale apartment complex in Kingsport. Completed in 1939, the apartments were situated on 11 acres.

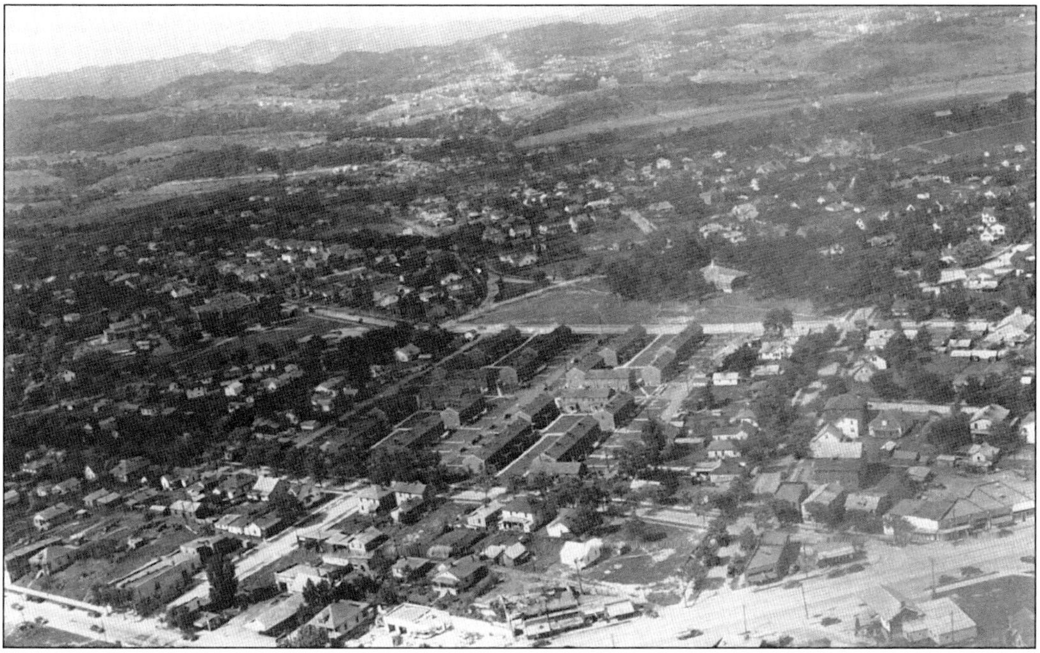

In the late 1930s, a group of Kingsport citizens led by J. Fred Johnson met with the U.S. Housing Authority and subsequently created a local housing authority to address the public housing needs of the community. The Kingsport Housing Authority oversaw the creation of two apartment complexes, which were segregated by race: Robert E. Lee Apartments for the white population and Riverview Apartments for the African-American population.

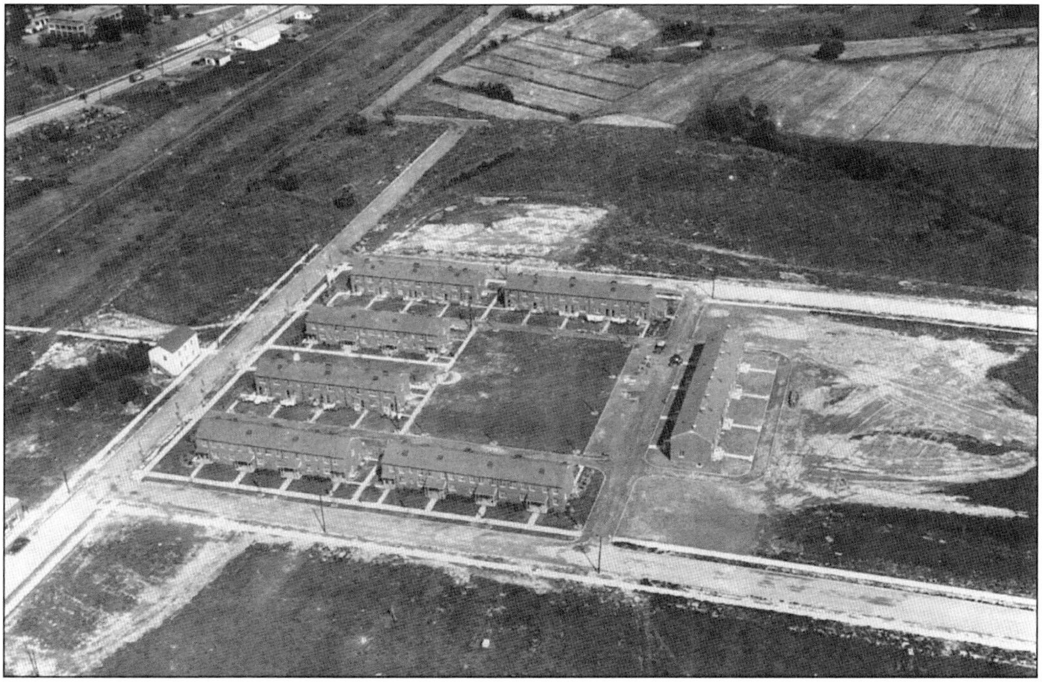

This image shows Riverview Apartments, housing for African Americans created by the Kingsport Housing Authority.

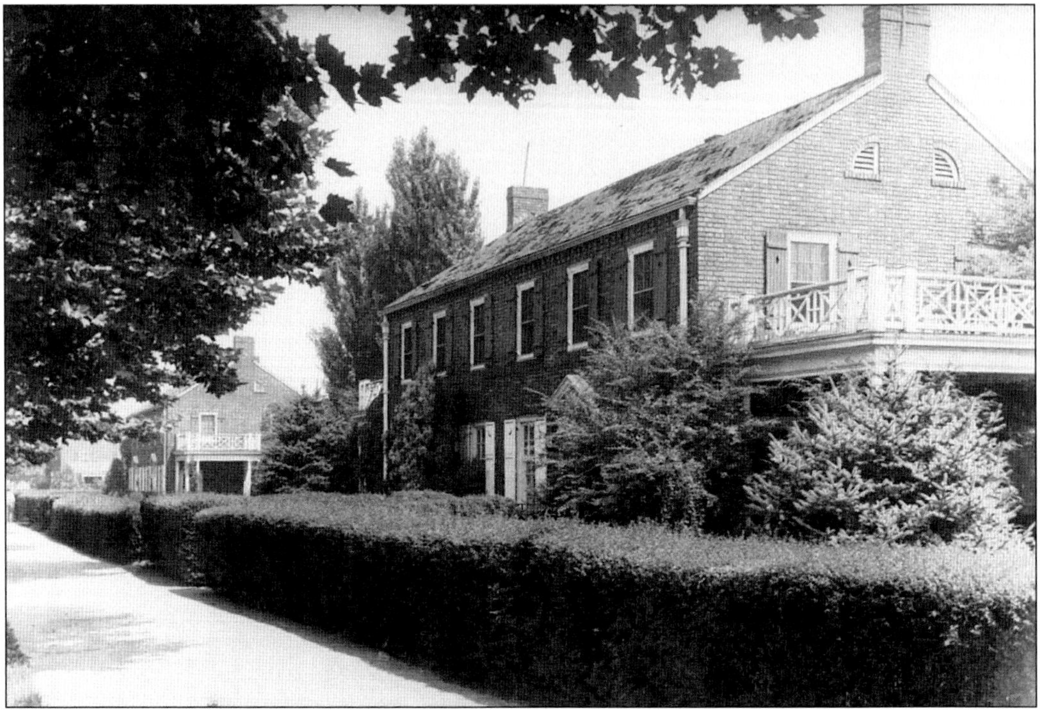

In the 1930s, beautiful duplex residential dwellings were built on Center Street. This housing section did not become a part of the commercial district until many years later.

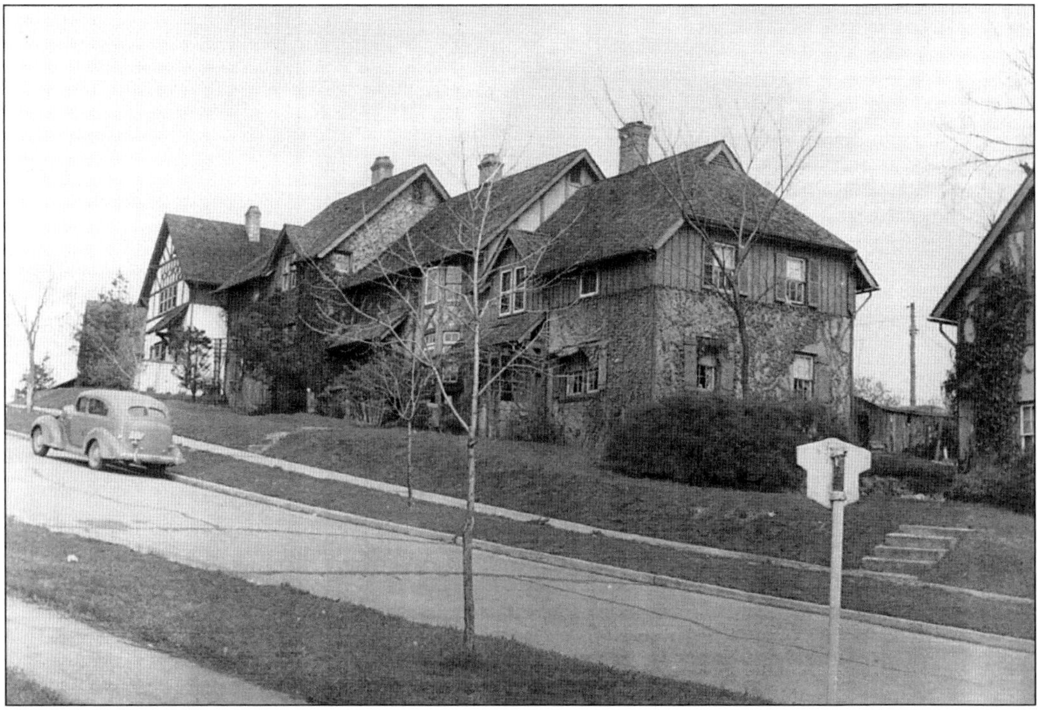

These West Wanola Street houses are remembered as the "Fifties," but have since experienced some renovation. In 1939, these dwellings were more than 20 years old.

Establishing the first architectural firm in Kingsport, Allen Dryden Sr. had been a student at the Art Institute of Chicago and the Armour Institute of Architecture of the Illinois Institute of Technology. In Kingsport, he designed churches, public buildings, housing developments, and many owner-commissioned houses on Watauga and Linville Streets. Pictured below is the house located on Orebank Road that he designed in 1926 for Kingsport businessman Harvey C. Brooks and his wife, Ruth Haire Brooks.

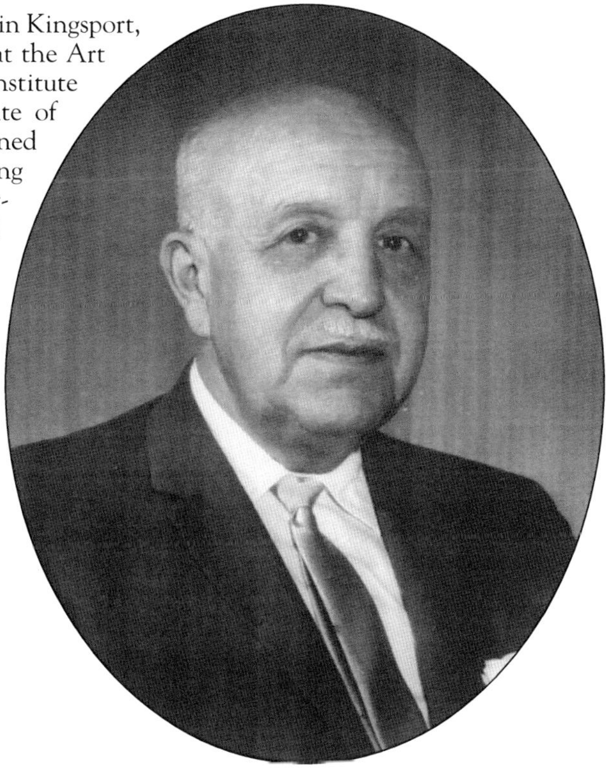

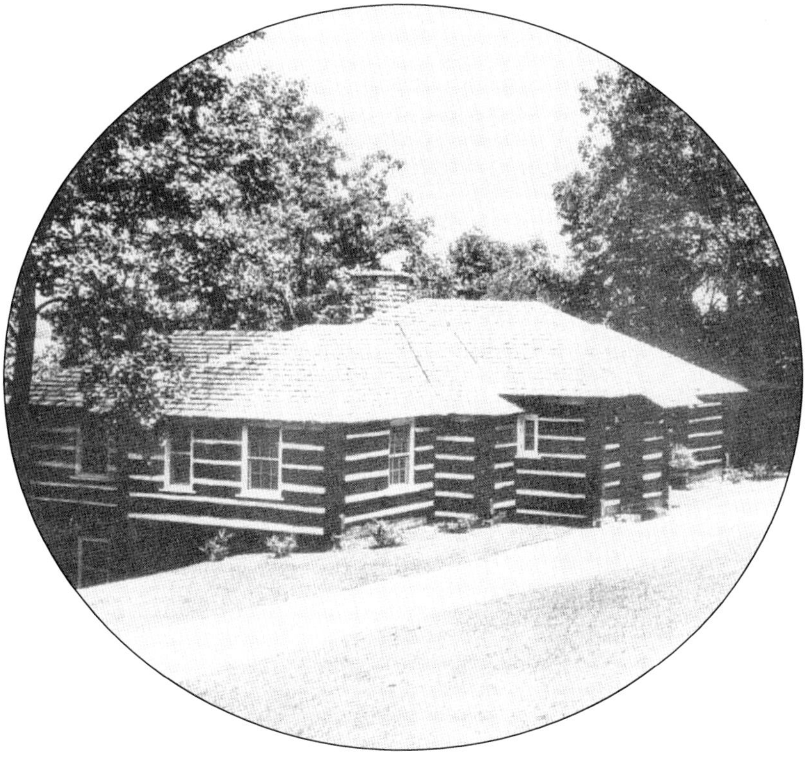

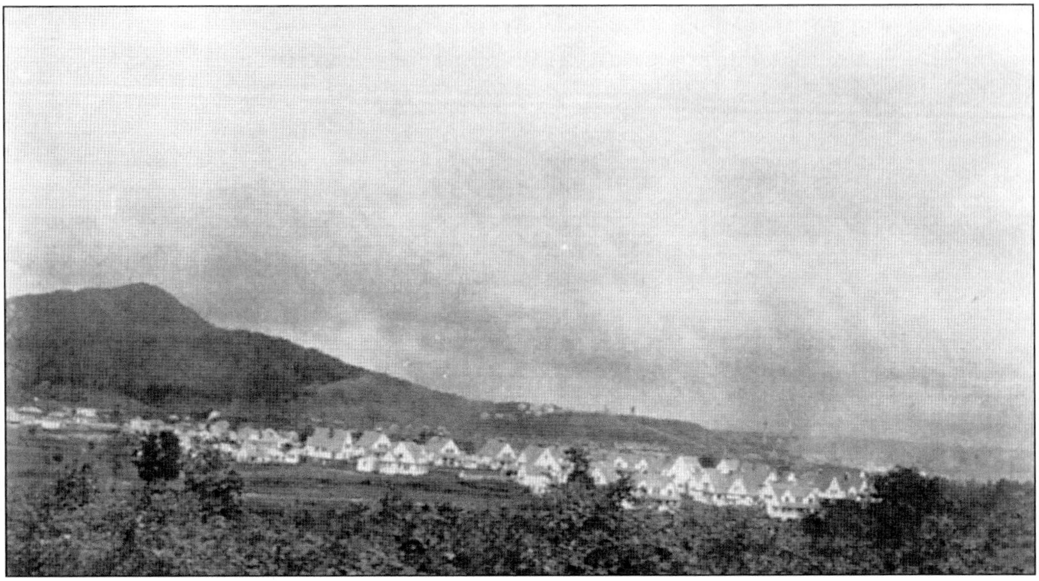

This long shot of White City, in the area of Yadkin Street, shows one of the original neighborhood developments in Kingsport. Some of these houses, so named because the deeds required that all the houses be painted white, were designed by Clinton Mackenzie.

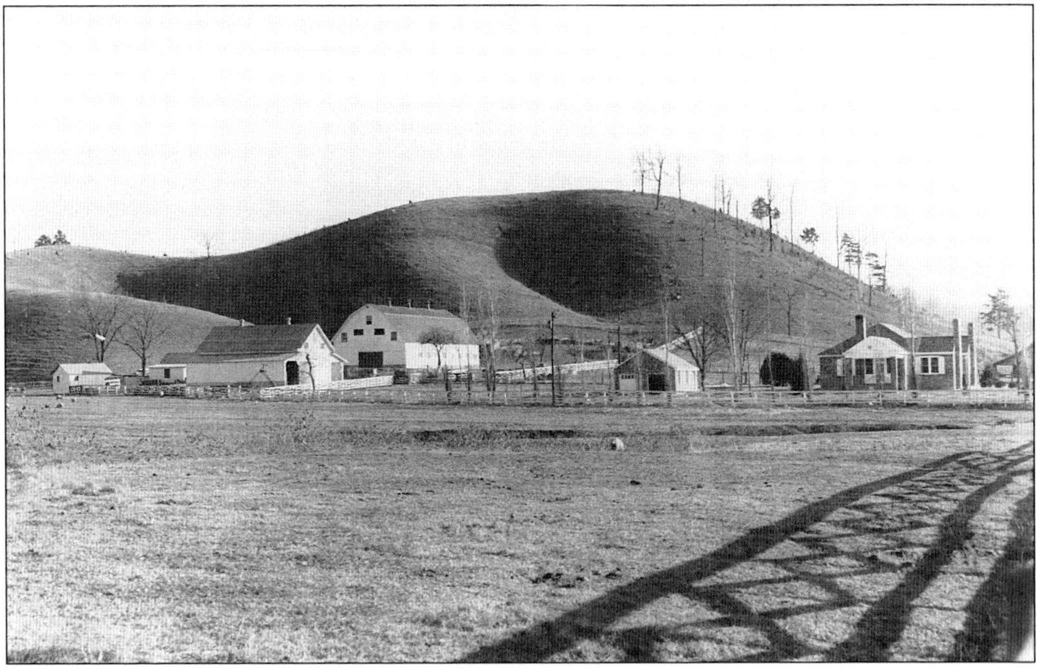

This 1939 scene of the Pierce family farm on Horse Creek Road pictures a significant area of land for both "old" and "modern" Kingsport. Native Americans, who valued it for its spring, traveled the land, located along Wilcox Drive near the MeadowView Conference Center. In the 18th and 19th centuries, it became farmland for Sullivan County residents.

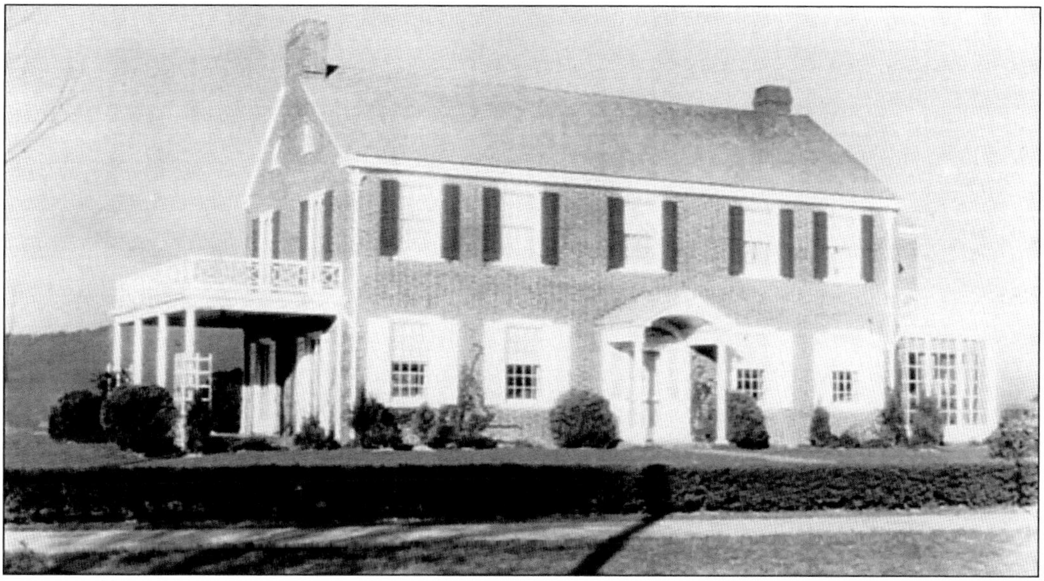

Designed by Clinton MacKenzie for TEC executive Perley Wilcox, this home is located at 1261 Watauga Street.

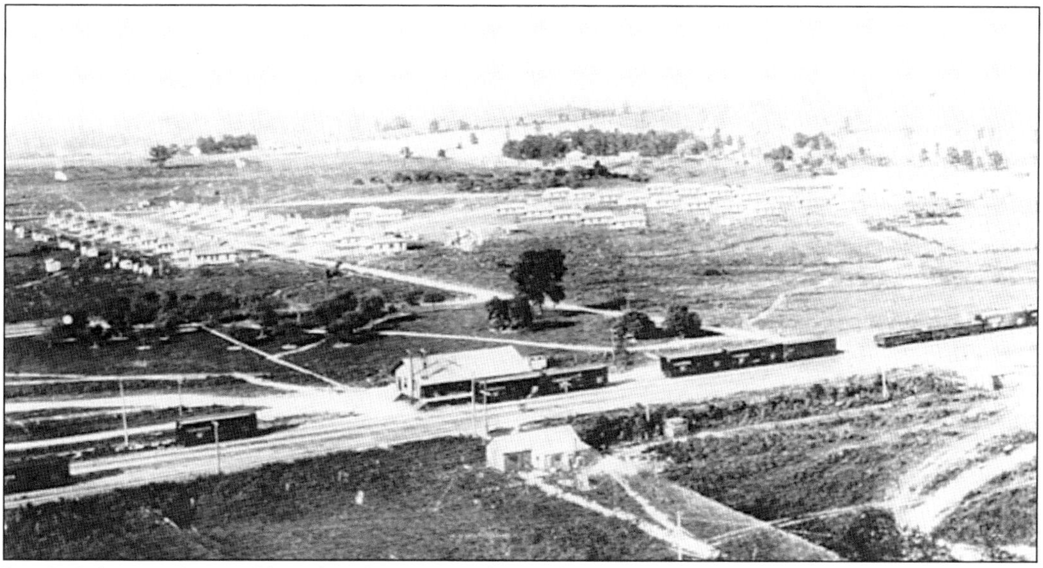

In 1912, houses facing Cherokee Street were located near the old Clinchfield Railroad passenger and freight station. Housing patterns in Kingsport had evolved from simple makeshift housing in the early part of the century and distinguished architectural achievements in the 1920s and 1930s to modern housing developments, public housing, and apartment complexes by 1950.

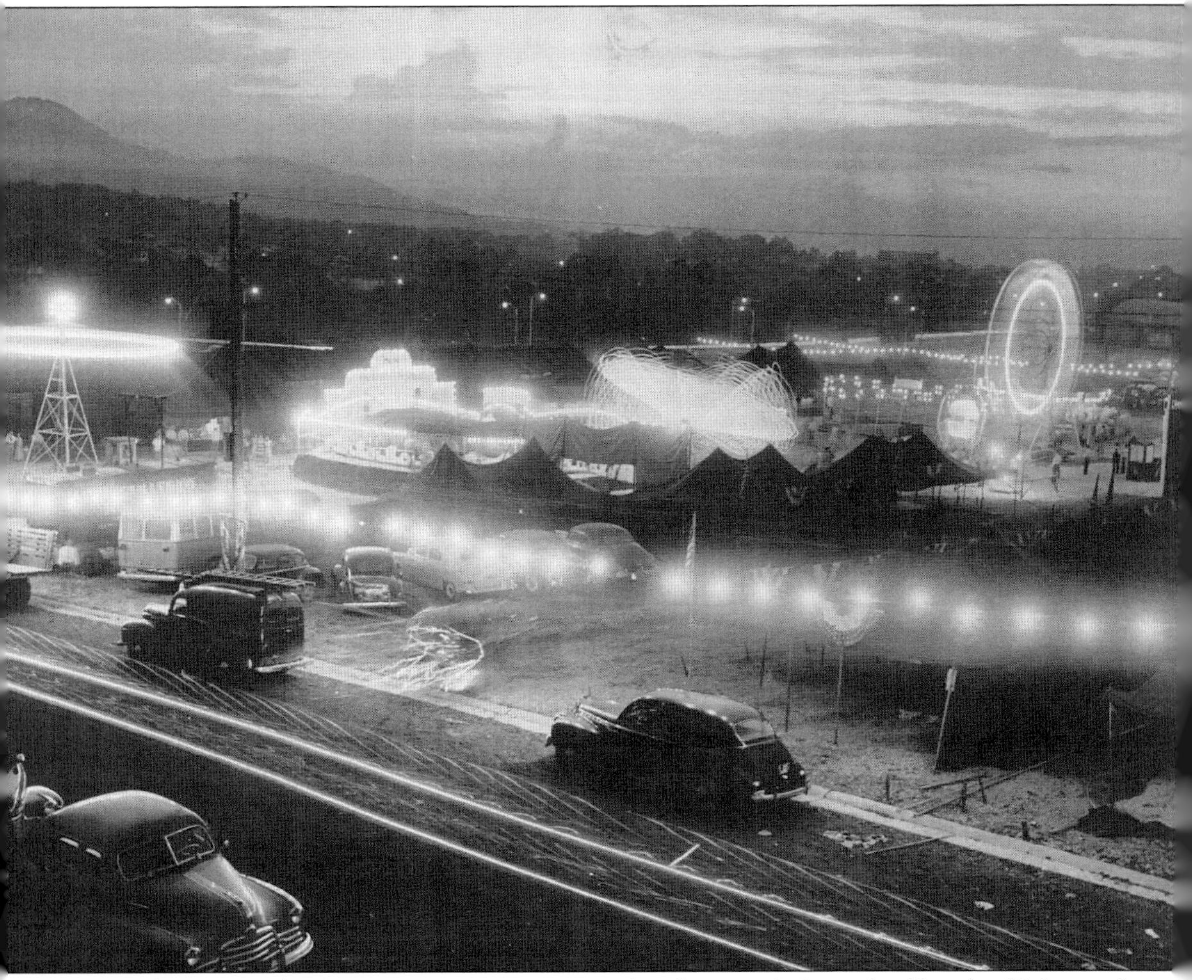

Each summer, the American Legion sponsors a fair that concludes with a Fourth of July parade. This picture, entitled "The Fair at Night" by Ellis Binkley, captures the carnival festivities when it was located in downtown Kingsport. Binkley had a long and distinguished career in journalism as a political correspondent, columnist, and editor for the Kingsport *Times-News*.

Five

People

Profiled in a post-World War II film produced by the U.S. State Department during the years of the Marshall Plan, Kingsport was presented as a model community demonstrating the value of "better living through voluntary planning." Necessary to Kingsport's success as a planned city with diversified industry was the "spirit of the community." Choosing Kingsport as their new "hometown," a diverse group of Americans, from inside and outside the region, located in Kingsport. The adoption of the "Kingsport spirit"—encouraging economic development while maintaining close community and family relationships—demonstrated how the people of Kingsport shaped the economic, social, and cultural growth of the city.

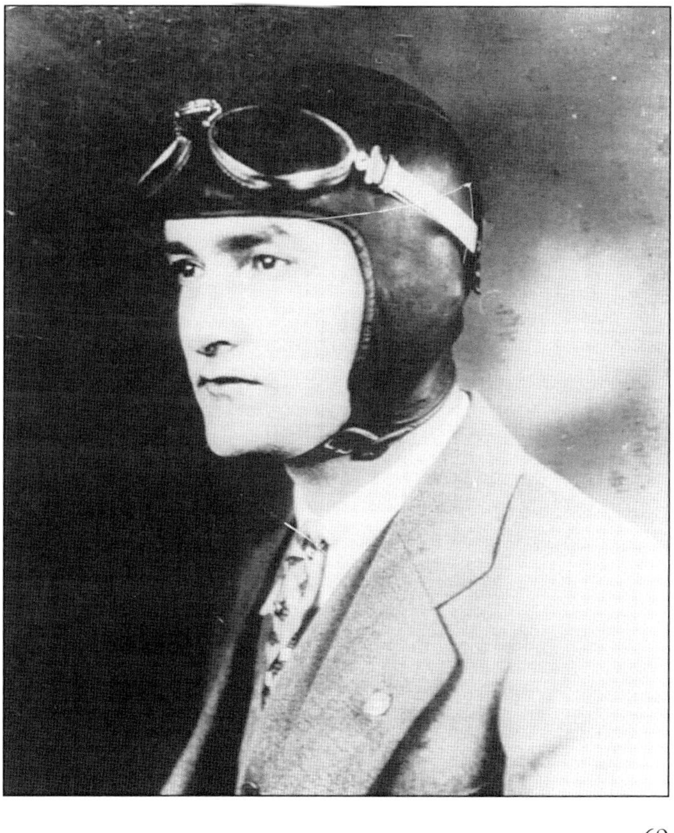

The first volunteer from Kingsport to serve in World War I was James Showalter.

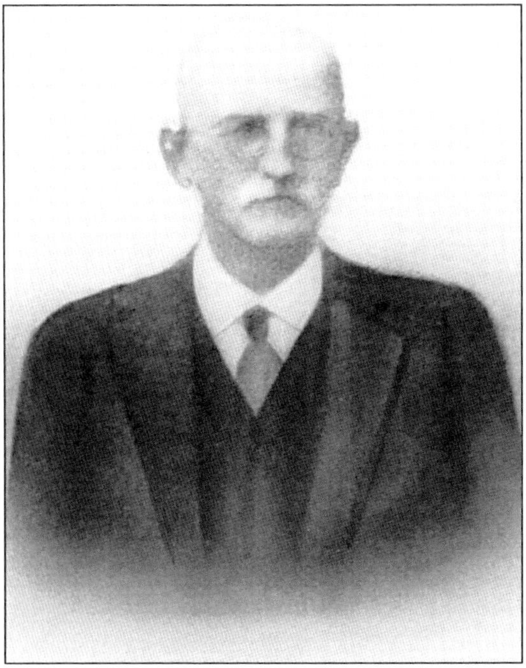

William R. Roller, the president of First National Bank of Kingsport, was the first head of that institution.

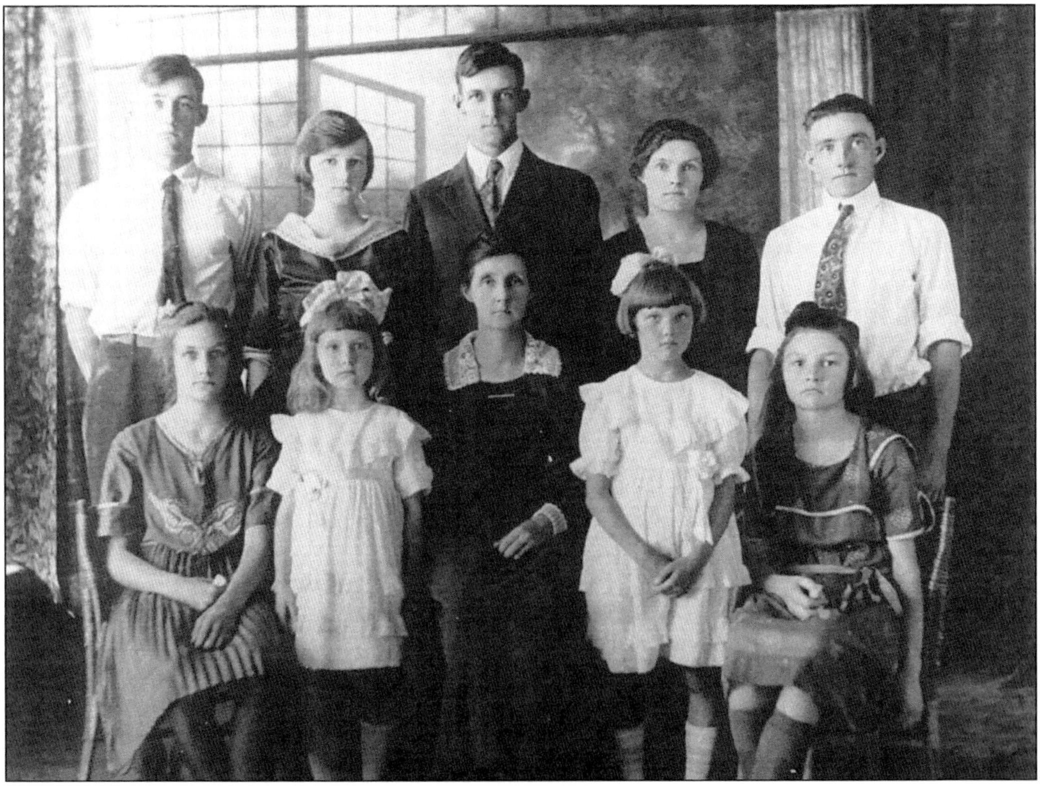

A gathering of the Blankenbecler family in 1922 shows the tenth Kingsport mayor, E.B. "Jitney" Blankenbecler (top row, left end). Blankenbecler served as mayor from July 1949 to July 1951.

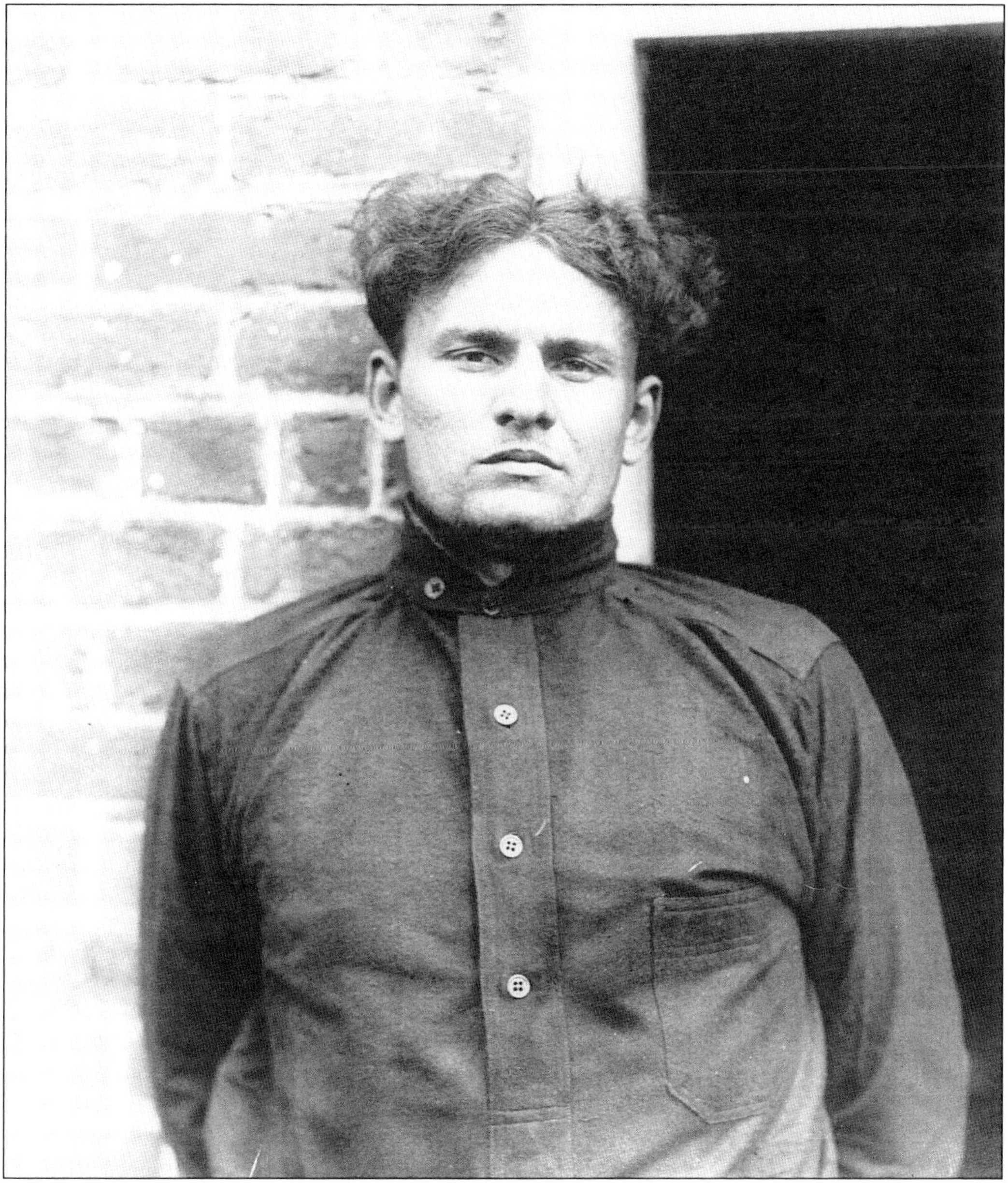

Legend mixed with fact surrounds the story of local desperado Kinnie Wagner, whose exploits were well known in east Tennessee and southwest Virginia. Born near Kingsport in Scott County, VA, Wagner joined the circus, where he learned to be an expert shot. His arrest for petty larceny in Mississippi in 1924 led to a series of escapes and murders which have become local legend. After his escape from a Meridian jail, Wagner fled to Kingsport, where a disturbance led to his killing a deputy and a policemen near the banks of the Holston River. His arrest the next day resulted in a Blountville trial, sentencing him to death by electrocution. While awaiting appeal of this death sentence, however, Wagner escaped from jail. Regarded as Mississippi's most-wanted killer and most-famous escape artist, Wagner had a criminal career totaling six escapes and five murders between 1924 and 1948. Captured the last time in 1956, Wagner died of a heart attack in a Mississippi penitentiary and is buried in Scott County, VA.

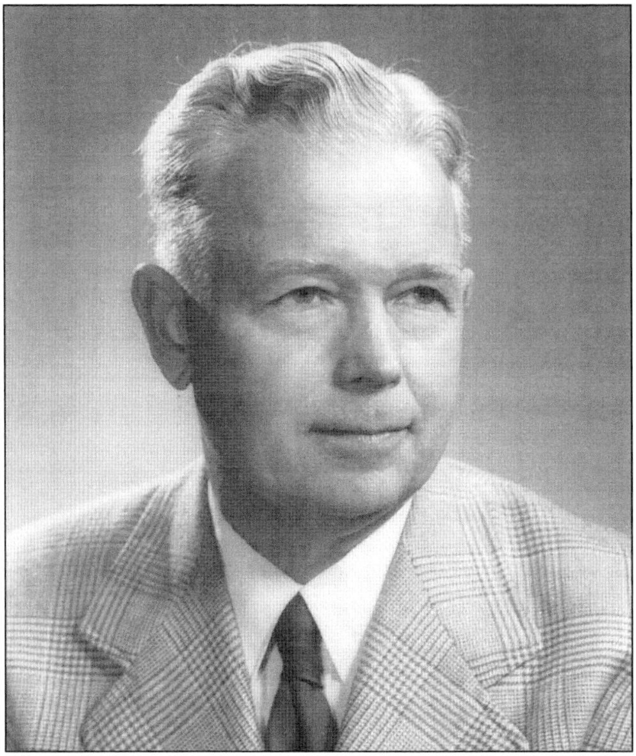

After locating in Kingsport as a manager of Holliston Mills in 1926, native Bostonian Max Y. Parker is remembered as a pioneer civic and business leader. Beginning his textile industry career in Lawrence, MA, with Pacific Mills, Parker next moved to Ramapo Finishing Company in New York before assuming the head post with the Holliston Mills organization. A navy lieutenant in the First World War, he was active in Kingsport government from 1957 to 1961 as an elected member of the board of mayor and aldermen.

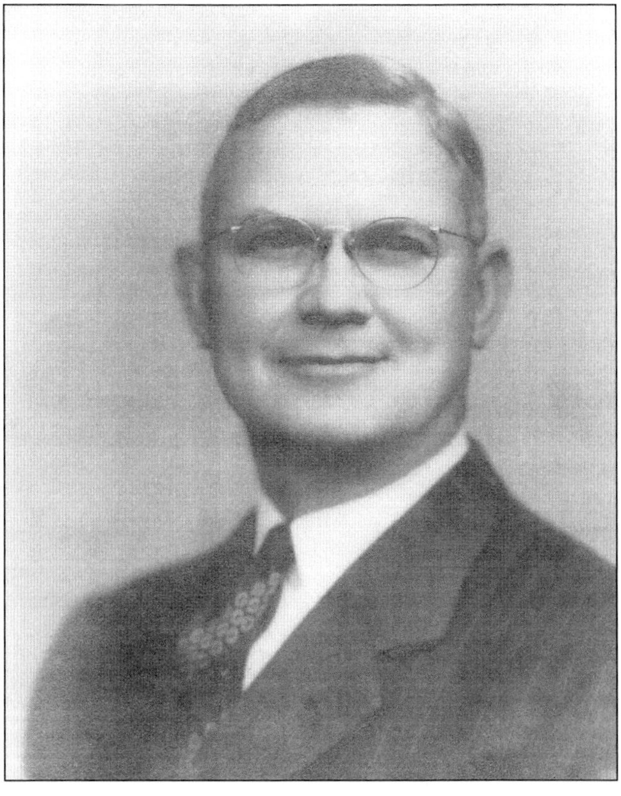

Recognized as a highly respected member of the first generation of Tennessee Eastman Company management, John S. McLellan Sr. came to Kingsport from his native Boston with the E.M. Badger Company, a construction firm contracting with TEC. Officially joining TEC in 1922, McLellan served as the production superintendent of all manufacturing operations and the general superintendent of the S&M division as well as the Koda and Teca Divisions. He completed a 44-year career with TEC as the assistant works manager and the first vice-president of Bays Mountain Construction.

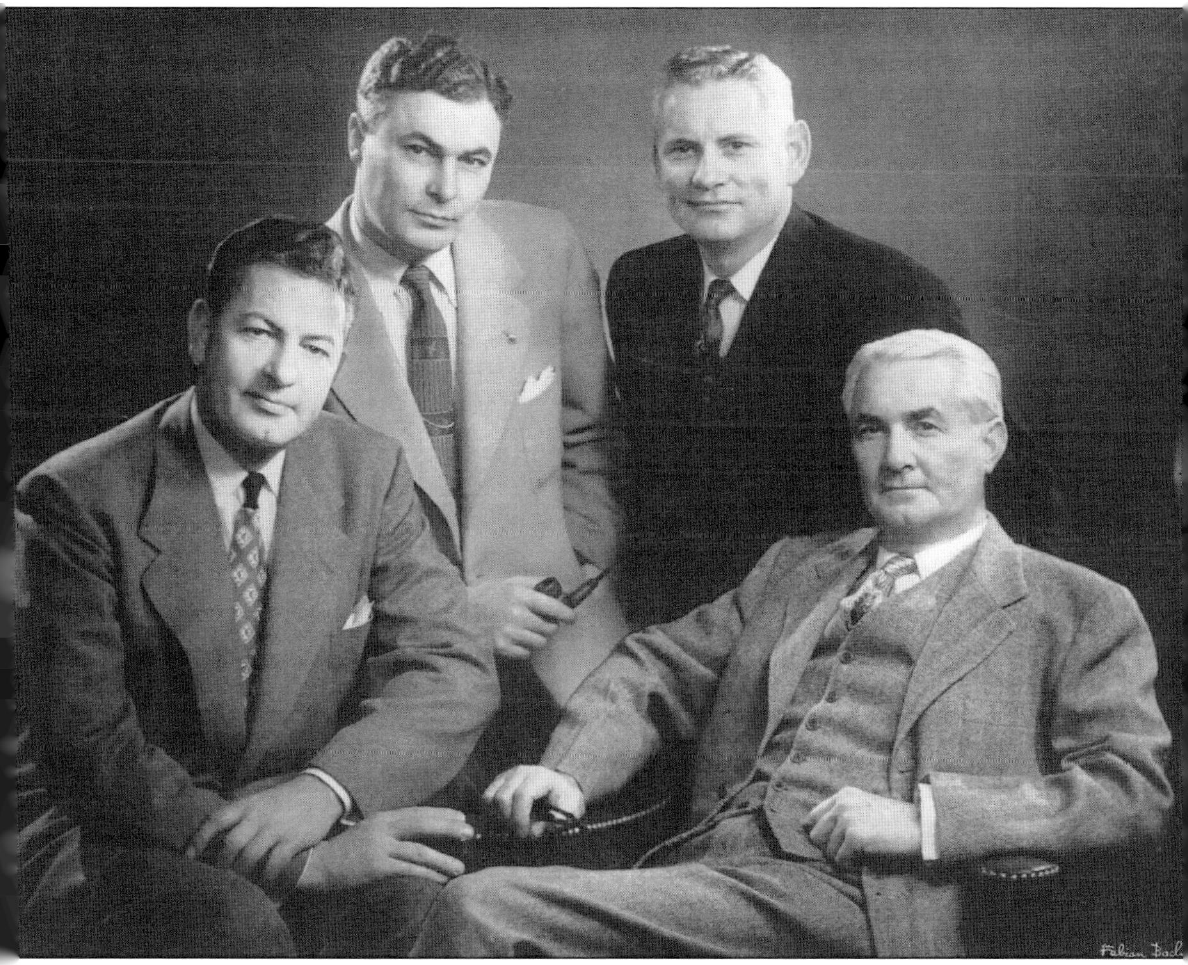

Key players in the Kingsport story for three generations, the influential Edwards family became established in Kingsport prior to World War I. Physician C.P. Edwards Sr. moved to the model city from Flag Pond, TN, and by 1919, in conjunction with Dr. E.W. Tipton, purchased Kingsport Community Hospital. The legacy of the Edwards family continues in the areas of banking, insurance, and real estate development. C.P. Edwards Jr. served as chairman of the board of the Bennett and Edwards Insurance Agency. Earle Draper planned Ridgefields subdivision on the Edwards's 2,000-acre tract of land, originally owned by the Roller family. For many years, Edwards owned the Kingsport Publishing Company. From left to right are James Edwards, L.L. Edwards, Val Edwards, and C.P. Edwards Jr.

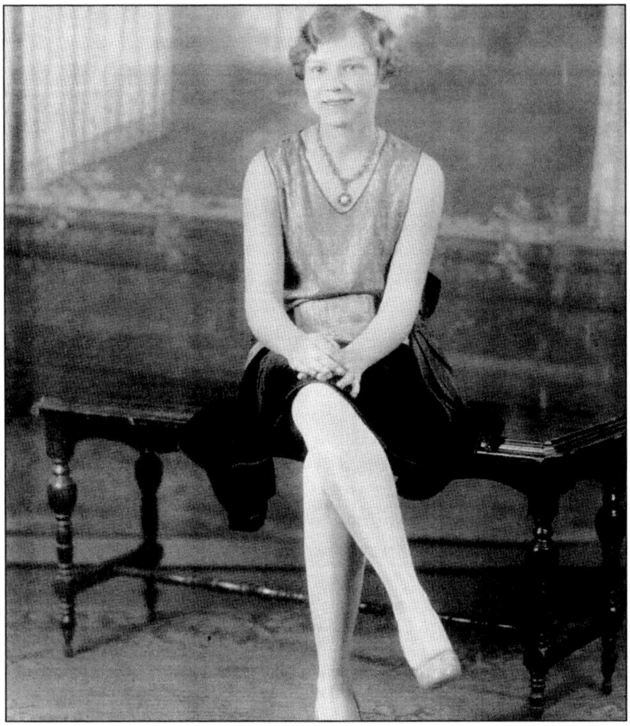

Large crowds were reported in attendance as the first Miss Kingsport was chosen in 1929 during a contest held at the Rialto Theatre. Miss Anna Lou Crumley was the winner of the competition sponsored by the Rialto and the Kingsport *Times-News*.

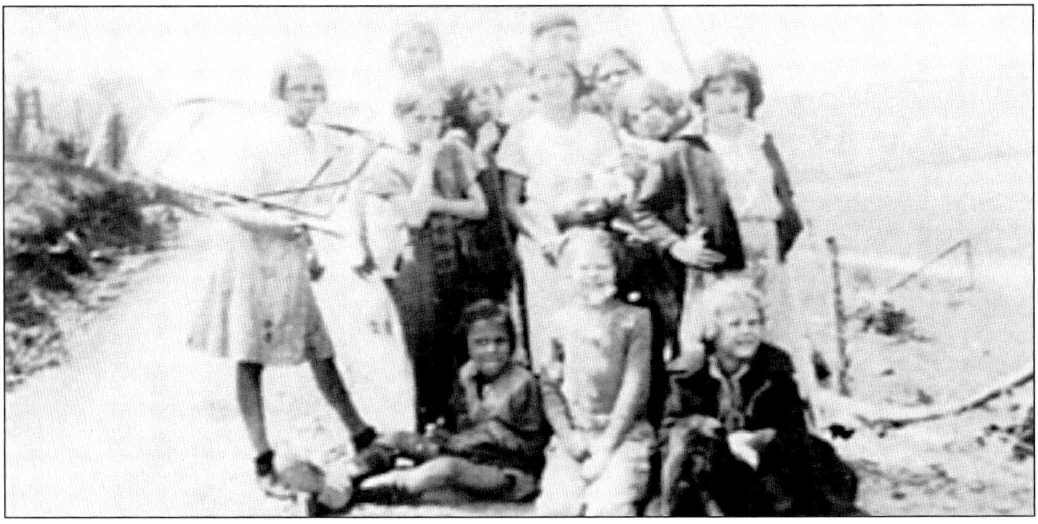

In the early years of modern Kingsport, the first troop of Girl Scouts was organized. This photograph recorded a two-day outing at Cloud's Ford. Twenty girls, ages 10 to 15, were involved in the trip, which was under the direction of troop captain Miss Rowena Watkins. The girls were taken to camp in five chartered cars. Those attending included Mattie Todd, Anna May Good, Peggy Campbell, Sarah Jane Hyatt, Ruth Huffaker, Virginia Hardin, Reba Sproles, Ruth Morehouse, Eleanor Jane Cusick, Evangeline and Pauline Showalter, Audrey Taylor, Ernestine Pyle, Roma Bedford, Mary Anne Smith, Margaret Qualls, Mary Ellen Bradley, Fay Smallwood, and Mildred Lady. Guests included sixth-grade teacher Clara Sawyer and students Sarah Huffaker, Nan Kagey, Sherry McLellan, Marjorie Taylor, Geneva Sproles, and Ruth Ann Hyatt.

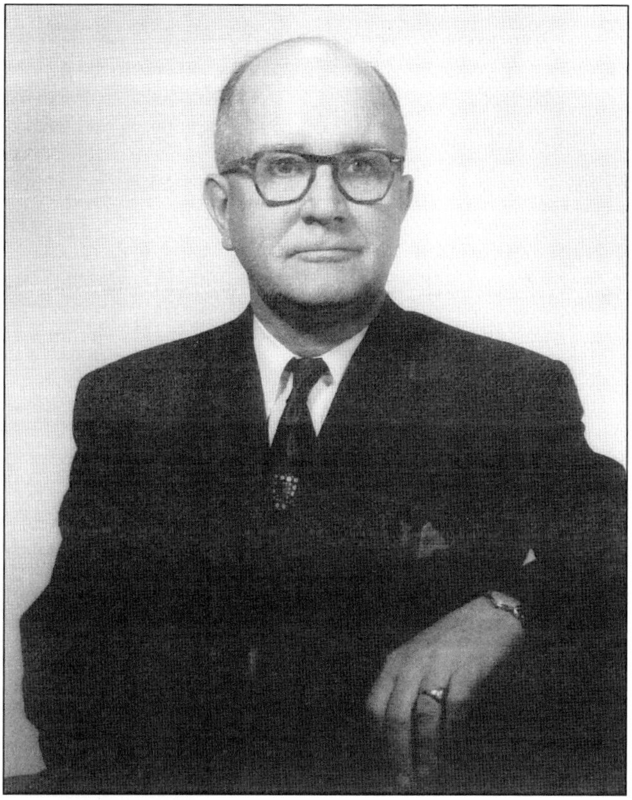

Glen Bruce began his Kingsport business career as the secretary-treasurer of the Kingsport Brick Company and then became the vice-president of the Kingsport Improvement Corporation. Serving General Shale as secretary-treasurer and as the firm's third president, Bruce was active in civic and governmental affairs. During the Depression years, from 1931 to 1938, he was a member of the board of mayor and aldermen and became the seventh mayor of Kingsport (1940–1944) during an era of rapid change and growth.

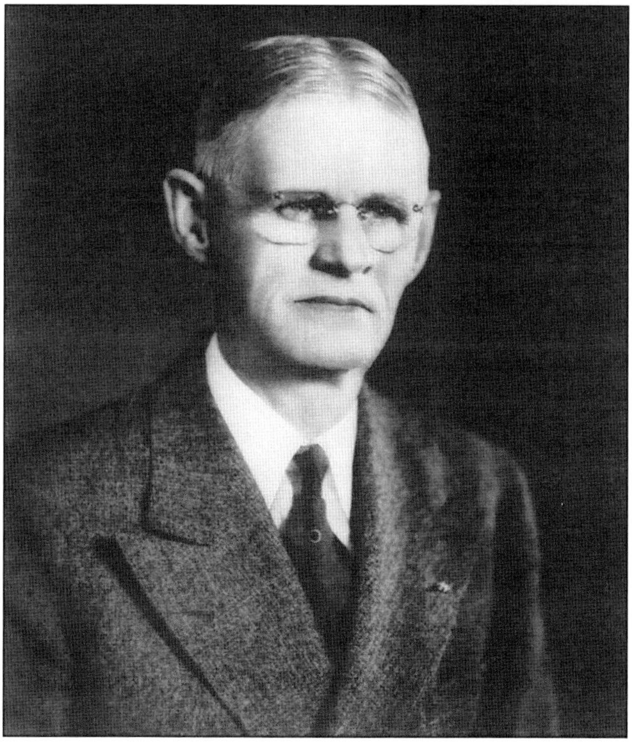

William Holyoke, a Plant engineer at Borden Mills, served on the board of mayor and aldermen beginning in 1931 and was the mayor from 1934 to 1939. During the Great Depression, President Franklin D. Roosevelt created programs to relieve the personal distress of millions of Americans. One such program was the Federal Emergency Relief Administration, which authorized an appropriation of $500 million in direct grants to cities and states. On October 17, 1934, the city manager of Kingsport was instructed to apply for $12,500 in assistance.

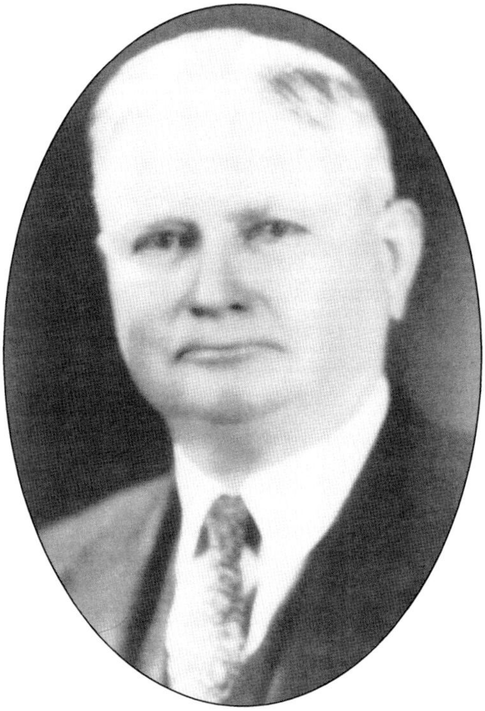

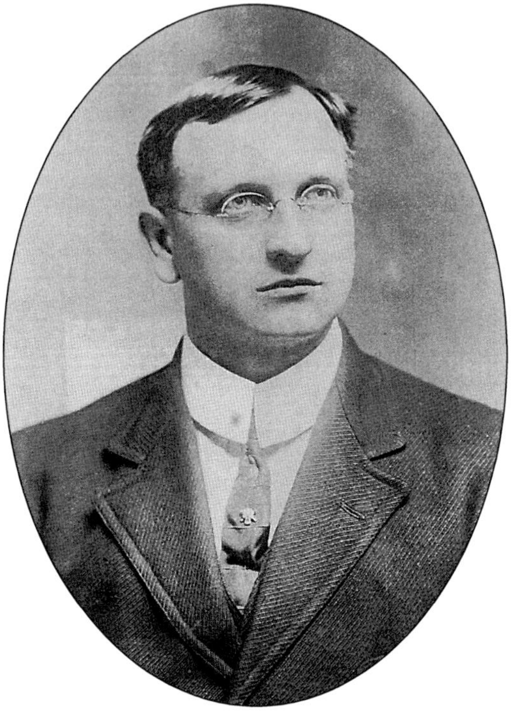

Dr. Enoch W. Tipton (left) served as the mayor of Kingsport from 1939 to 1941. Along with Dr. W.H. Reed (right), Tipton and other Kingsport physicians, including T.B. Yancey, Lemuel Cox, J.H. Clifford, George G. Keener, Paul Marsh, Thomas McNeer Sr., and Thomas Gannaway Sr., played a prominent role in Kingsport's civic and political affairs from the town's genesis through the World War II era. Illustrative of Progressivism in both spirit and practice, the lives of the first generation of Kingsport physicians exemplified the professionalization of medicine and the growing social authority of the medical community. Prior to the establishment of Holston Valley Community Hospital (1933), private facilities such as Riverview Hospital and March Clinic served citizens of Kingsport. Riverview Hospital faced the Holston River on Netherland Inn Road. Marsh Clinic was located on Holston Street near Church Circle.

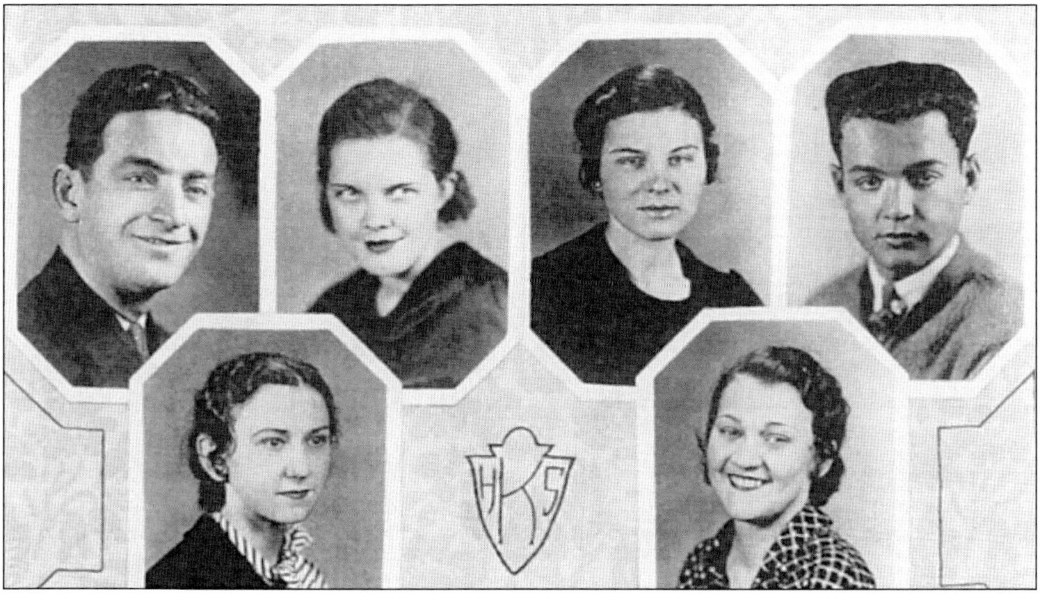

James H. Quillen, the First District congressman for over three decades, graduated from Dobyns-Bennett High School in 1934. After graduation, Quillen worked at the Kingsport Press, Inc. and the Kingsport *Times-News* before beginning his own newspaper, the *Kingsport Mirror*. As a student at Dobyns-Bennett, Quillen participated in the national Forensic League, Debate, and Glee Clubs, and worked as a school reporter. He is pictured in the top row, fourth from left in the 1934 *Maroon and Grey* annual.

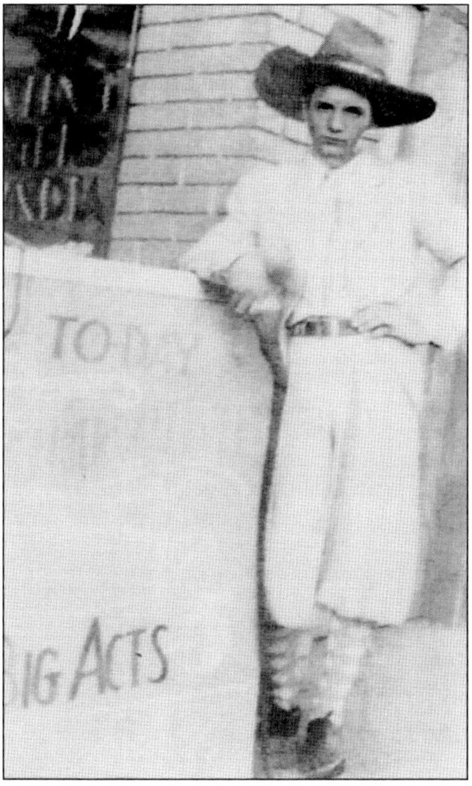

In the early 1930s, James H. Quillen worked as an usher at Kingsport's Gem Theatre, located on Main Street.

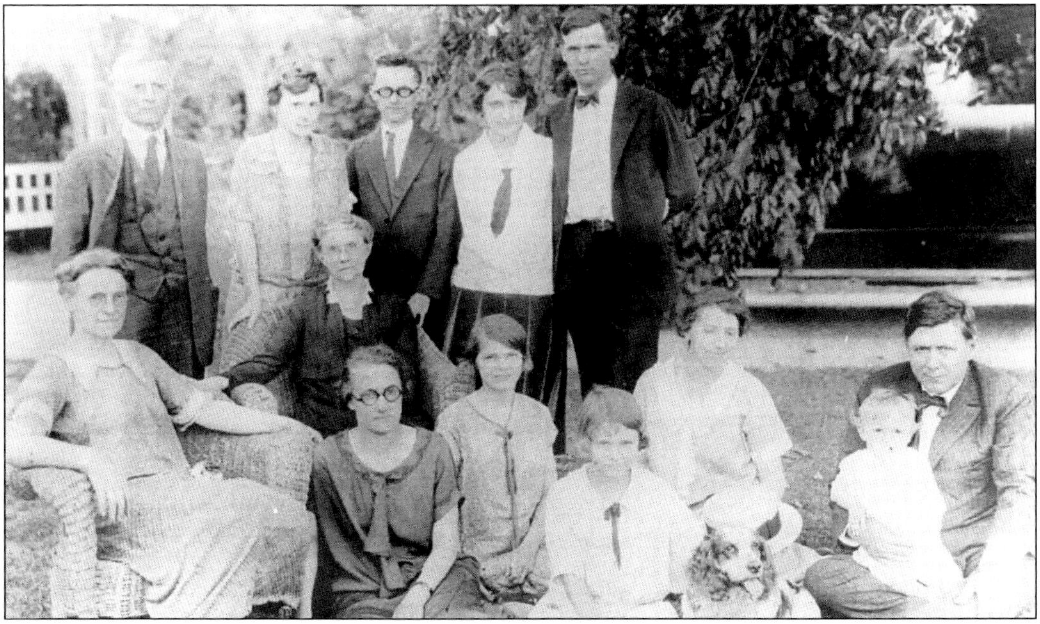

The J. Fred Johnson and Arthur Doggett families came together for this group portrait in 1924. From left to right, they are as follows: (on ground) Eleanor Doggett, sister of Arthur Doggett and Elizabeth D. Johnson; Mary Early Hart Shumate, niece of J. Fred Johnson; Grace Hart King, holding J. Fred Johnson's cocker spaniel; Bobby, niece of J. Fred Johnson; Ruth Carter Johnson, wife of J. Fred Johnson and sister of George L. Carter; and J. Fred Johnson, holding Ruth Doggett Todd (daughter of Arthur Doggett and niece of Elizabeth D. Johnson); (front row, seated in chair) Berta Carter Doggett, wife of M.W. Doggett and sister of Ruth Carter Johnson; (middle row, seated in chair) Mary Pierce Early Johnson, mother of J. Fred Johnson; (back row) Dr. Marshall W. Doggett, a Presbyterian minister; Estelle Reid Doggett, wife of Arthur Doggett; Arthur Jackson Doggett; Elizabeth Doggett Johnson, sister of Arthur Doggett and second wife of J. Fred Johnson; and Marshall W. Doggett Jr.

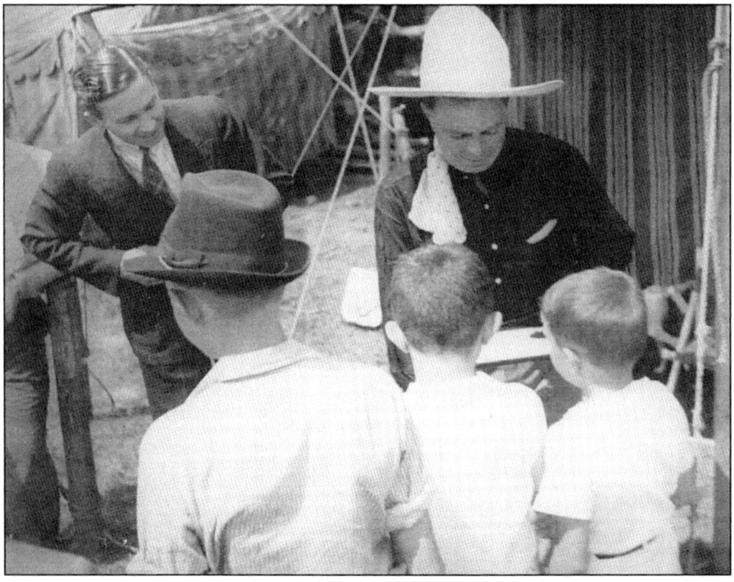

Signing autographs for admiring fans, cowboy movie star Hoot Gibson was a featured attraction when the circus came to Kingsport in 1936.

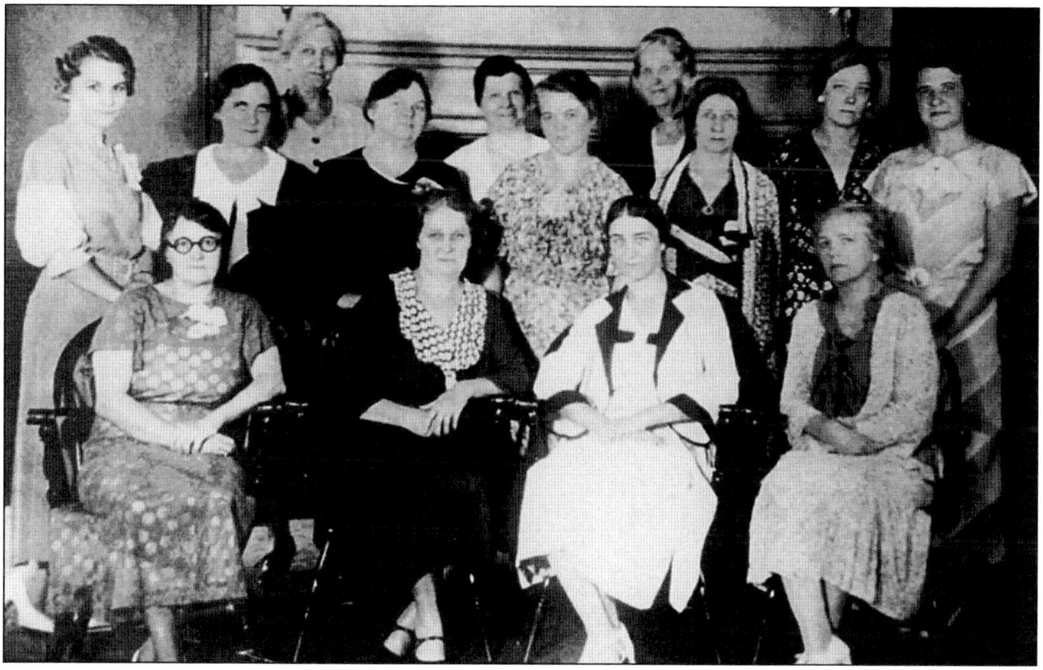

This photograph, from the late 1930s, features members of the Virginia Club, a group of Kingsport residents whose Virginia birthplace made them eligible for membership in this civic and social group. They are, from left to right, as follows: (seated) Mmes. Walker Nelms, William Highsmith, Robert L. Peters, and George Penn; (standing) Mmes. B.K. Bright, Glen Bruce, Guy Hillenberg, George Wilkerson, Wallace Hufford, Will Jennings, J.W. Dobyns, G.D. Black, W.H. Reed, and Sam Anderson.

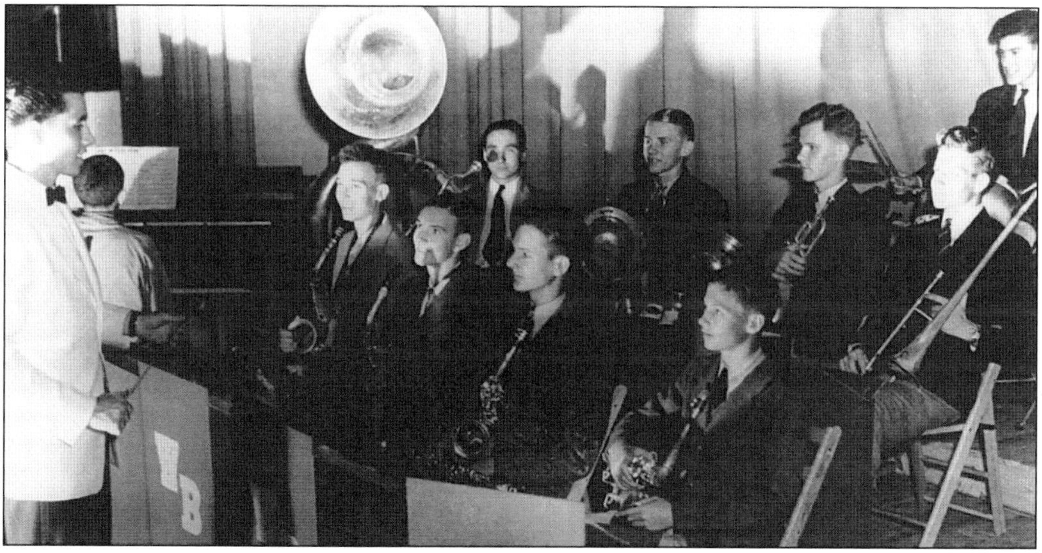

Director Warren Brown leads a 1941 dance band comprised of Kingsport musicians. The musicians are as follows: (first row) Charles Church (piano), Winston Pannell, Kenneth Hultin, Kenneth Cox, and Barney Pendleton (saxophone); (second row) Vernon Fueston (bass), Tom Shipley and John I. Cox Jr. (trumpets), and W.L. Cavin (trombone); (third row) J.C. McDavid (drums).

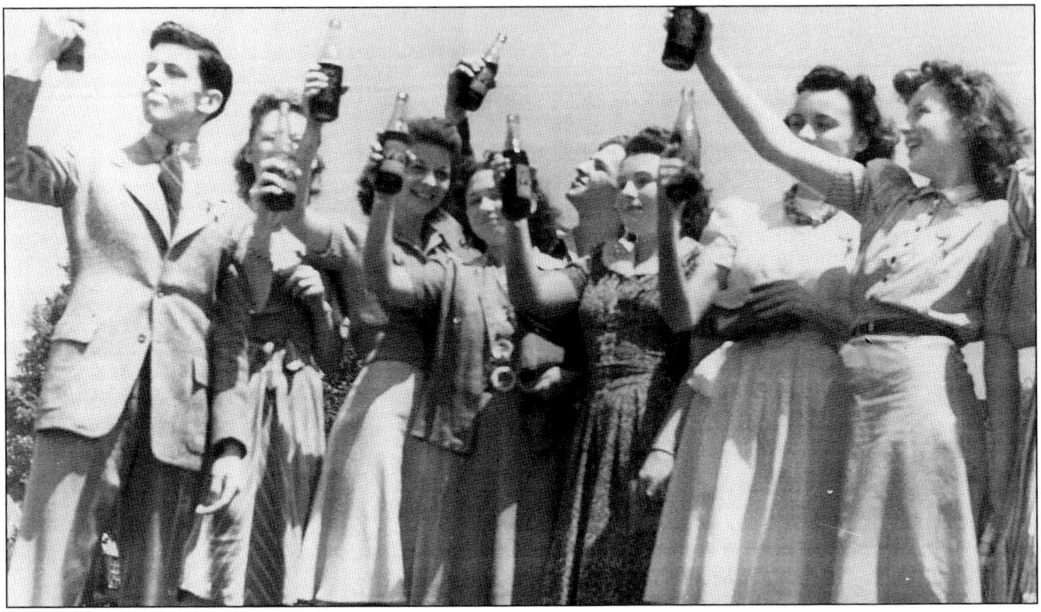

Kingsport teens were featured in this 1941 "Dough Boy" soft drink advertisement. From left to right, they are Mark Hargrave, Ann Showalter, Elizabeth Shuey, Louise Terry, Rudolph Kiss, Virginia Cannoy, Cora Evelyn Bell, Estelle Penn, and Lillian Von Bramer.

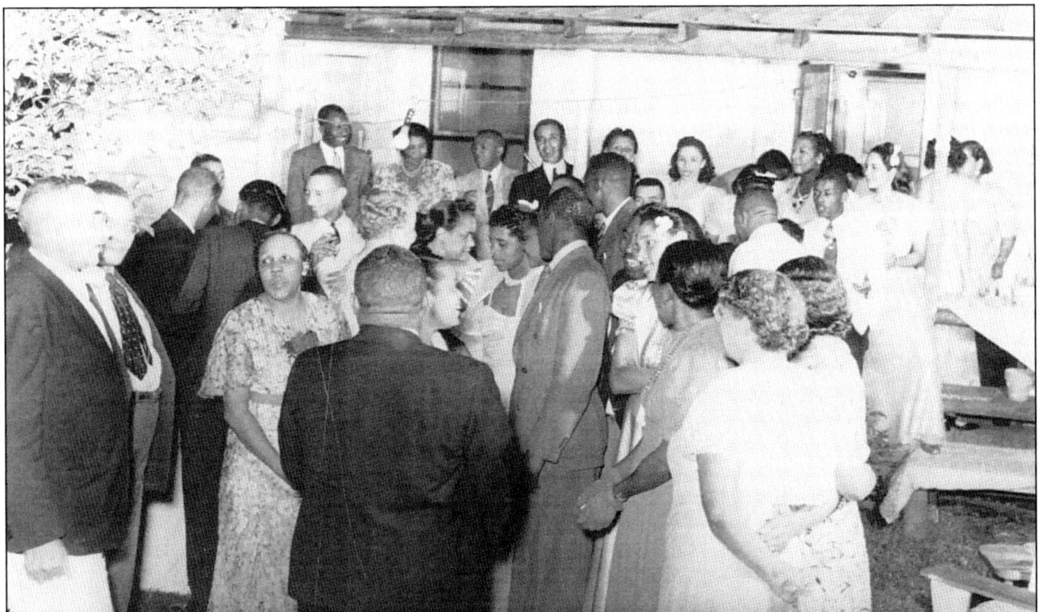

The guest list of Elsa and John Turner's 1940 Garden Party included, from left to right, the following: (next to the house, in back row) Dr. Roland Faust, Elsa Turner (hostess), unidentified, Reverend Thomas Hendricks, unidentified, Minerva Taylor, Gladys Byrd, and Hazel Lindsay. Among the party-goers are Nathan Byrd, Paul Taylor, Harvey T. Stacy, Ada B. Stinson, Brun Long, Annie Lawson, Joseph Stinson, Gertrude Smith, Sudie Patton, Cora Cox, John Turner (the host, with his back to the camera), Reverend Nelson Smith, and Reverend Hamilton (on the left front side).

In World War II, Sullivan County and Kingsport sent 4,930 sons and daughters into military service. Nationwide, 891,000 members of the African-American combat units included the 92nd and 93rd divisions and a group of air force pilots. Pictured here are Douglass High School students who served their nation. Among those are, from left to right, as follows: (first row) Bill White, Wilbur Hendricks, Kelsie Davis, Eugene Davis, and Junior Davis; (second row) Richard Watterson, Philip Cartwright, unidentified, June Thompson, and Thomas Cartwright; (third row) Jack Walton, James Phipps, and Leroy Bradley; (fourth row) Buddy Cain, William "Bud" Hickman, unidentified, Earnest Ligon, Jack Pierce, and unidentified; (fifth row) Billy Hipps, Clevcland Rutledge, ? Griffin, and Buddy Lee.

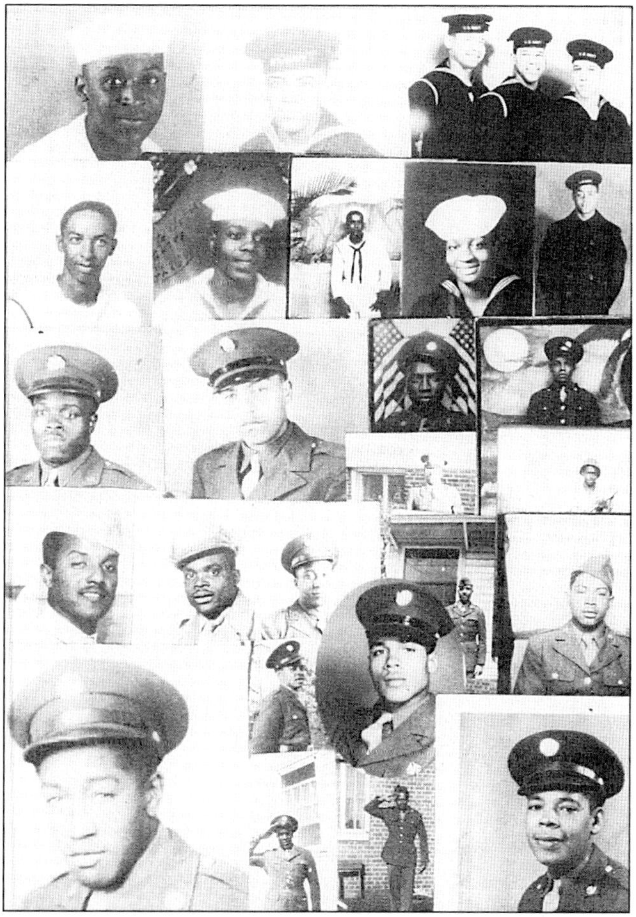

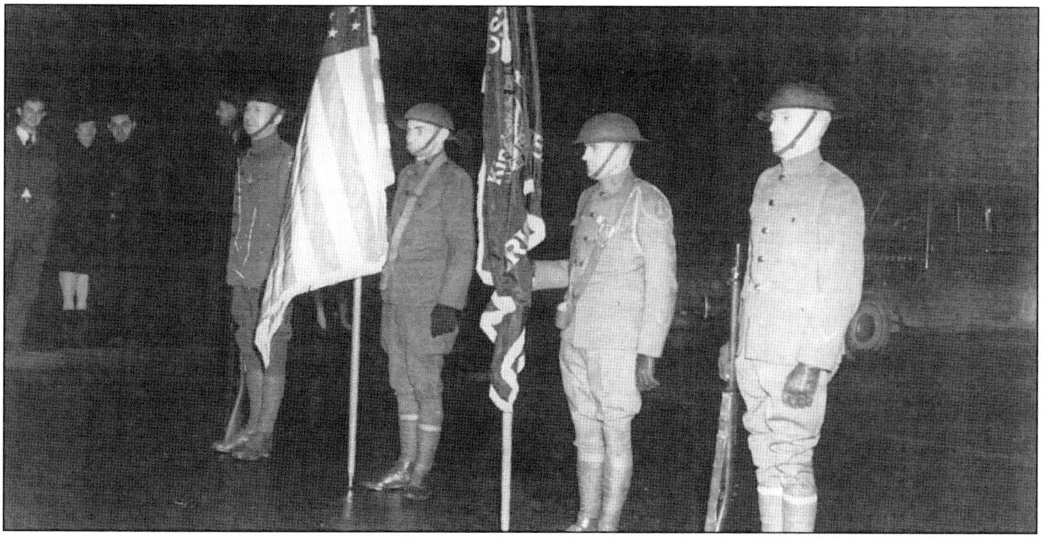

Kingsport's American Legion was formed in the 1920s and continues today as an active community organization. In this photograph, the American Legion Color Guard honors Kingsport's World War II draftees.

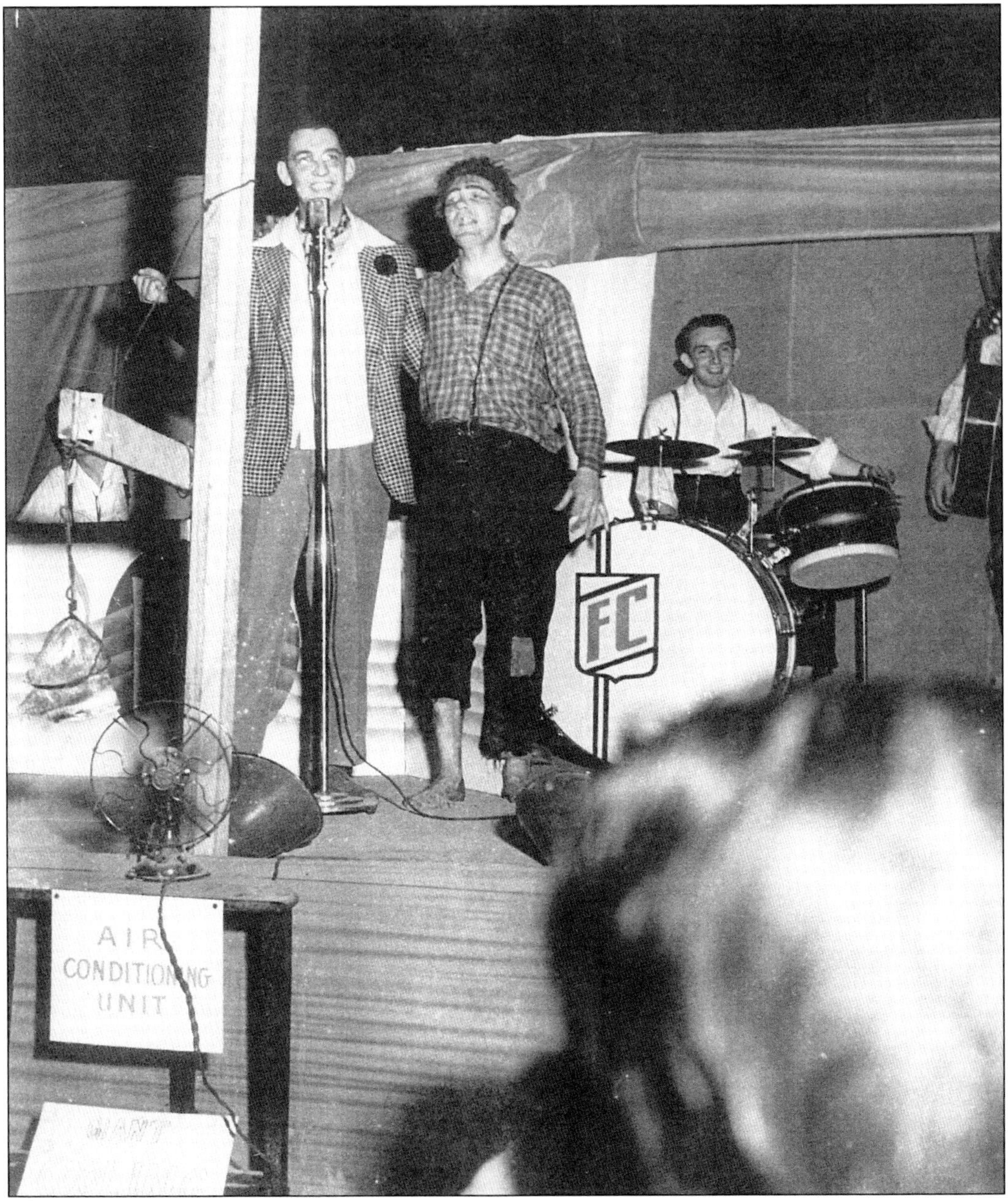

Beloved entertainers for over four decades, Frank Taylor and Mack Riddle thrilled Kingsport audiences with their comedy routines. Performed at the American Legion Fourth of July carnival, the "Frank and Mack Show" became the big-tent attraction, drawing a large and dedicated audience from across the region. Participation in Kiwanis Kapers, a fund-raising effort for local projects, resulted in the civic club honoring Frank and Mack for their performances on behalf of those in need.

Six

People at Work

The distinctive pattern of industrialization in Kingsport attracted an energetic generation of workers who, in combination with business and professional elements, pursued common goals based upon a middle-class attitude toward life and economic opportunity. Some of the people who migrated to Kingsport had previous experience in industrial work, while numerous others were directly transposed from an agrarian way of life. Many chose factory work, yet were successful at maintaining a tie to the land. Factory labor in a rapidly developing world changed lives forever. These new Kingsport residents demonstrated that ordinary life has extraordinary significance.

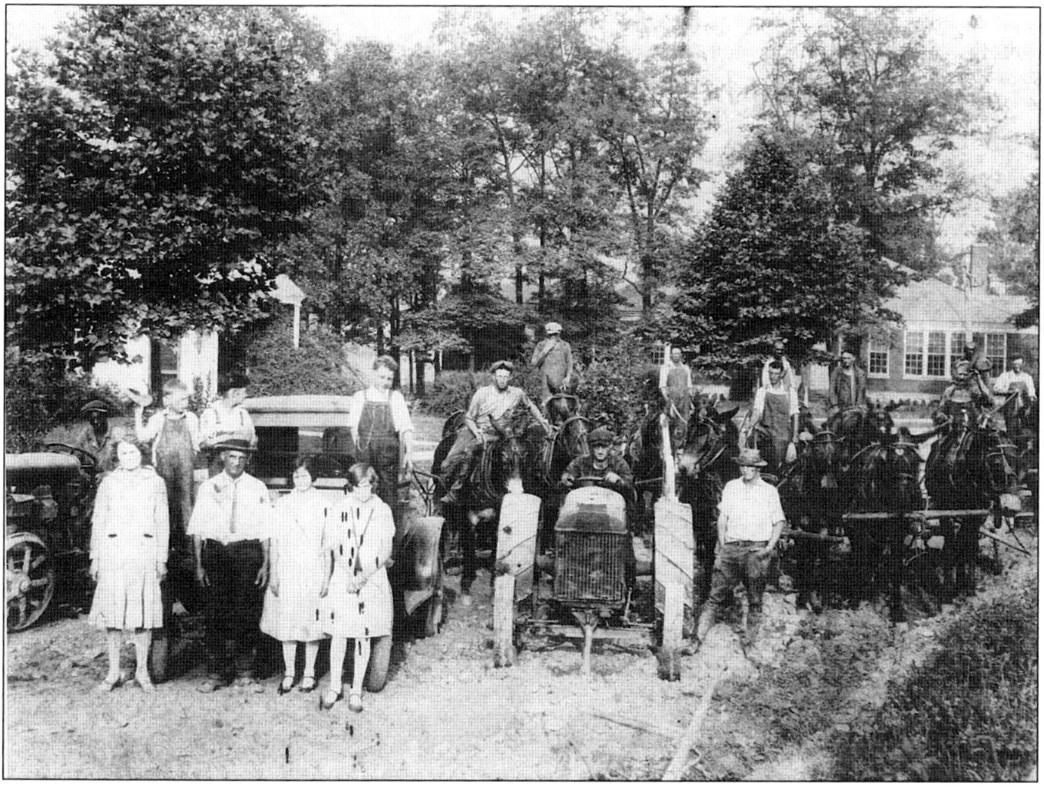

A city of Kingsport workcrew is pictured in this 1927 scene on Wateree Street. The Robert E. Lee School is visible in the background.

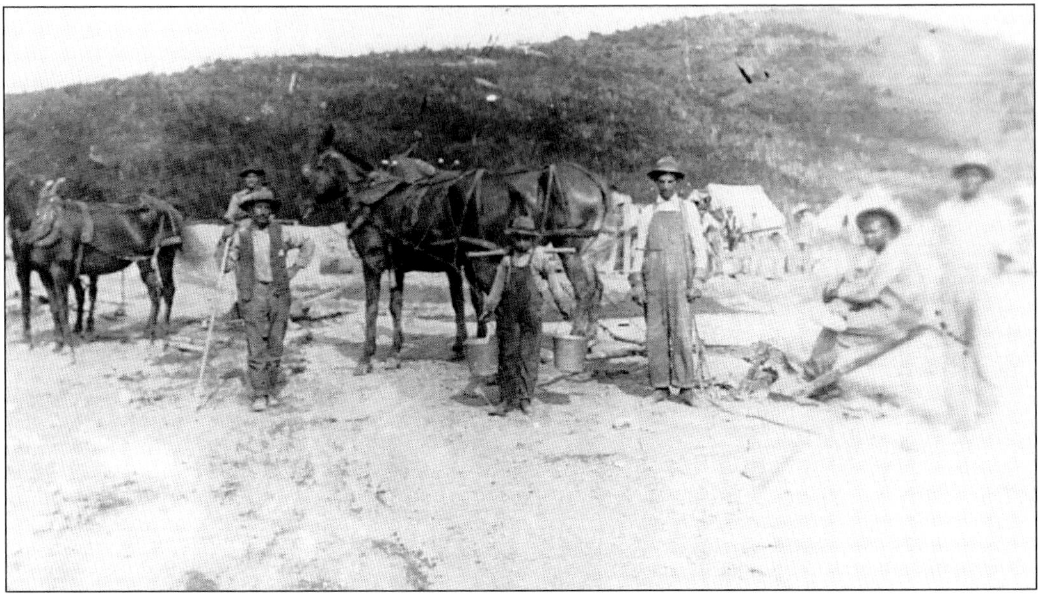

Ground was broken for the construction of Kingsport Portland Cement Company in 1910. Beginning the manufacture of cement in 1911, the Kingsport plant, which came to be known as the Pennsylvania Dixie Corporation, ranked at one time as one of the largest cement plants in the country.

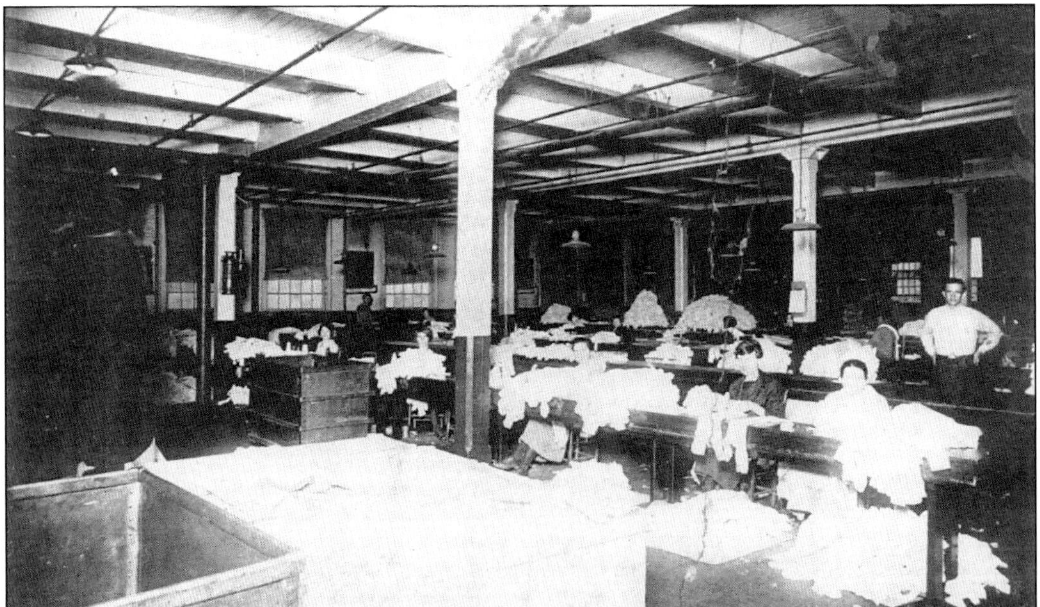

Labor-intensive industries producing durable goods and using primarily a female workforce were located throughout the region and the South during the 1910s and 1920s. Beginning soon after the incorporation of Kingsport in 1917, Kingsport Hosiery Mills, Inc., located on Reedy Street, began with 85 employees and produced 300 dozen pairs of finished hose daily. Ten years later, the plant employed 417 workers, of whom 296 were women, and 2,200 dozen pairs of finished hose were manufactured daily.

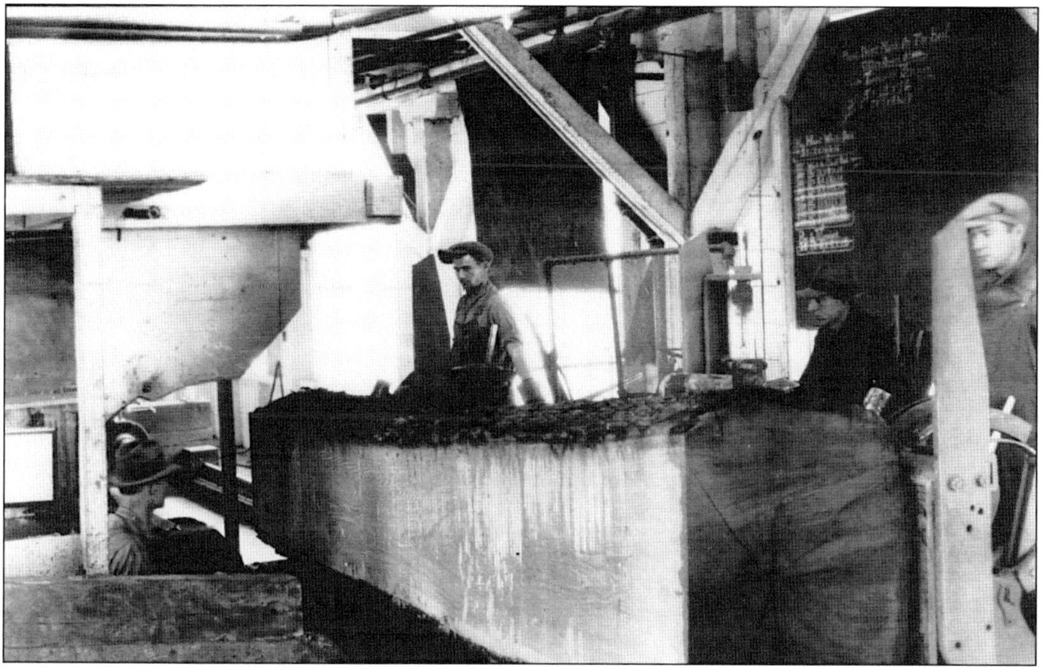

In the 1920s, a large band sawmill at Tennessee Eastman was central to the operations of the subsidiary, which depended on the harvesting of area hardwood forests. Skilled sawyers and block setters were recruited from within the region and elsewhere. Operational in 1927, by the following year the sawmill was producing 35,000 board feet per ten-hour day. Kodak at Rochester received a certain amount of the lumber to be used in the manufacture of film. Foreign and domestic markets purchased the lumber not utilized by the parent plant. Among the men pictured in this 1927 TEC photograph is Auburn Kennedy Egan (second from right).

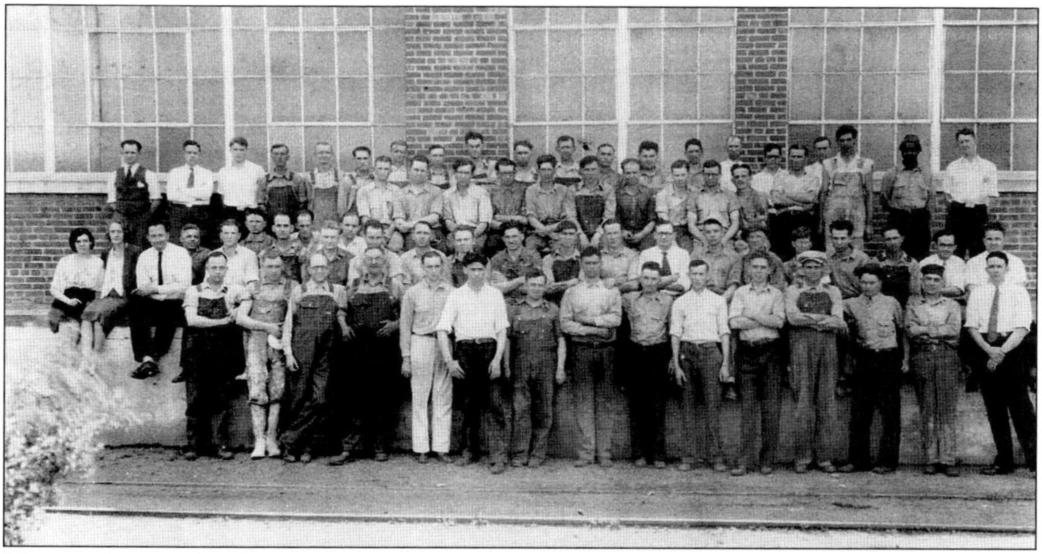

The employees of Holliston Mills pose for an official company portrait in the early 1930s. In the late 1930s, the company was one of the three largest producers of book-cloth in America. Employees were involved primarily in two processes: the first function involved the bleaching of the cloth; the second duty was the finishing, or dyeing, process.

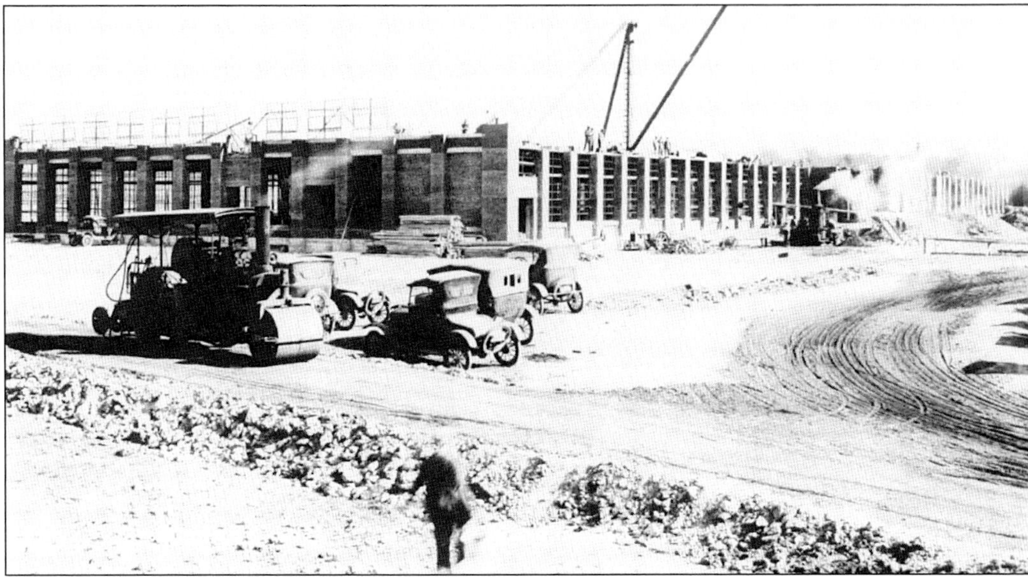

On August 16, 1924, the construction of the Borden Mills plant began. The company routinely created a photographic record of its construction. Tennessee Governor Austin Peay attended the ceremony when the cornerstone for the main building was laid on October 11, 1924.

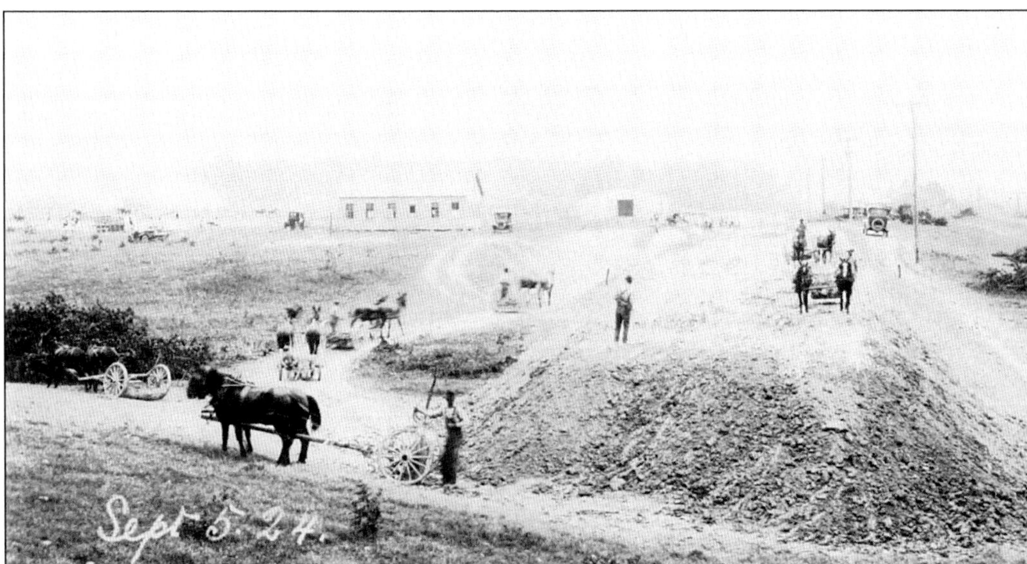

The New South crusade for industrial development often took the form of Northern textile firms locating subsidiary plants in the Appalachian South of northeast Tennessee and the Piedmont region of North Carolina. Borden Mills, Inc. was a subsidiary of the American Printing Company of Fall River, MA.

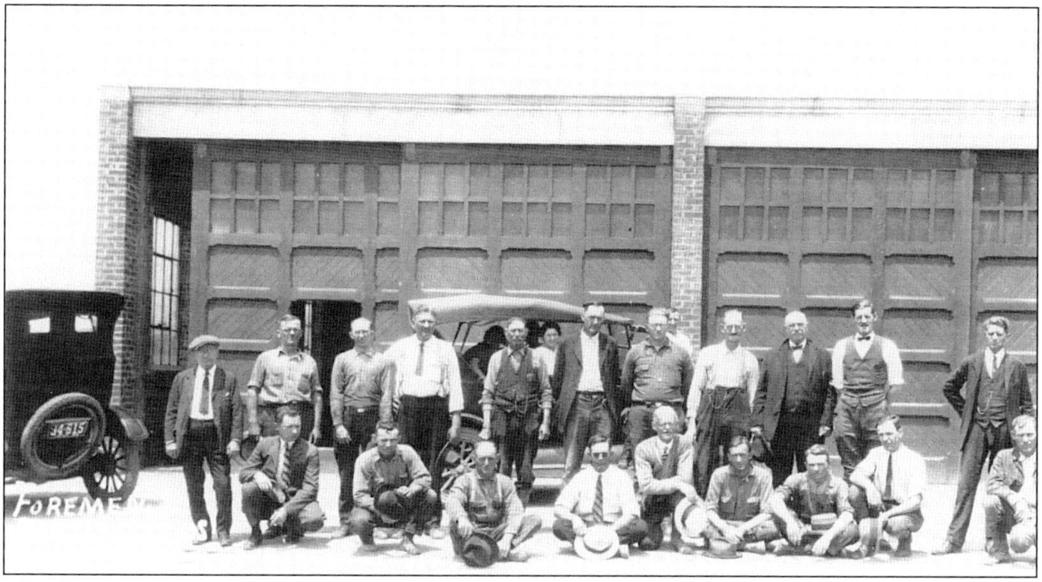

The foremen of Borden Mills gather for a portrait during the first year of operation. By the late 1920s, the textile firm employed 758 men and 469 women. One of the few Kingsport industries that operated company housing, Borden Mills began a residential village of 277 single houses for employees.

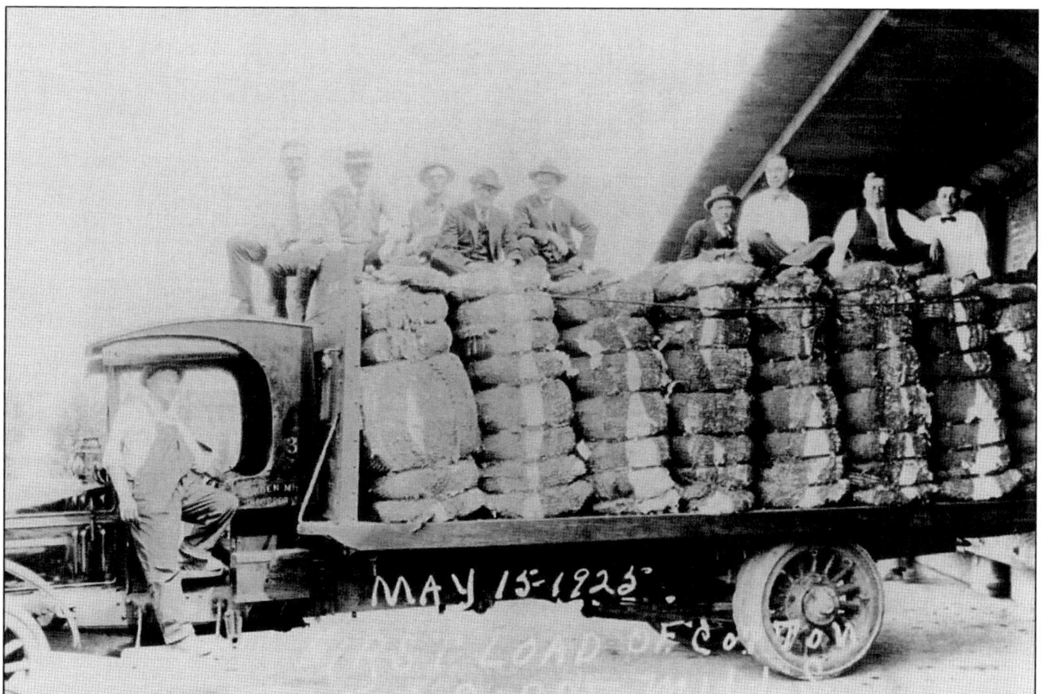

The first truckload of cotton was shipped to Borden Mills on May 15, 1925.

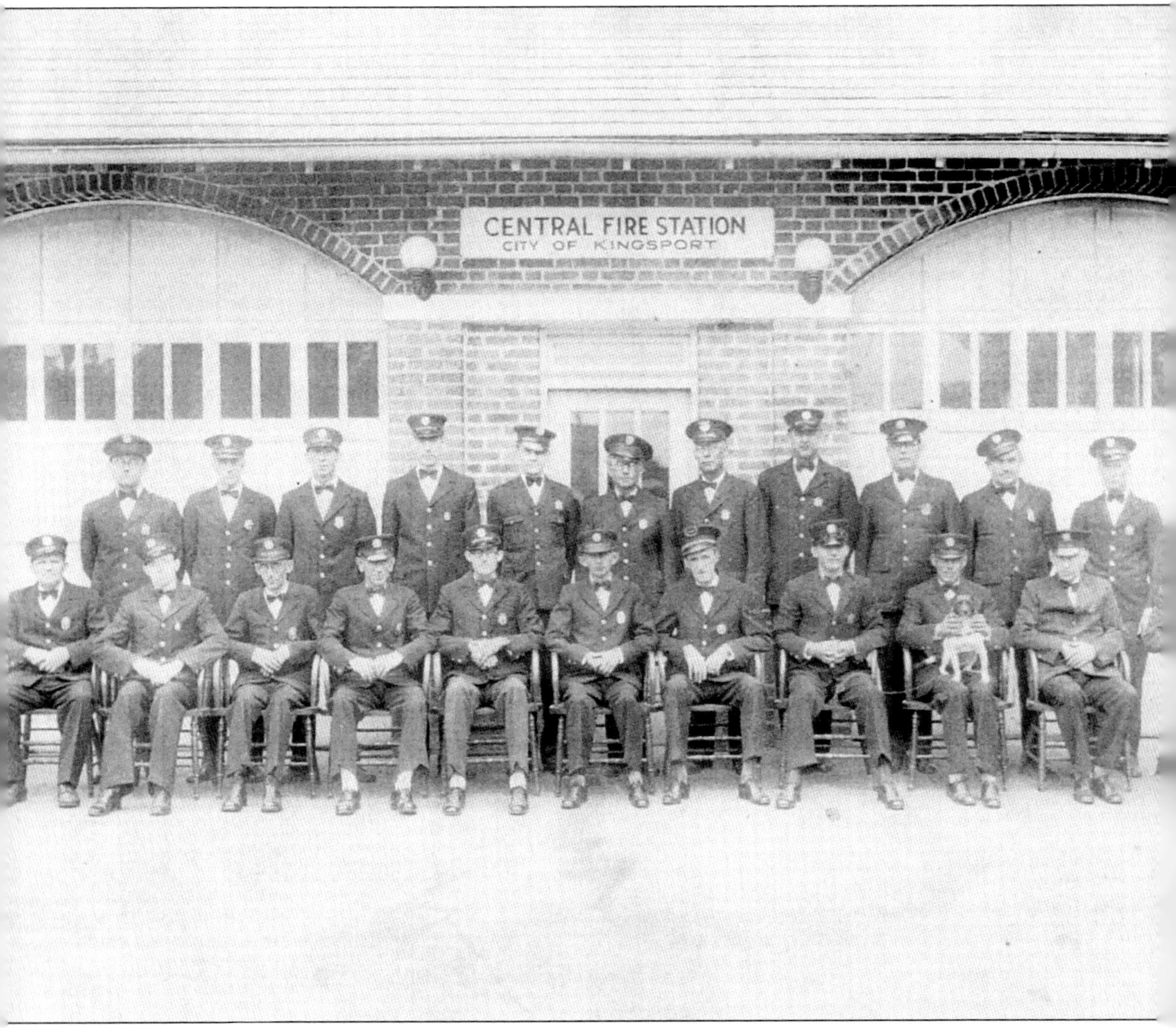

The fire department was established by the 1917 Kingsport Charter. Pictured in this 1931 photograph are, from left to right, as follows: (sitting) Worley J. Butler, Ivan King, H.O. "Tad" Pyle, Walter H. Brown, Mack M. Jones, J. Roy Pyle, Tom C. Warrick, C.H. "Jack" Bostic, Ray V. Barger, Gus Caton, and "WG"; (standing) E.B. "Jitney" Blankenbecler, Joseph R. Pectol, Lark M. Minton, Luther E. Salyer, Elton Herrin, J.M. Reams, J.D. McCrary, Hershel B. Johnson, M.H. Hensley, C.M. McCormick, and Parker S. Grills.

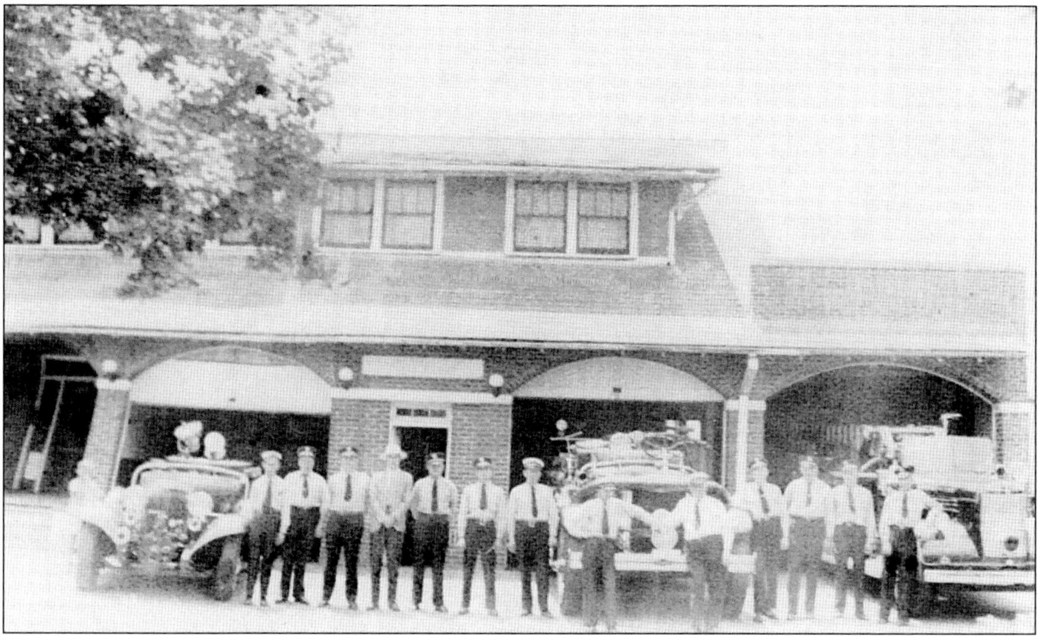

Fire Station Number One was located on Watauga Street as shown in this picture during the 1940s.

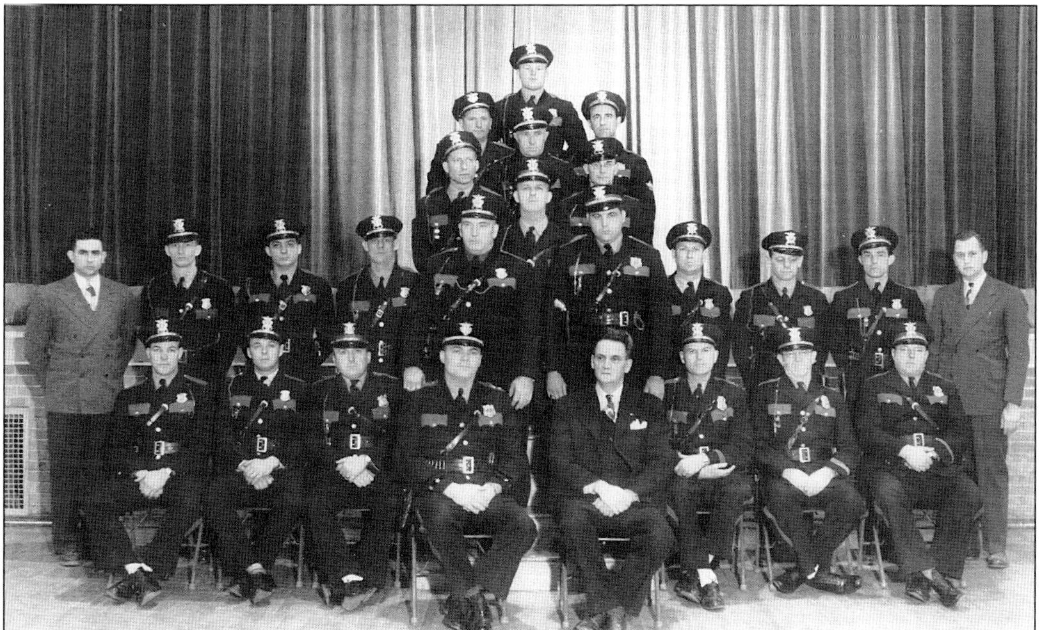

The 1950 Kingsport Police force included, from left to right, the following: (front row) Harold Fleming, Paul Fleming, Bill Taylor, Chief Charles Still, D.W. Moulton, Bill Fletcher, Tyler Anderson, and John Martin; (second row) William Burchfield, Cecil Ammons, George Rogers, Bill Rucker, C.H. McInturff, Clarence Rogers Jr., Hal Crumley, Robert Jobe, Everette Dykes, and Cecil Durham; (third row) Paul Porter, Max Lee, and Jim Broyles; (fourth row) B.F. Cutshaw, Ira Burgess, and Sam Davis; (back row) J. Fred Hall.

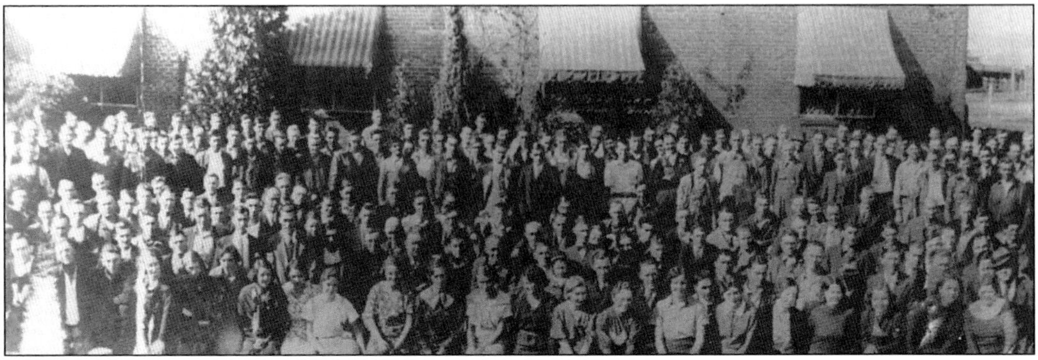

This 1933 gathering of Mead Corporation employees was taken at the company on Center Street in downtown Kingsport. By the mid-1940s, Mead was comprised of 14 divisions and subsidiaries for the manufacture of pulp, paper, paperboard, and chestnut extract. With plants in eight states, Mead had a workforce totaling 4,100.

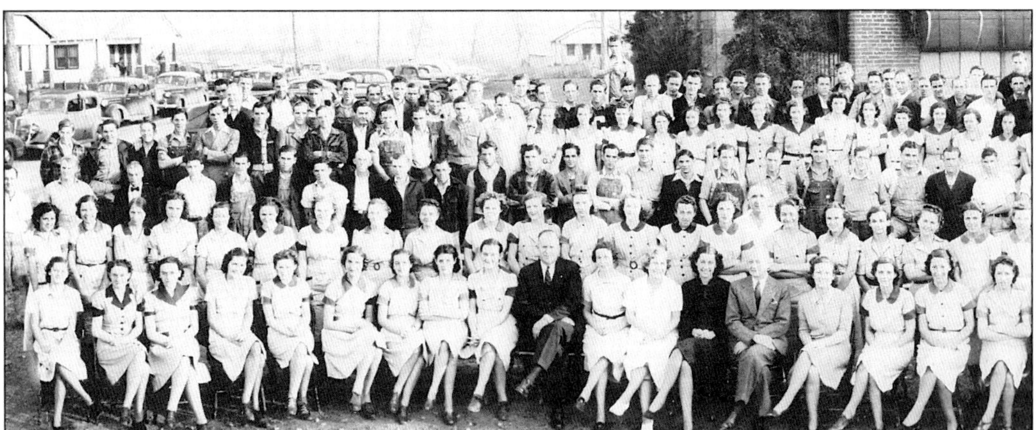

Located on Berry Street in Highland Park, Smoky Mountains Hosiery Mills began operation in 1936 and during the years progressed from producing a line of quality pure silk hosiery to the manufacture of nylon and other fibers. Production at the plant was marketed under the brand-name of "Quaker" as part of the "Quaker" curtains and dinner cloths produced by the Quaker Lace Company of Philadelphia, PA. This photo of employees was taken at the plant in 1939.

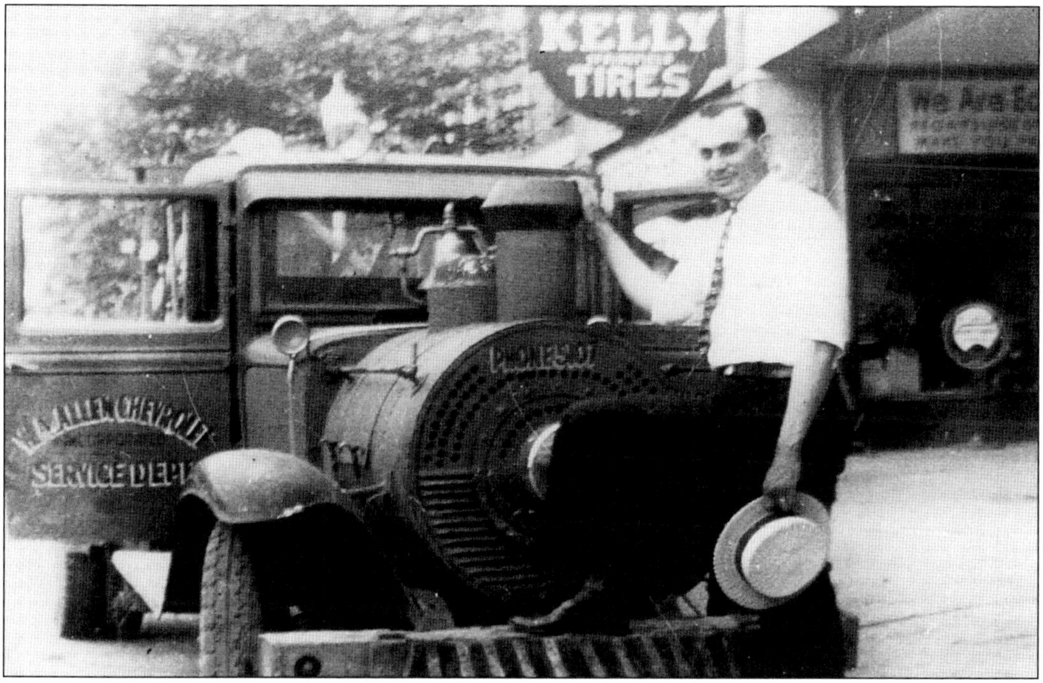

The W.A. Allen Chevrolet Company of General Motors, located at 315 Cherokee Street, was one of the three automobile retailers in Kingsport in the late 1930s. The number of automotive dealerships and service agencies increased five-fold by the end of World War II. The scene above shows the W.A. Allen Chevrolet wrecker service in 1934. Below are workers involved in auto ramp construction at the Allen Garage in 1937.

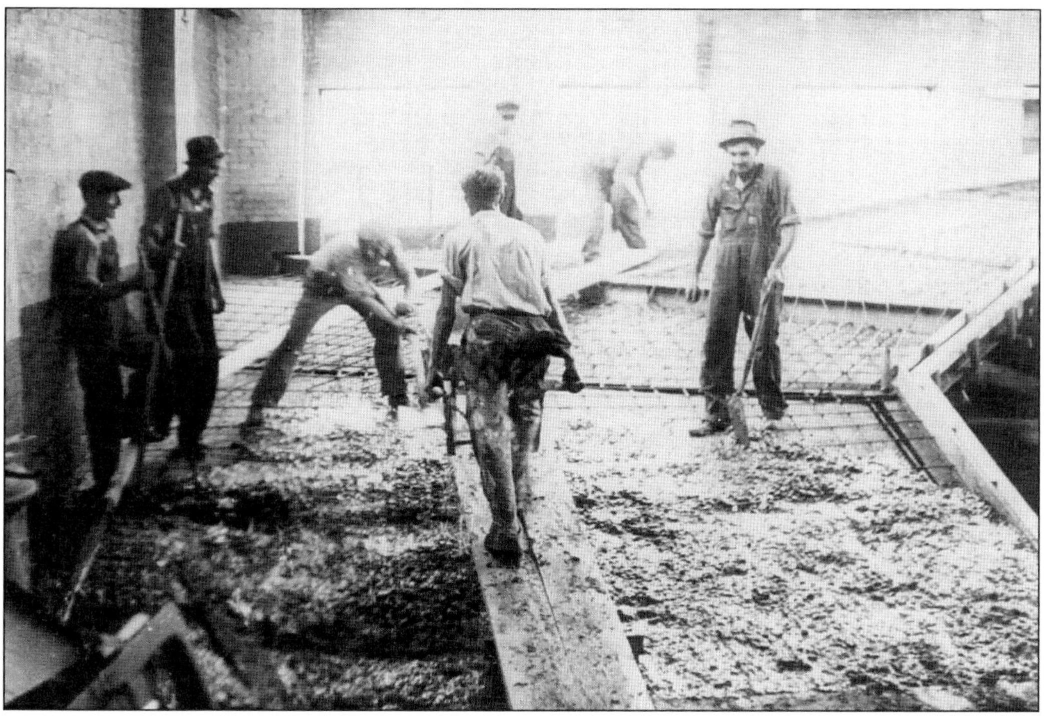

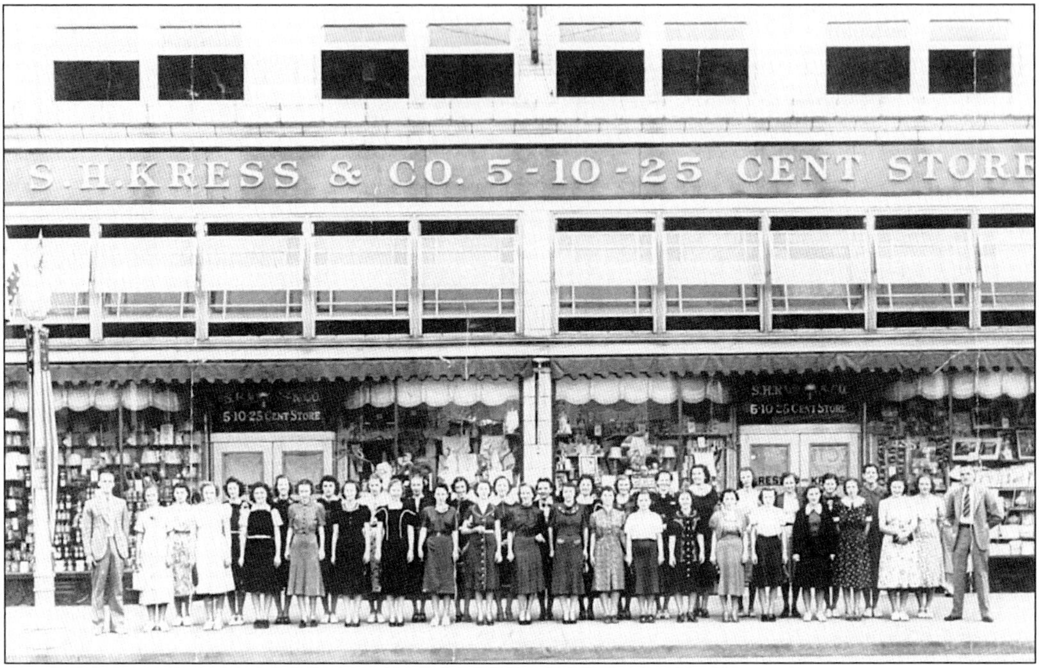

A "5 and 10 cents store," S.H. Kress and Company was located at 218–220 Broad Street in downtown Kingsport. Employees pose in front of the store in 1935.

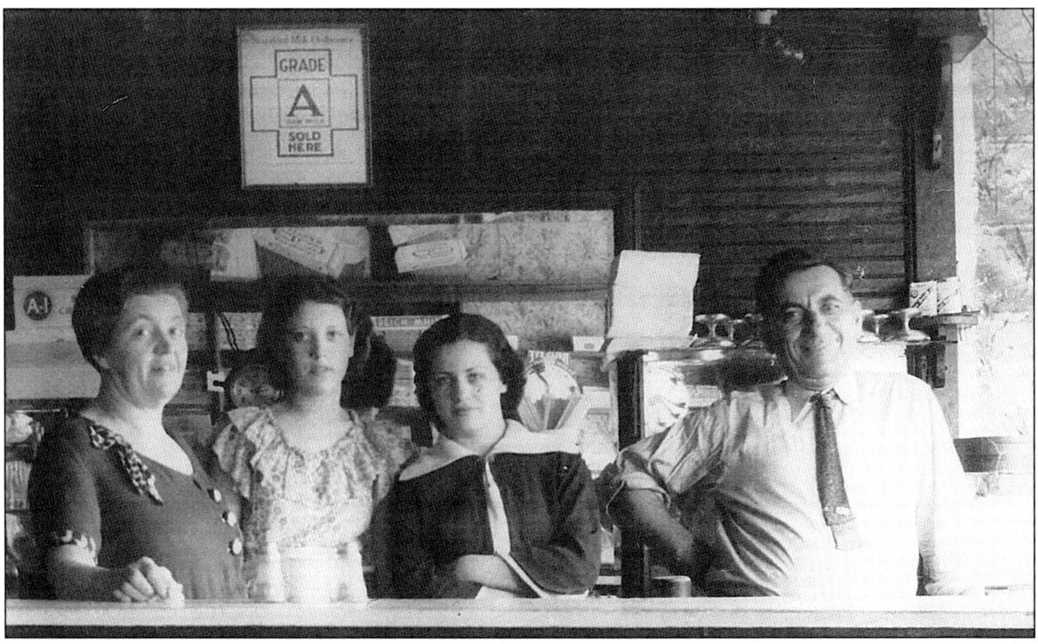

Haney's Place, a well-known confectionery located at 405 Cherokee Street, was owned by Salman and Della Haney.

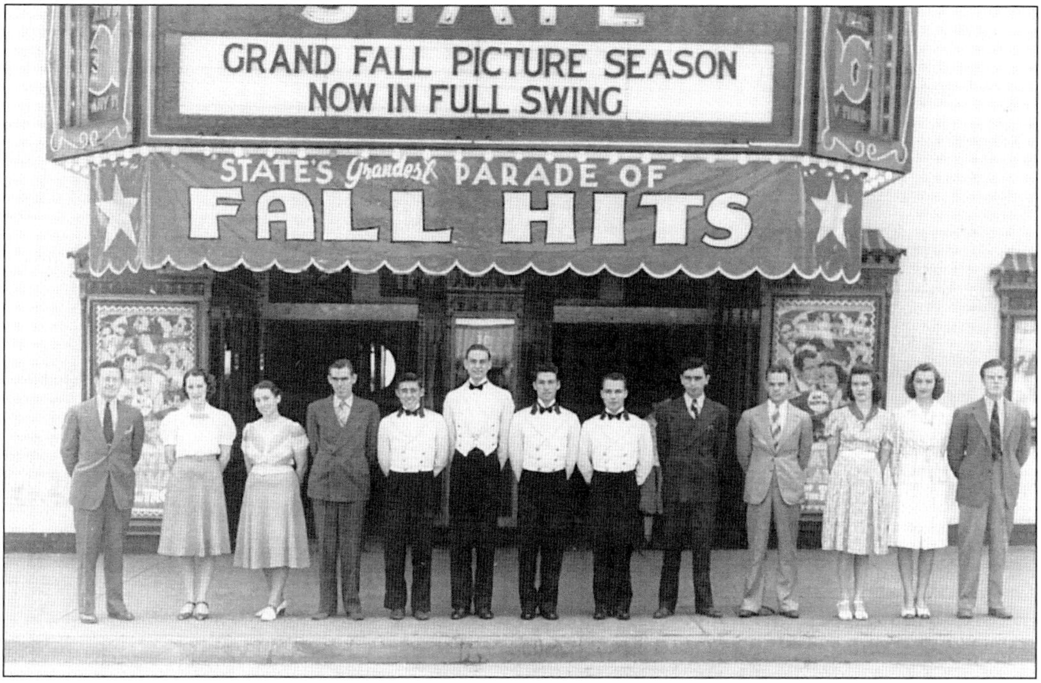

Employees of the State Theatre pose in front of the Kingsport movie house in 1938. Located on the corner of Broad and Market Streets, the State Theatre began showing films in 1936. L.J. "Jimmy" Pepper was the theater manager.

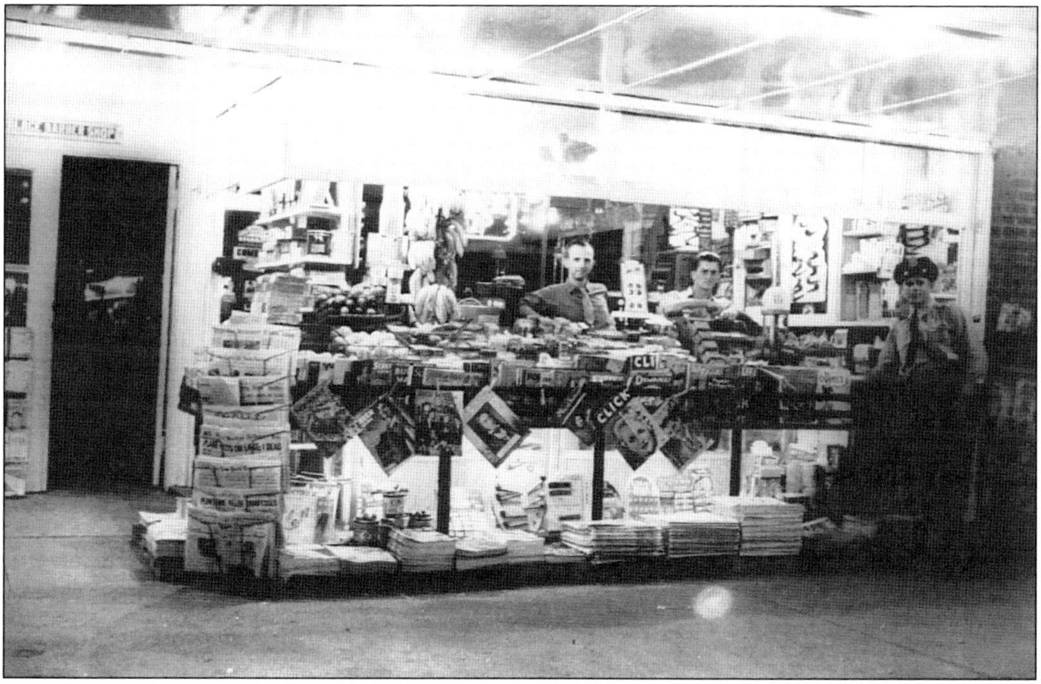

At 156 Broad Street, Palace Fruit and News could be found near Palace Barber and Dry Cleaning, Inc. The president of the business was J.R. Tranbarger and the secretary-treasurer was P.T. Nottingham.

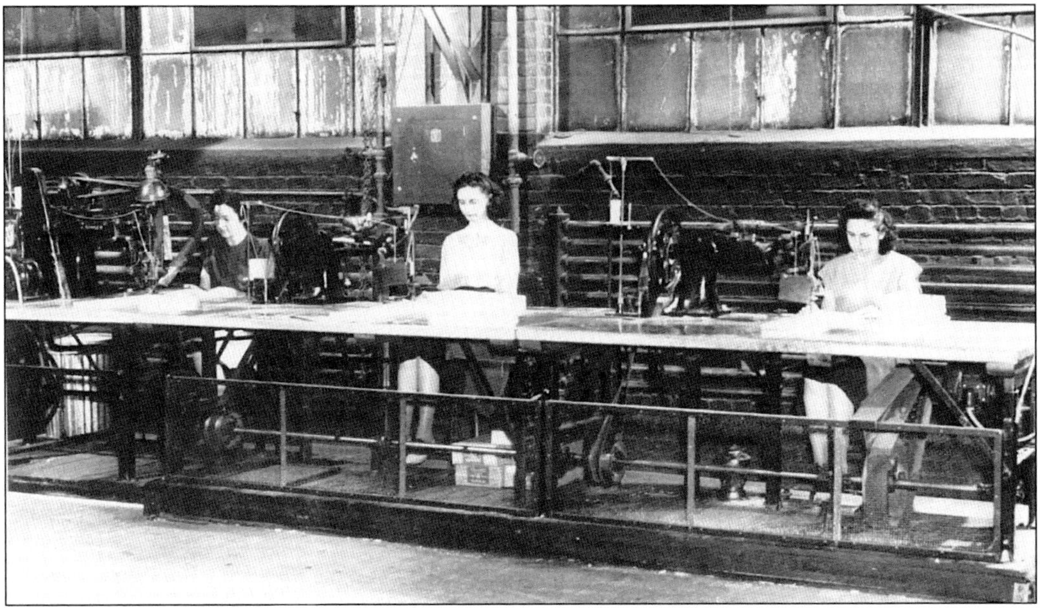

During World War II, when E.W. Palmer was deputy director of the printing and publications division of the War Production Board, the Kingsport Press manufactured such materials as Bibles and equipment instruction manuals for U.S. troops.

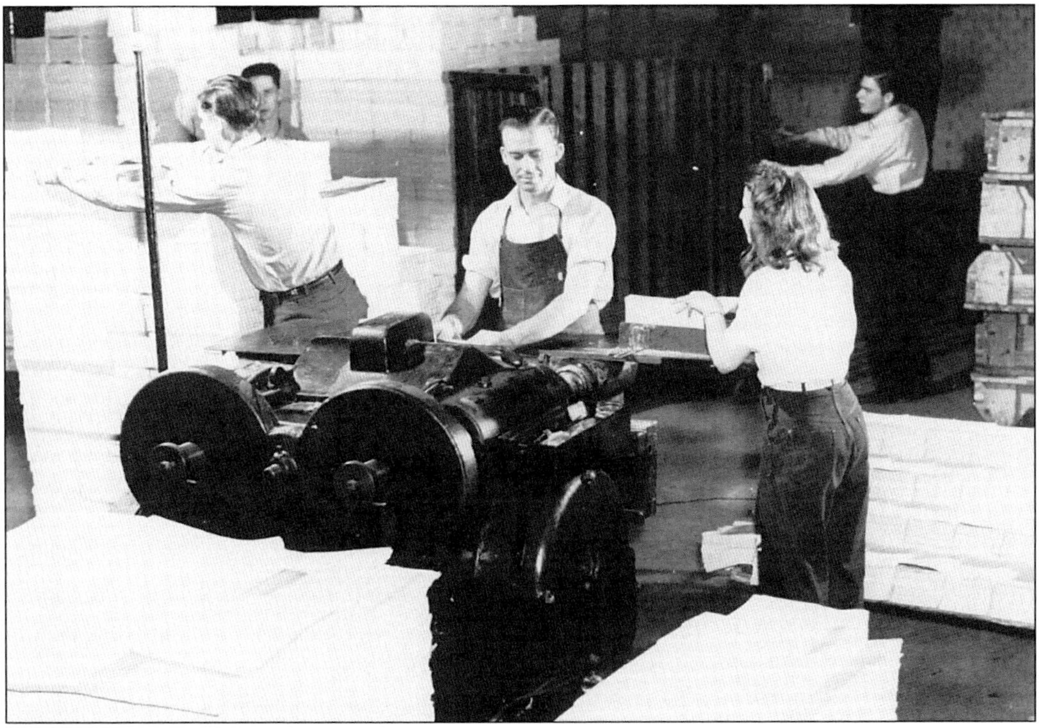

During the 1930s and 1940s, Palmer diversified the fields of publications at the Kingsport Press to include textbooks and encyclopedias, increased company floorspace from a few hundred square feet to 12.5 acres, and added additional shifts, making the press operational 24 hours a day.

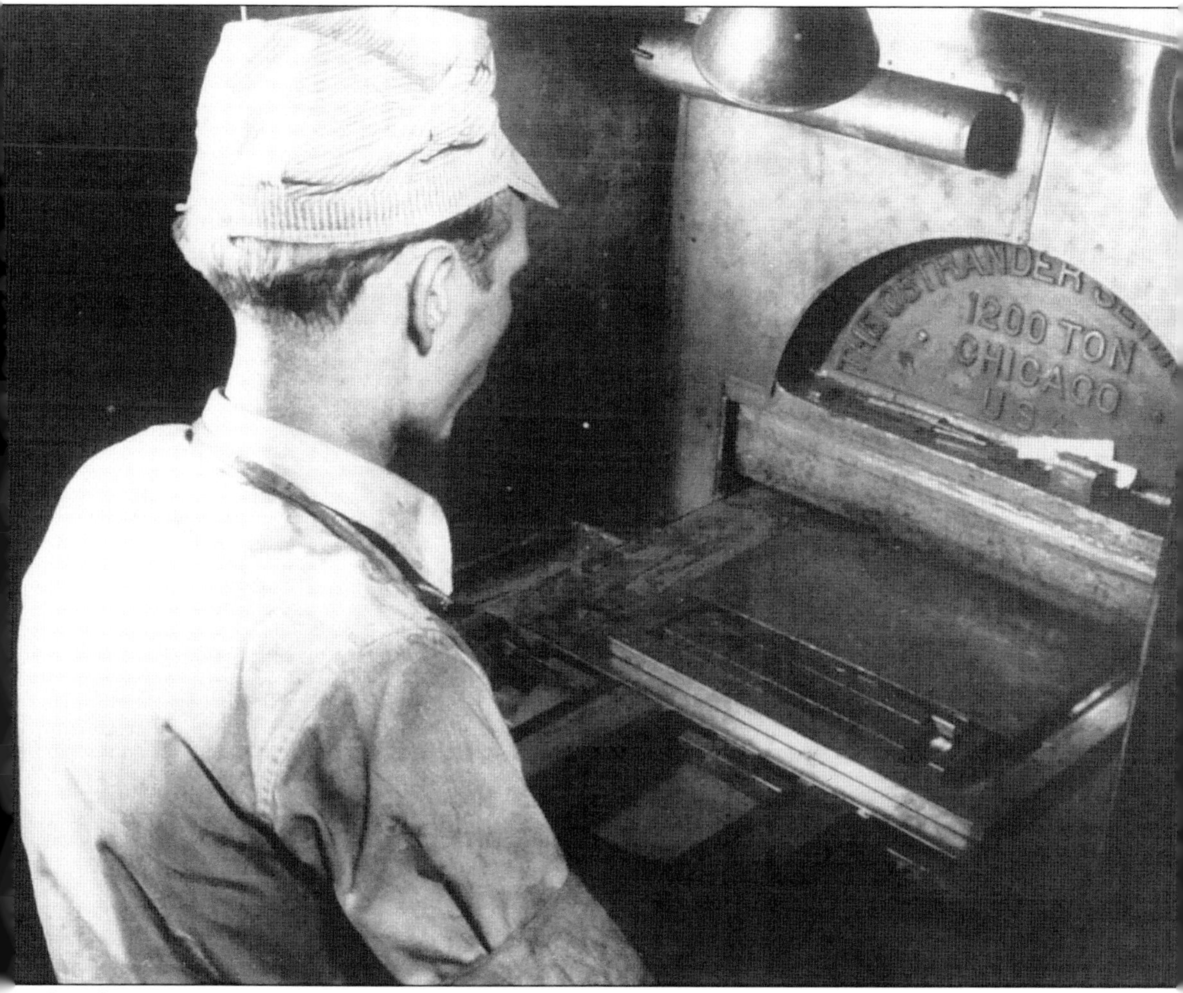

The first contract secured by the Kingsport Press was with the Woolworth chain for the mass production of a miniature clothbound series of the classics. These photographs of the Kingsport Press, Inc. were taken by professional photographer Thomas McNeer Jr. in 1946. McNeer (d. 1991) led efforts to establish an archives to preserve the history of Kingsport. His large photographic collection is now housed in the archives of the Kingsport Public Library.

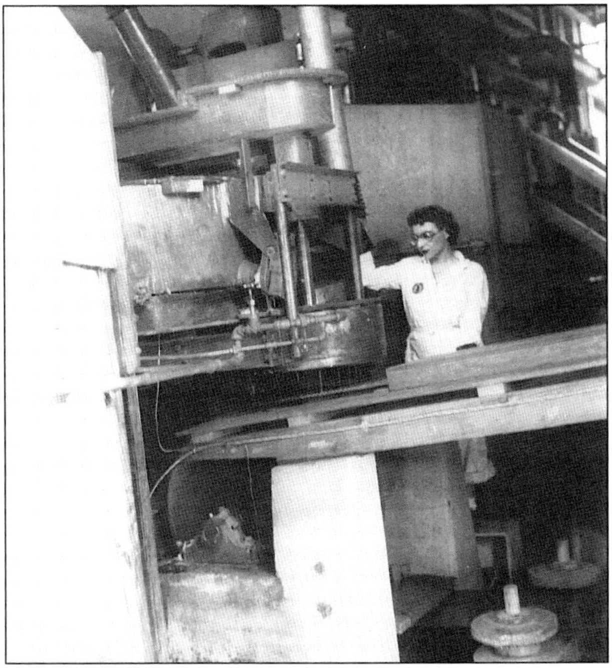

This Holston Ordnance Works operator works in an incorporation building where molting explosives are dropped on a casting belt to cool. She is opening a valve on the bottom of the melt pot, allowing the product to drop into the pellet pot. After the material hardens into a finished product at the end of the belt, it is transferred to a packing operation.

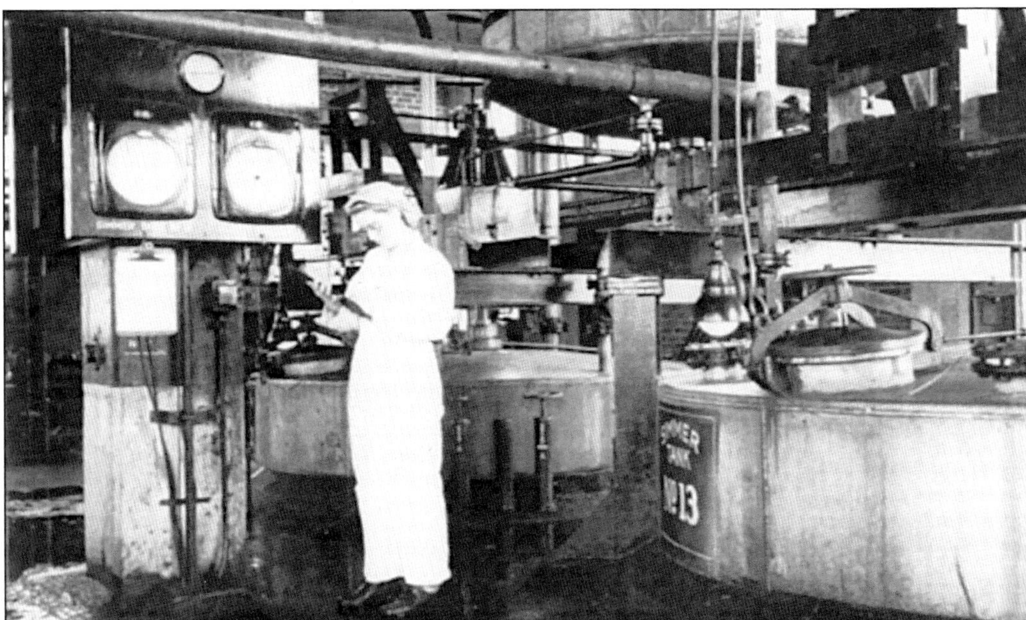

World War II created an unprecedented need for new workers. In response to that need, more than 6 million women entered the workforce, increasing the female labor force by 50 percent. The most profound changes in the employment of women happened in regions of the U.S. with a concentration of defense industries. The number of women in the manufacturing force grew 110 percent overall during the war compared to the number of women in war industries, which skyrocketed 460 percent nationwide. Seen here, D-building (Nitration) was where different chemicals were combined to form high explosives. The operator in this picture is checking temperature recorders on the second floor of D-building.

Seven

EDUCATION

Historically a priority of both government and residents, the educational system of Kingsport was designed to create schools that were superior to systems inside and outside the region. Viewed as critical to the overall success of the economic and social plan of Kingsport, the school system consciously fostered the "Kingsport spirit" and modeled itself after noted educational systems existing across the nation. In particular, founders of modern Kingsport, steeped in Progressive-era concepts of quality education, emulated the school system of Gary, Indiana.

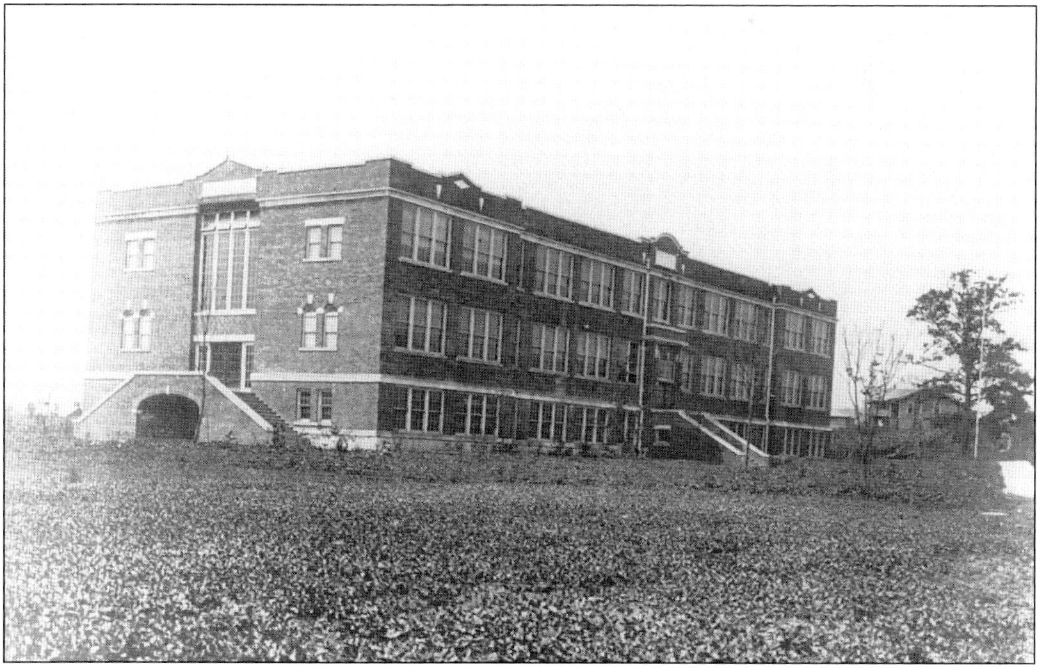

Plans for a city high school were approved by the board of mayor and aldermen on July 24, 1917. D.R. Beeson served as the architect for the Central School Building, which officially opened on September 18, 1918.

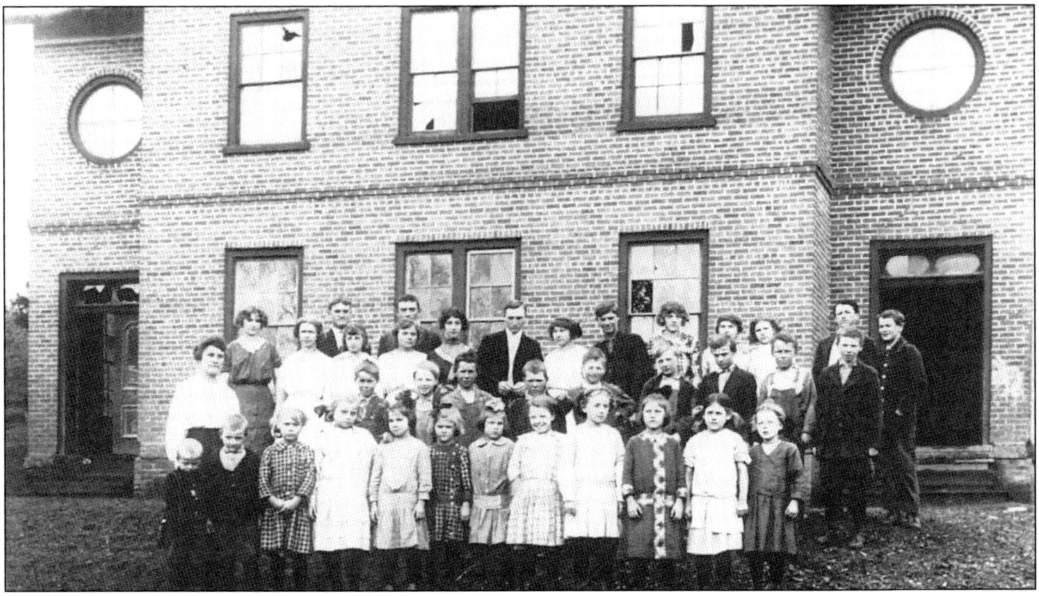

An emphasis on education in Sullivan County and Kingsport was evident well before the incorporation of Kingsport in 1917. By the early 1900s, five schools were located in the Kingsport area: Cedar Grove, Cloud's Bend, Kingsport Academy (Old Kingsport), Oklahoma, and War Path. Seen here is a 1907 picture of Kingsport Academy, which was constructed near the Fort Robinson Baptist Church.

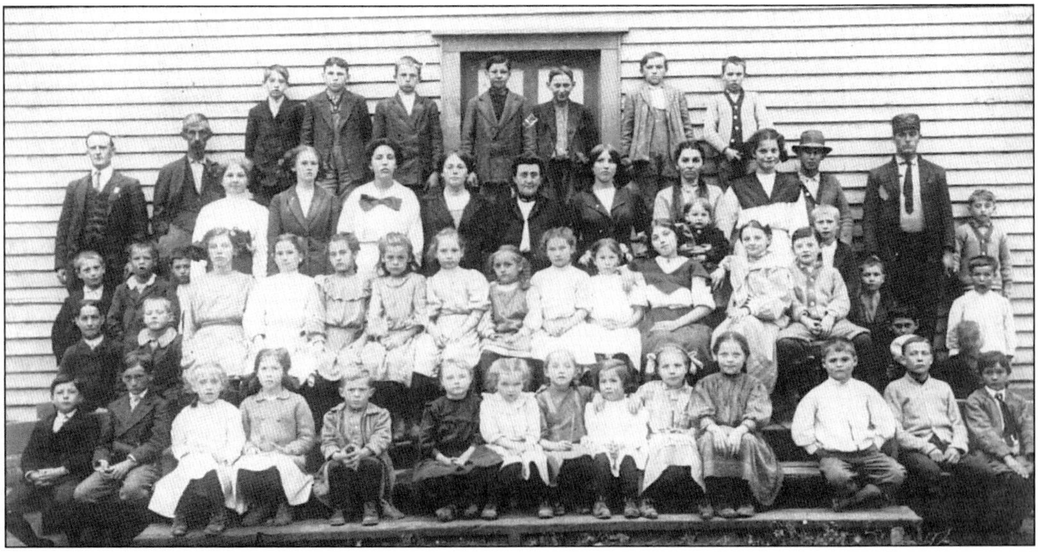

Oklahoma School, pictured here with some of its students in 1910, became a part of incorporated Kingsport in 1917. It was located on the site that later became the Robert E. Lee School.

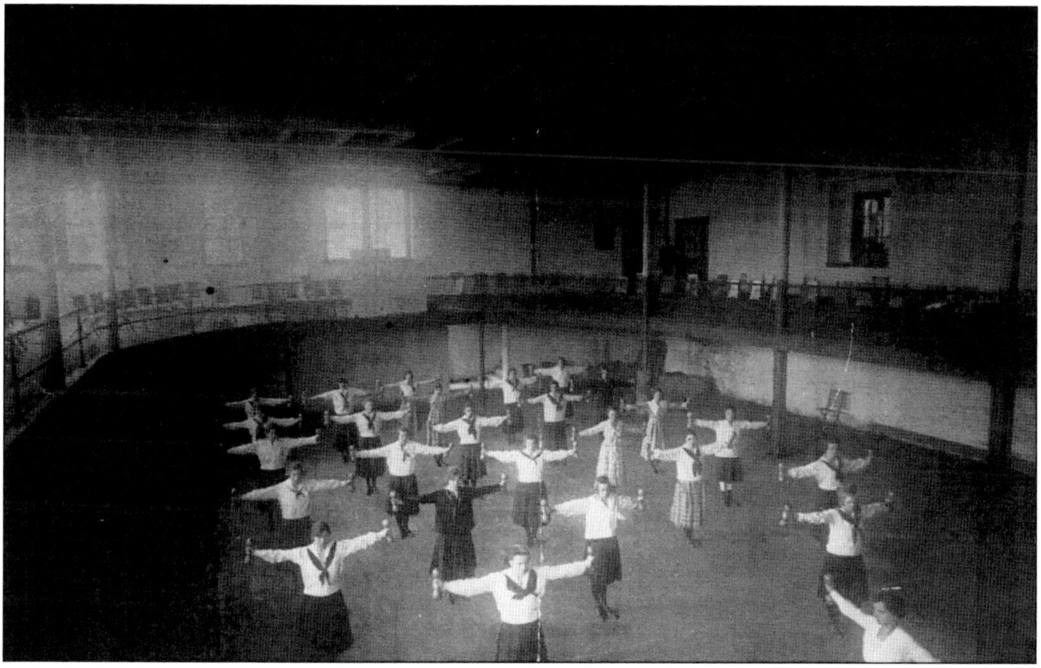

The Central School Building set a high standard for the new city school system. The school included 20 rooms, a large auditorium, and a full-size gymnasium. With a master's degree from Columbia University, Eugene M. Crouch became the first superintendent of Kingsport City Schools. Pictured here is the 1919 girls' gym class.

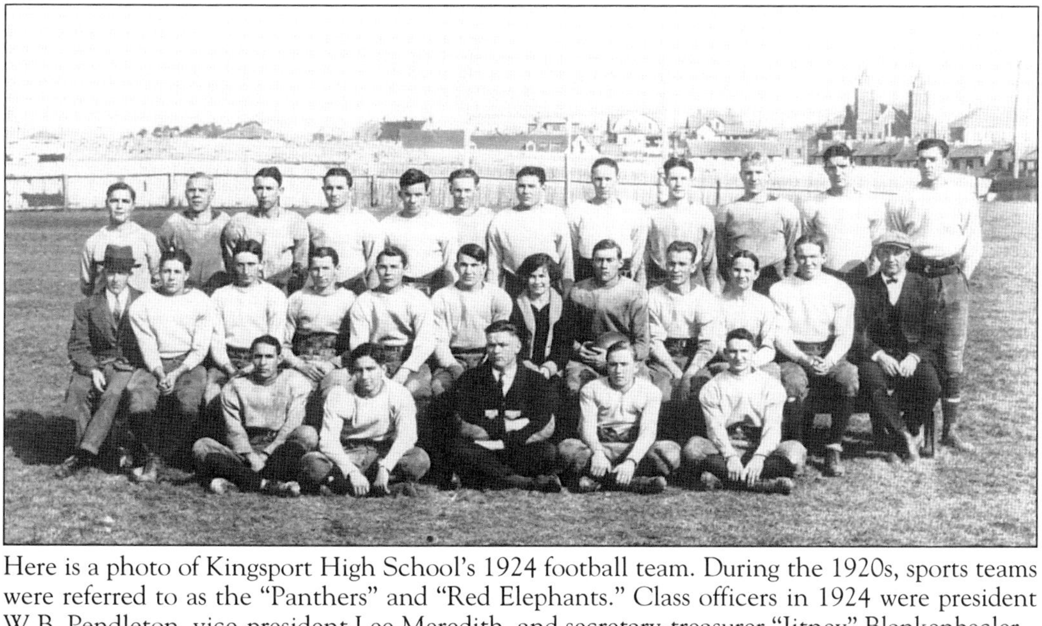

Here is a photo of Kingsport High School's 1924 football team. During the 1920s, sports teams were referred to as the "Panthers" and "Red Elephants." Class officers in 1924 were president W.B. Pendleton, vice-president Lee Meredith, and secretary-treasurer "Jitney" Blankenbecler.

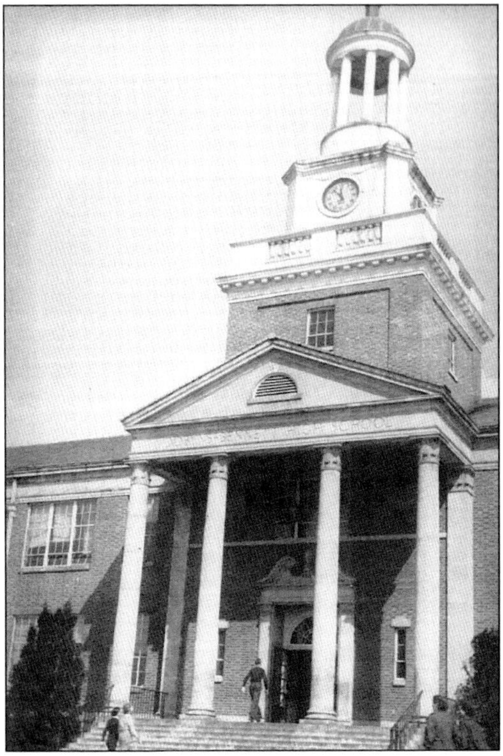

Named in honor of the first mayor of Kingsport, James W. Dobyns, and the first president of the board of education, W.M. Bennett, Dobyns-Bennett High School, with a 500-student capacity, was established between Oak and Yadkin Streets and Wateree and Catawba Streets. Architects Allen N. Dryden Sr., A.L. Bandy, and Clinton Mackenzie designed a building that was created at an estimated cost of $250,000. Opening in September 1926, Dobyns-Bennett housed grades 7 through 12 until 1937.

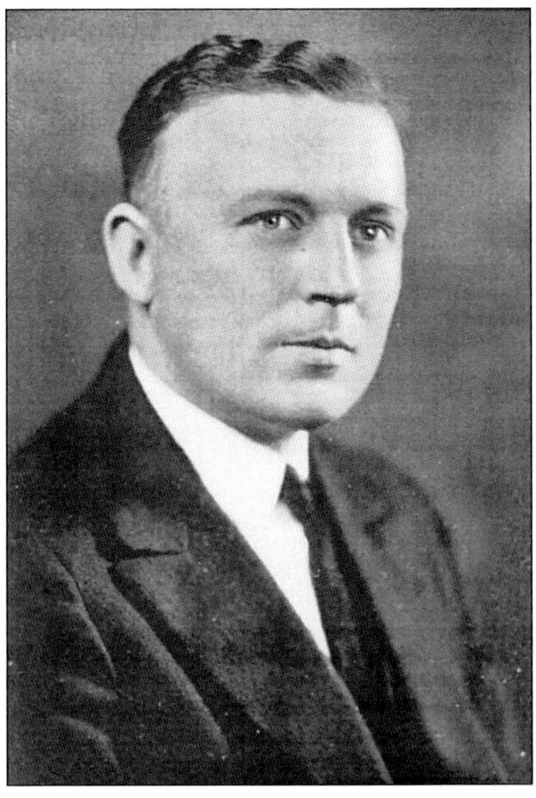

Over the years, Dobyns-Bennett High School principals have proved to be some of the most respected individuals of the community. Union University graduate Charles K. Koffman began a distinguished 20-year tenure at Central High/Dobyns-Bennett in 1925. A former principal in Morristown, Koffman married local teacher Frances Nelms and obtained a master's degree from the University of Wisconsin. During a life of dedicated service to Kingsport education, Koffman received a 1950 appointment to the board of education and served as chairman of that body from 1956 to 1962.

Appointed as superintendent of Kingsport schools in 1924, Columbia University graduate Ross N. Robinson led the school system for 29 years. During his administration, Kingsport schools earned a national reputation for academic as well as athletic excellence.

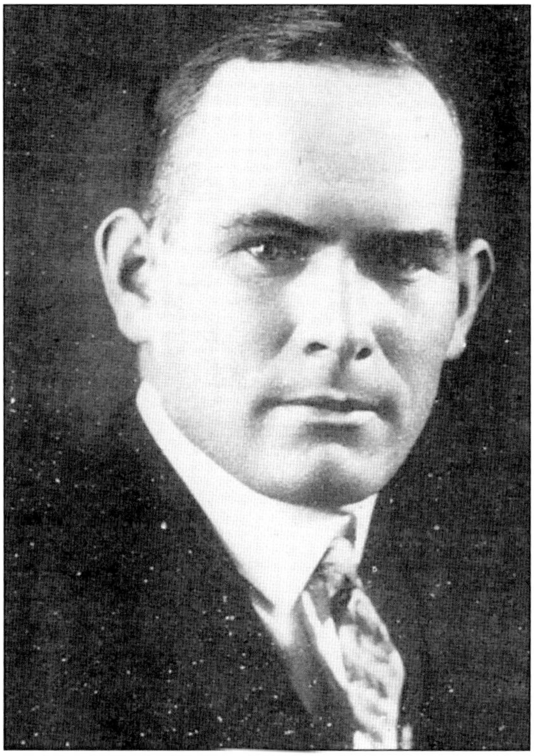

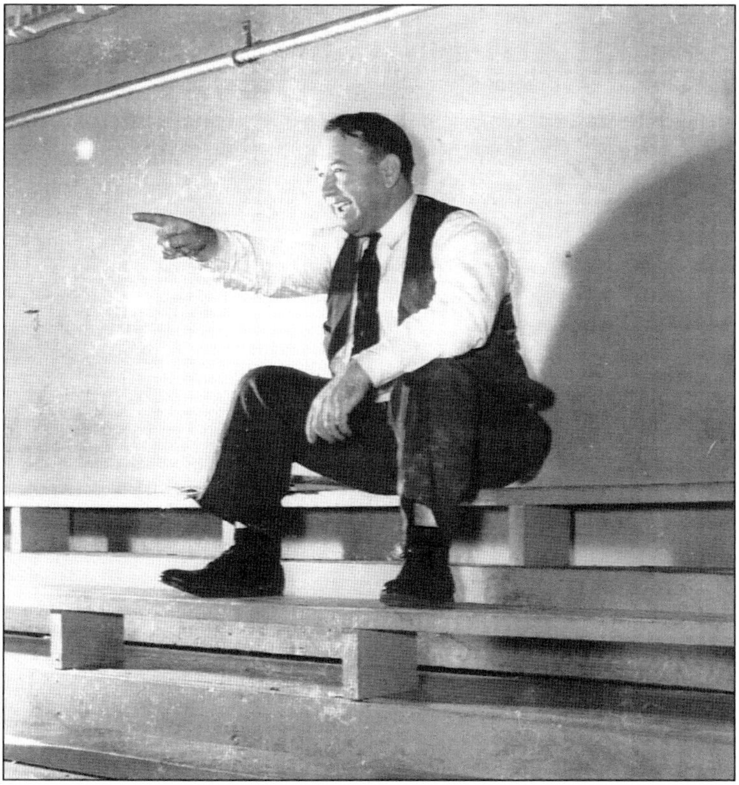

Known as the "father of Kingsport athletics," Canton, Ohio native Leroy Sprankle was hired by Superintendent Ross N. Robinson. Sprankle coached basketball, baseball, football, and track. Before accepting another position in Florida, Sprankle established the athletic program in Kingsport as a member of the Tennessee Secondary Schools Athletic Association (TSSAA) and coached such notable athletes as University of Tennessee All-American quarterback Robert Lee "Bobby" Dodd.

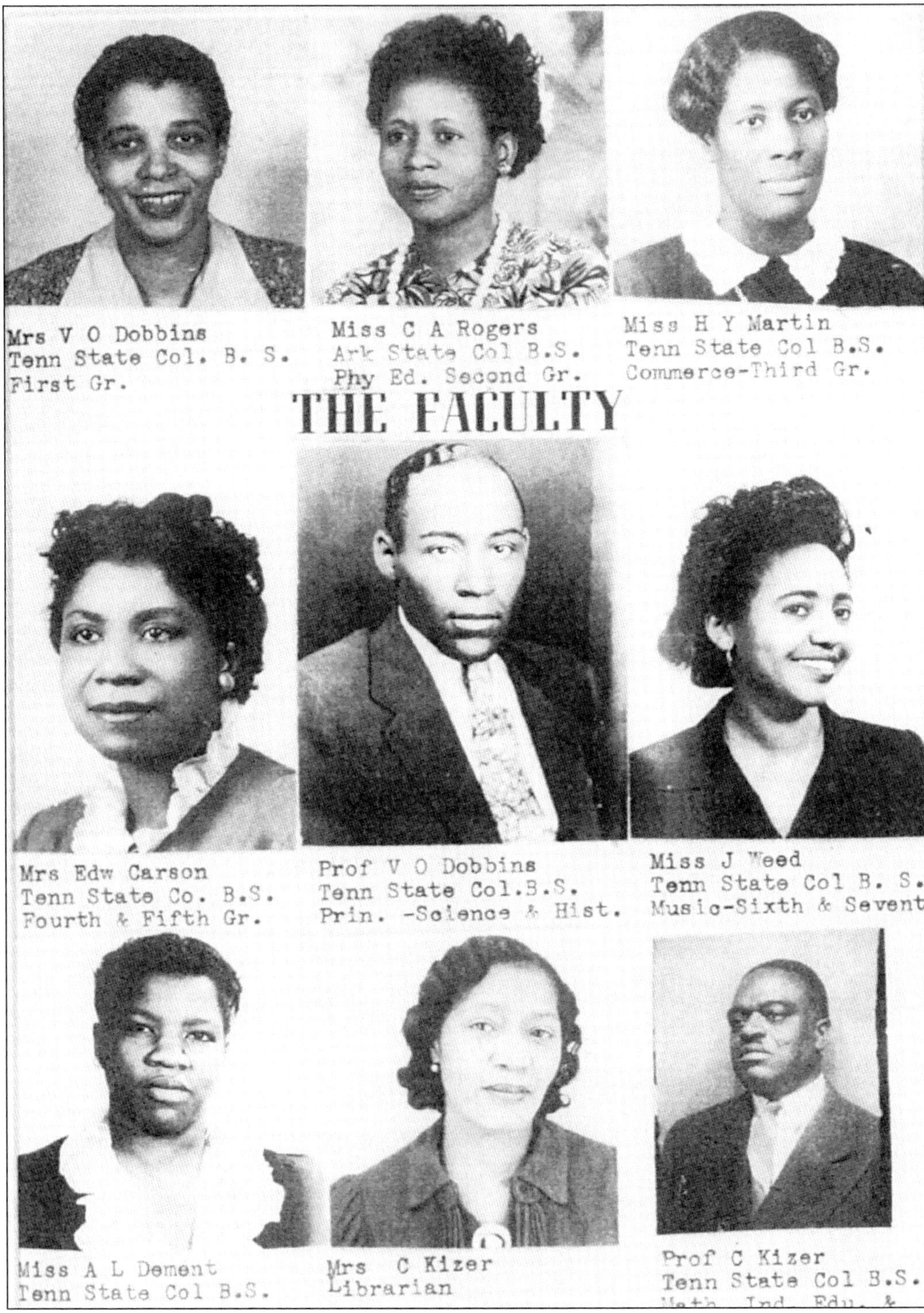

Kingsport City Schools were racially segregated until 1966. Douglass School was the site of education for the African-American student population of Kingsport from the late 1920s until desegregation was achieved. Above is the 1944–45 Douglass School faculty.

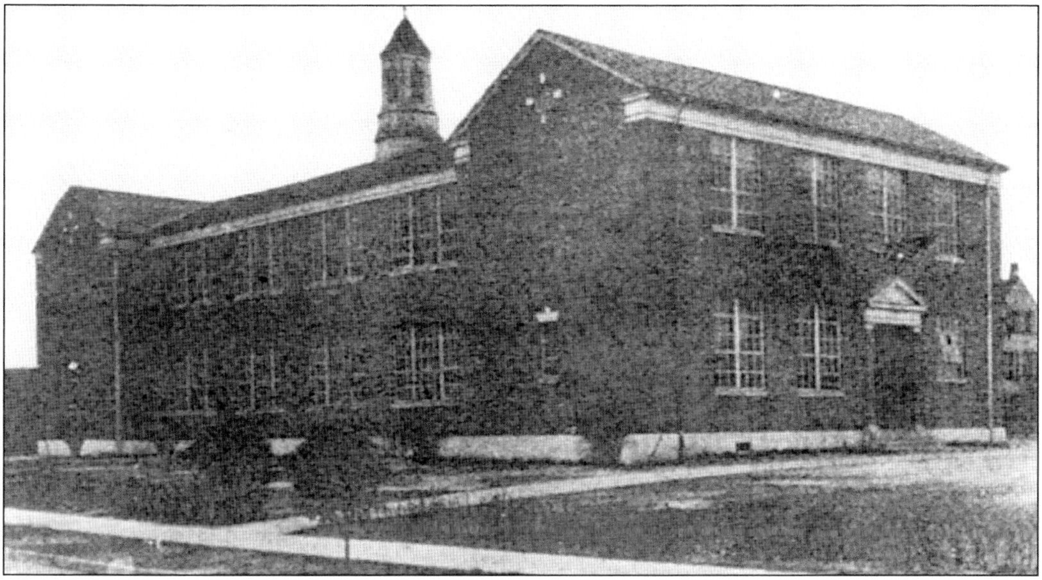

Douglass School was located on the corner of Center Streets and East Sevier Avenue. For 18 years, principal Albert H. Howell led successful efforts to establish a winning athletic program combined with strong emphasis on academics.

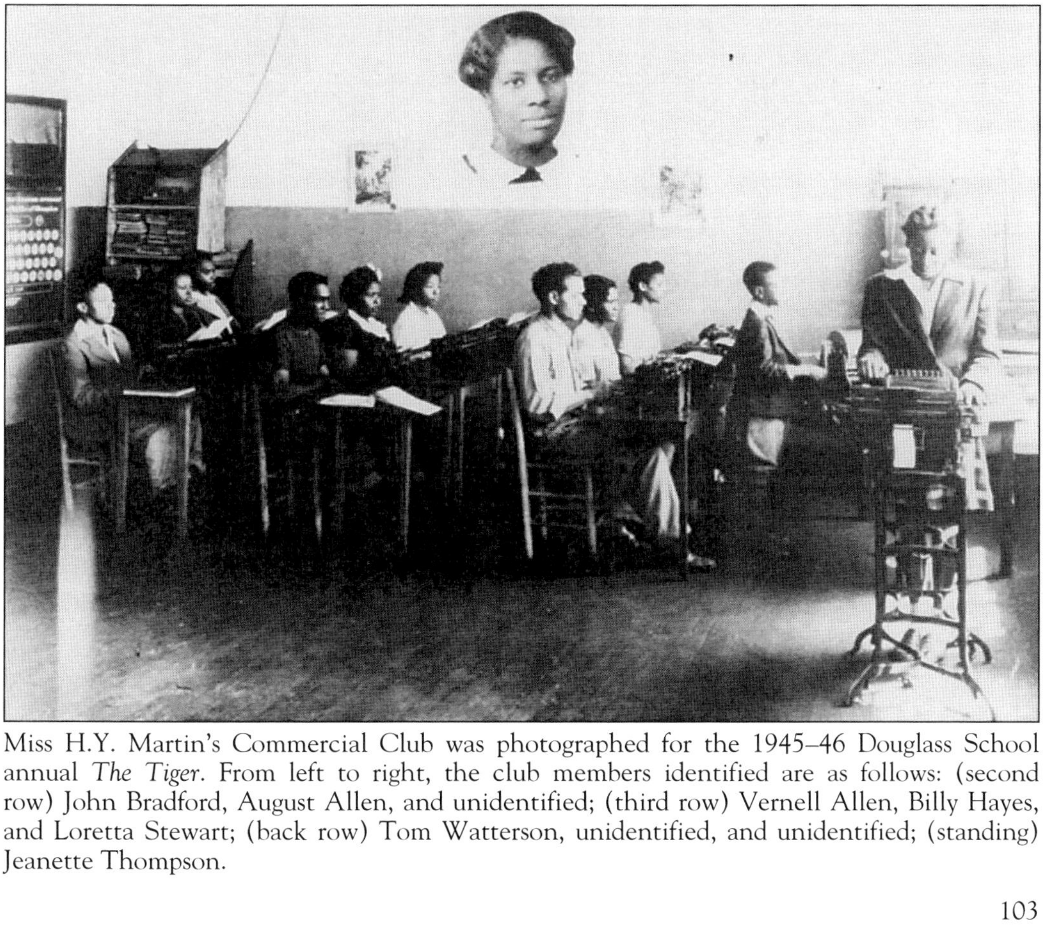

Miss H.Y. Martin's Commercial Club was photographed for the 1945–46 Douglass School annual *The Tiger*. From left to right, the club members identified are as follows: (second row) John Bradford, August Allen, and unidentified; (third row) Vernell Allen, Billy Hayes, and Loretta Stewart; (back row) Tom Watterson, unidentified, and unidentified; (standing) Jeanette Thompson.

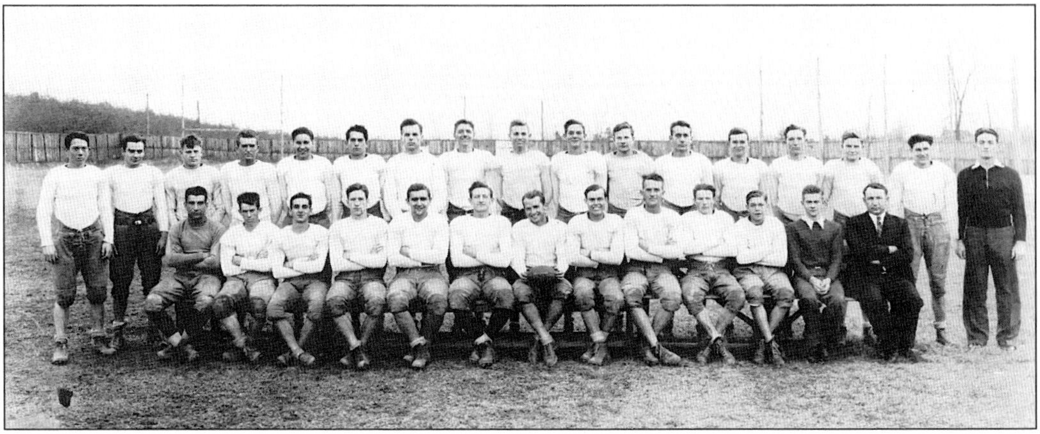

The Kingsport "Red Elephants" preceded the "Indians" as the name of the football team. In this 1933 photo, Coach Leroy Sprankle is pictured on the far right.

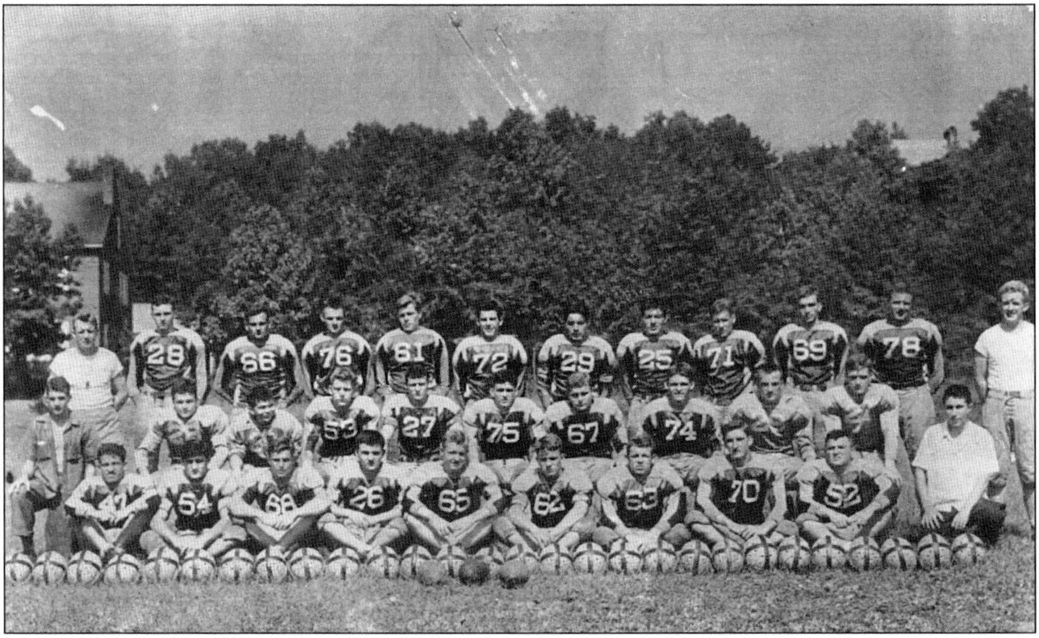

In 1945, the Dobyns-Bennett (D-B) football team earned the title "State Grid Champs of '45." This was the first perfect season in 26 years of football at D-B, with ten wins and no defeats. Pictured are the following: (front row) Joe Halton (manager), Robert Archer, Charlie Frye, Bert Shanks, Harry Belk, Doe Hood, Buster Brown, Clyde Groseclose, Cecil Maddux, George Gruber, and John Eachus (manager); (middle row) Ira Rathburn, Don Isley, Bill Christopher, Darrell Crawford, P.T. Nottingham, Kyle Shipley, Jack Patterson, John Campbell, and Bill Haynes; (back row) Coach Ed Shockley, Hal Miller, Sherrill Linkous, Ivan Cole, Bob Bingham, Cecil Puckett, D.W. Salley, J.W. Salley, Buck Anderson, Jack Moneyhun, Jack Fulkerson, and Coach Red Yancey. Team members not pictured are Tommy Howard, L.V. Boyd, Preacher Bullion, Doc McConnell, and Ike Neeley.

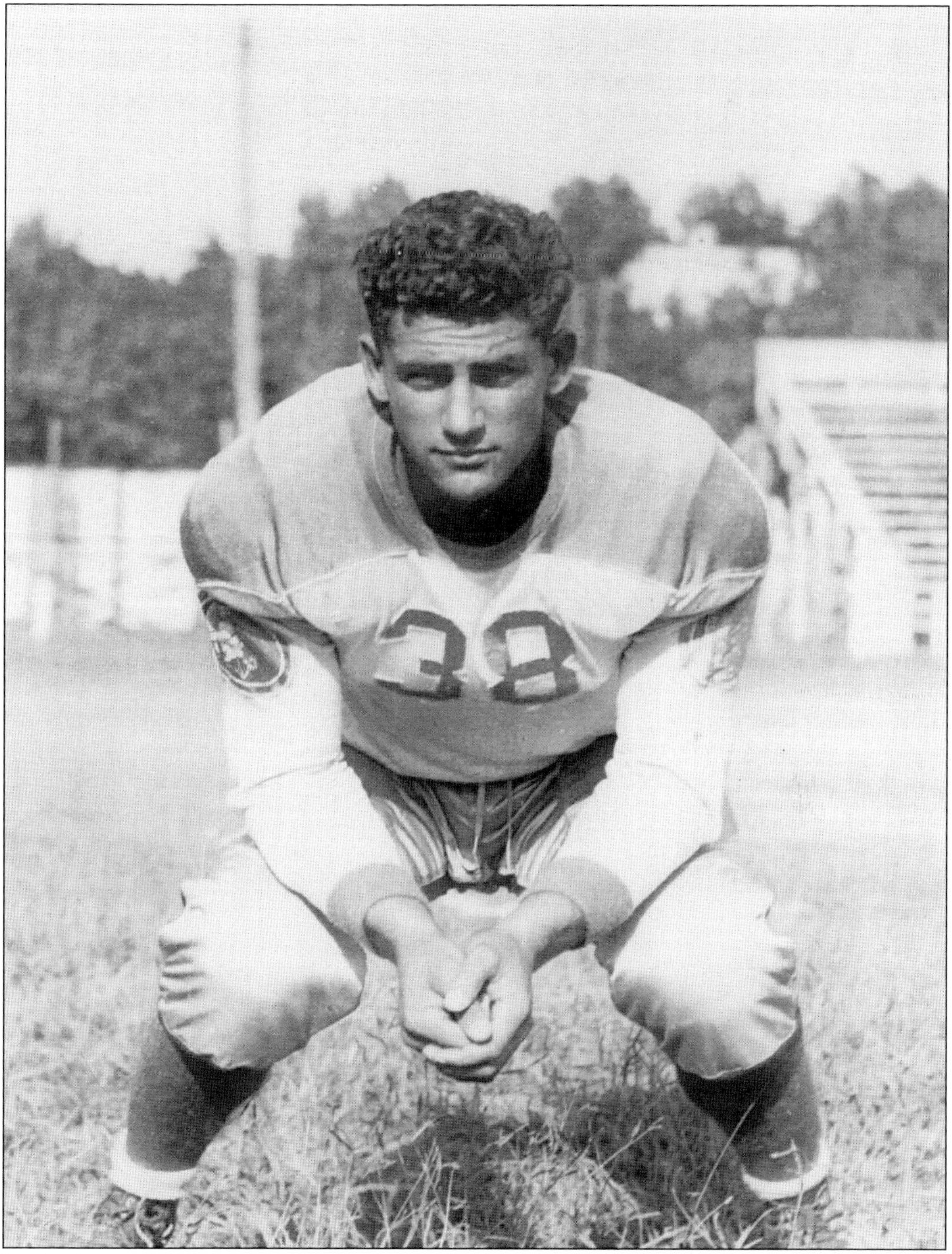

Ranked as one of the greatest high school athletic stars of all time, Bobby Cifers, a member of the Tennessee Sports Hall of Fame, played multiple sports at Dobyns-Bennett High School and was a standout in football and track at the University of Tennessee (UT). Cifers set a national scoring record in Kingsport football during the late 1930s and early 1940s and continued on to play football at UT. He enjoyed a five-year pro football career with the Detroit Lions, Pittsburgh Steelers, and Green Bay Packers.

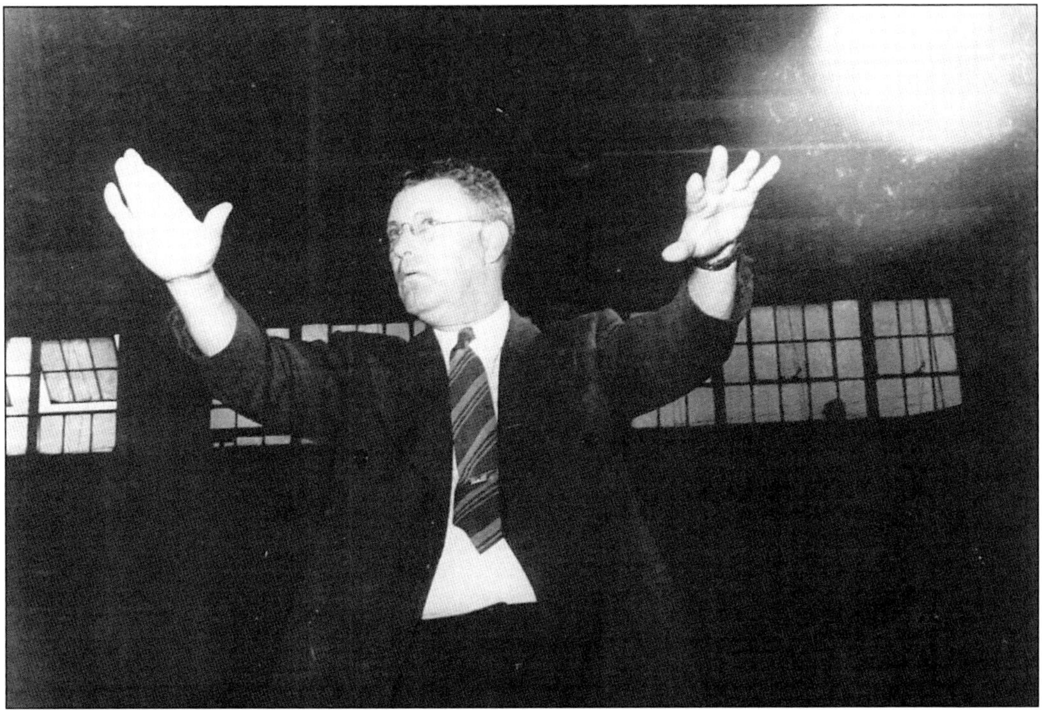

Professor S.T. Witt established a tradition of musical excellence in 1926 at Dobyns-Bennett High School. During "Fess" Witt's tenure, the band received wide recognition for musical achievement. Until 1952, Witt served as the director of both the band and the orchestra. Pictured here is the 1941–42 Dobyns-Bennett High School Band.

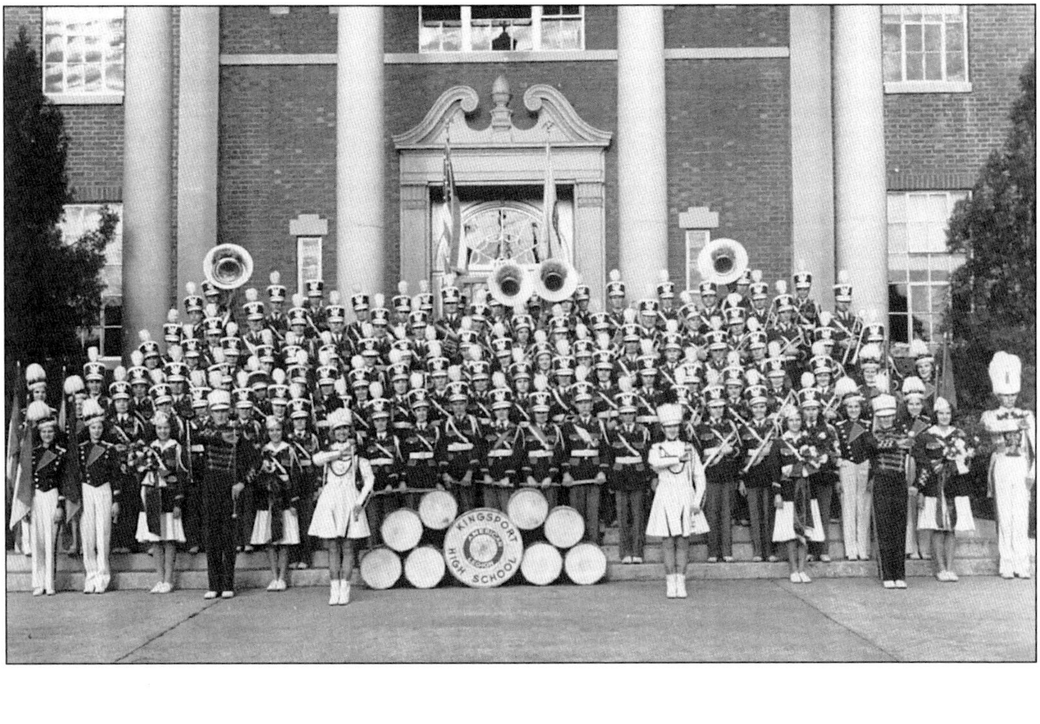

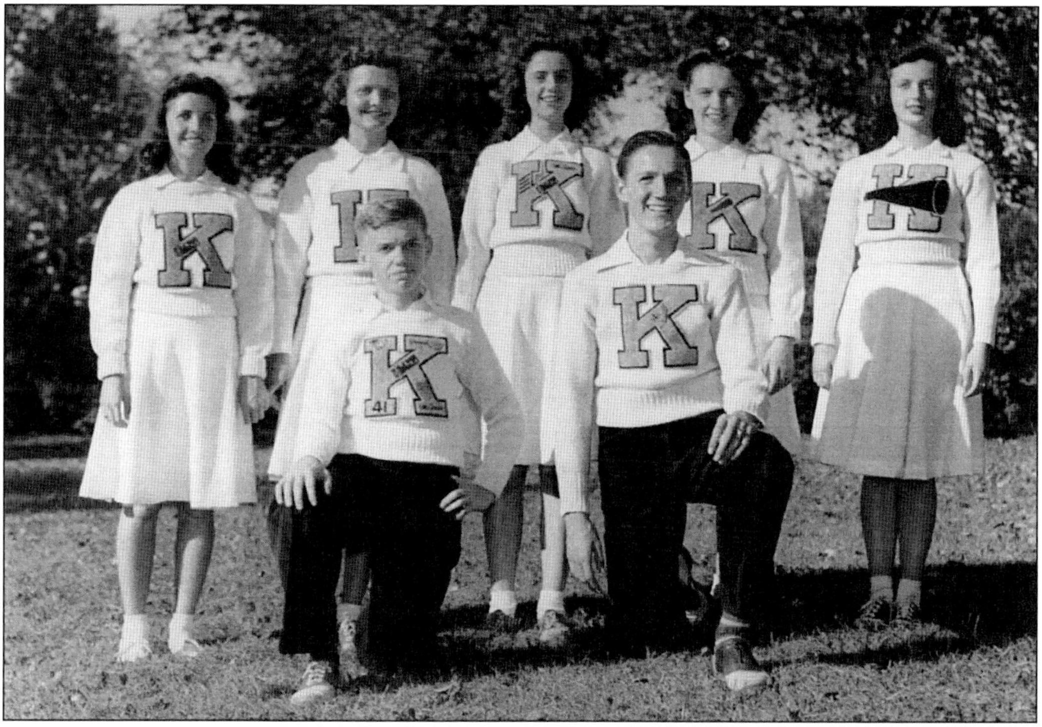

Featured among the 1942 Dobyns-Bennett High School cheerleading squad are the following: (front row) Marvin Simpson and Bill Todd; (back row) Velma Coats, Vivian Daniels, Gussie Lee Barrett, Margaret Kiss, and Shirley Pyle.

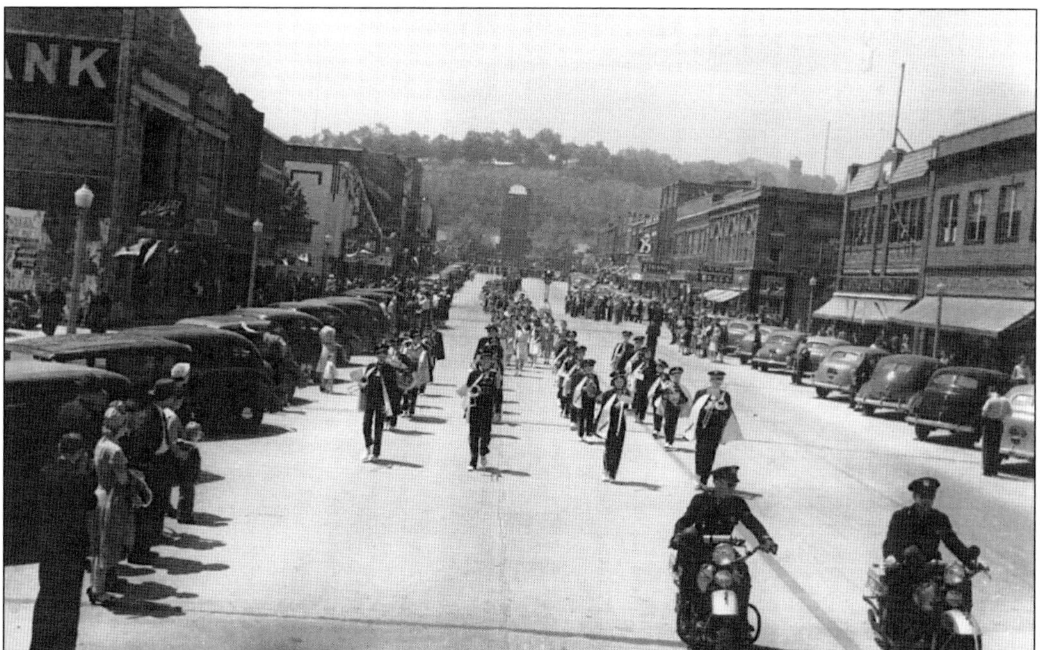

During each spring for many years, Kingsport High School graduates celebrated with a parade down Broad Street in the center of downtown.

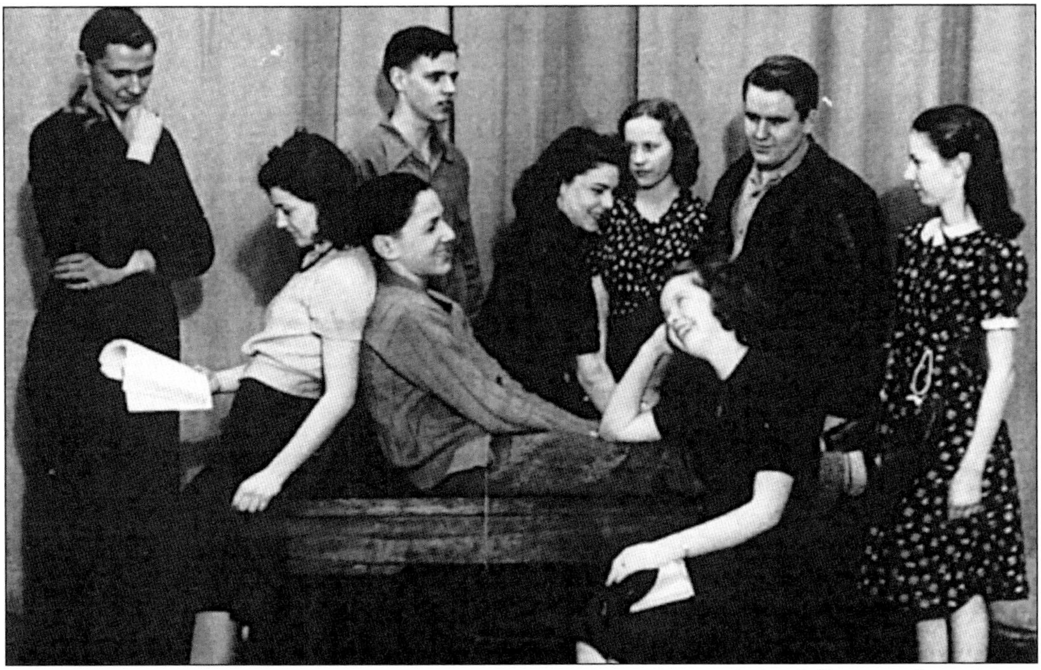

The 1940 Dobyns-Bennett sophomore play, *June Madness*, featured the following, from left to right: Kenneth Fincher, Jane Shivell, James A. Brockman, Bill Todd, Valda Stone, Angela Brown, Helen O'Toole, Lyons Westmoreland, and Laurena Billington.

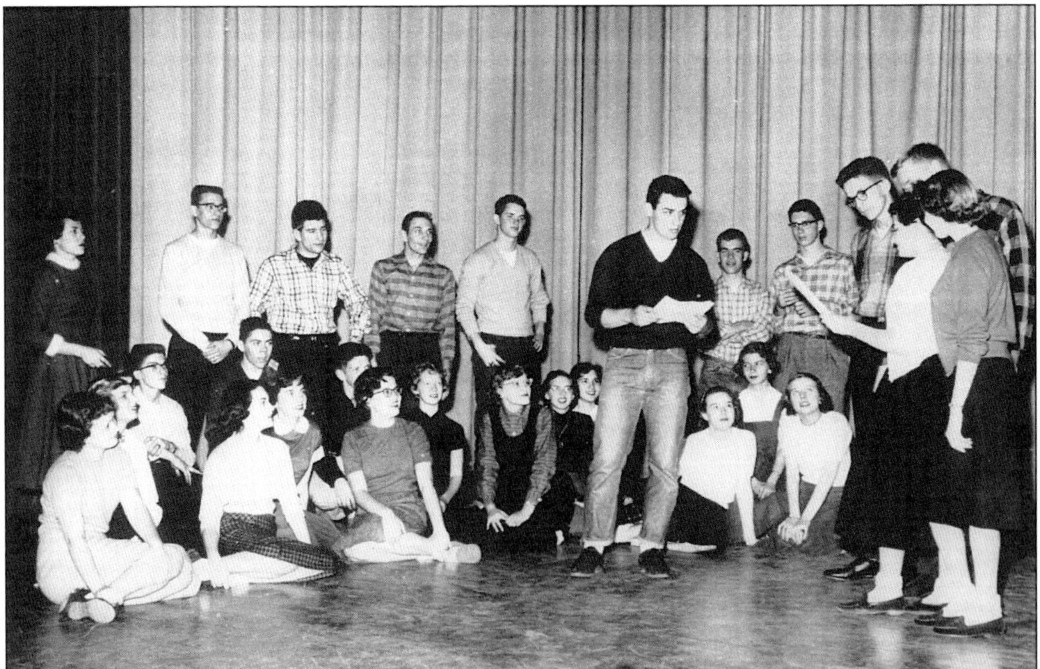

In this photograph from the late 1940s, Dobyns-Bennett High School drama and speech teacher Nancy Necessary Pridemore (far left, standing) is pictured rehearsing with her class. Pridemore directed the speech and drama program for 39 years.

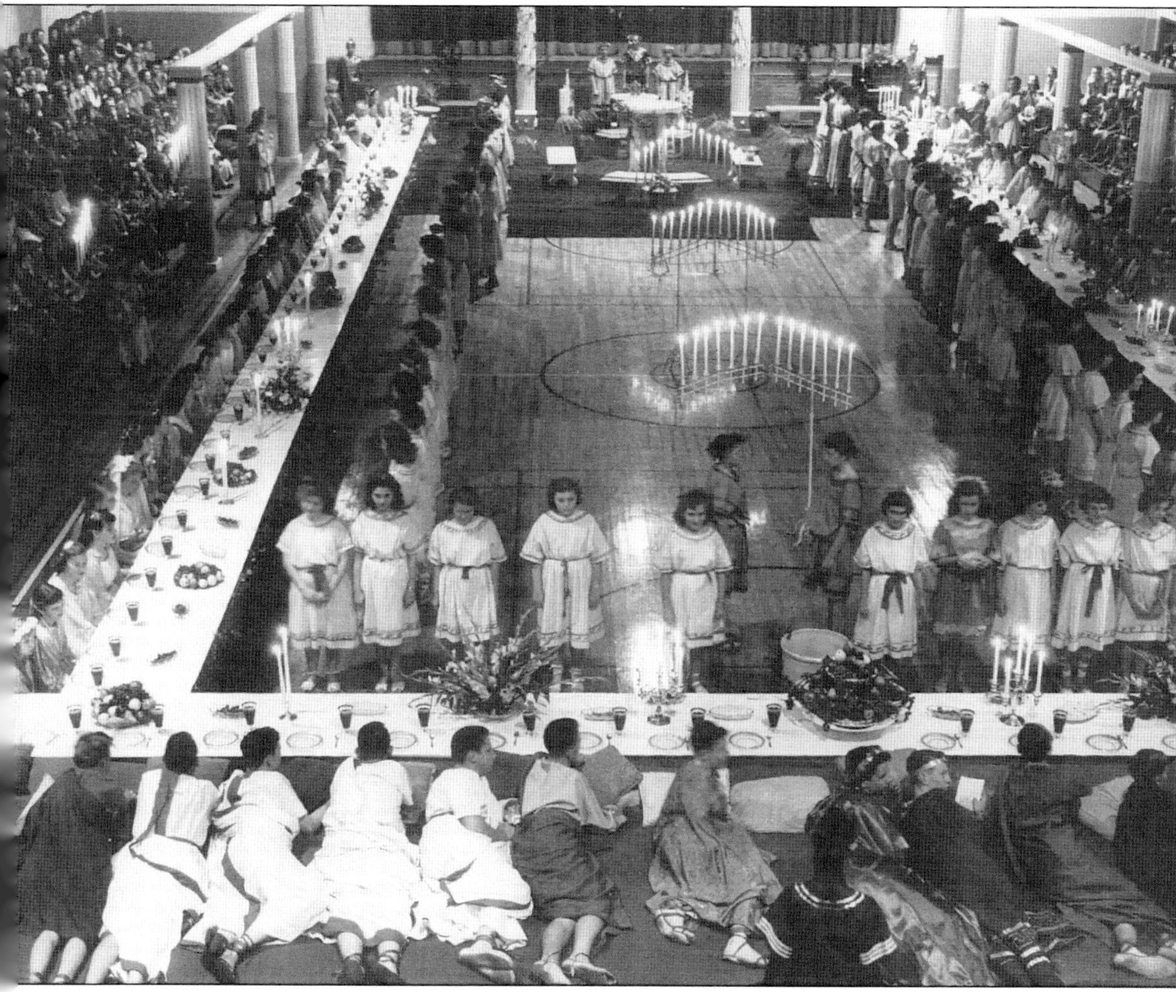

On November 22, 1948, Latin teacher Grace Elmore produced an extravagant Roman banquet for her students at the Civic Auditorium. *LOOK* magazine sent a reporter and a photographer to profile the festivities. Accompanied by Kingsport pianist Will George, Metropolitan opera singer Helen Jepson sang in Latin while wearing her costume from *Thaïs*.

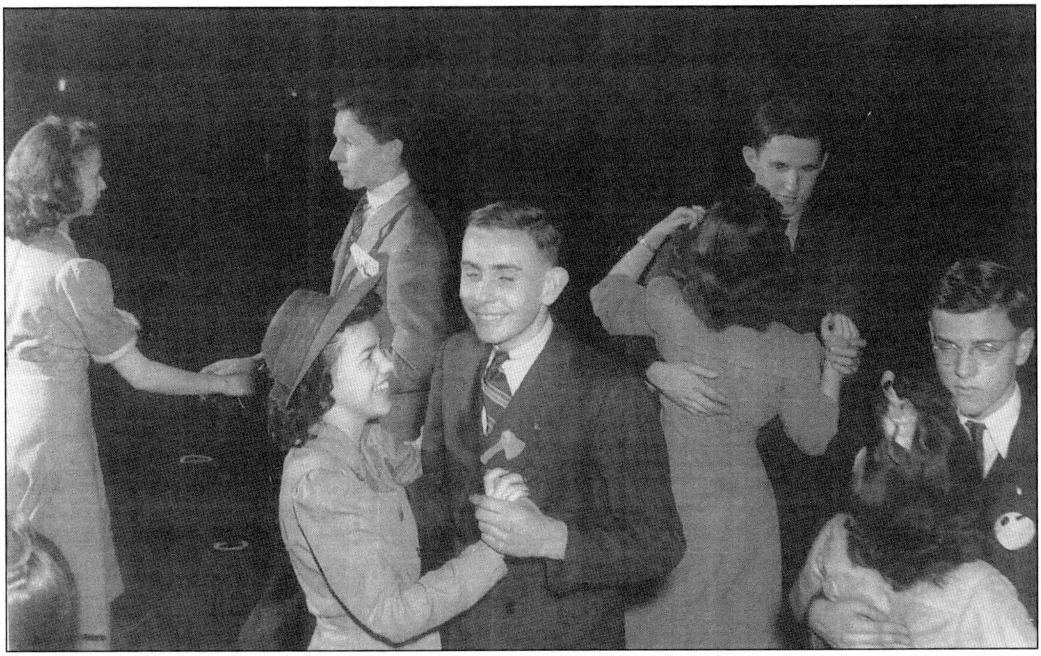

Among those present at the 1939 junior-senior dance at Dobyns-Bennett were Bill Todd, Kenner Lyons, Jim Brockman, and Peggy Rollins.

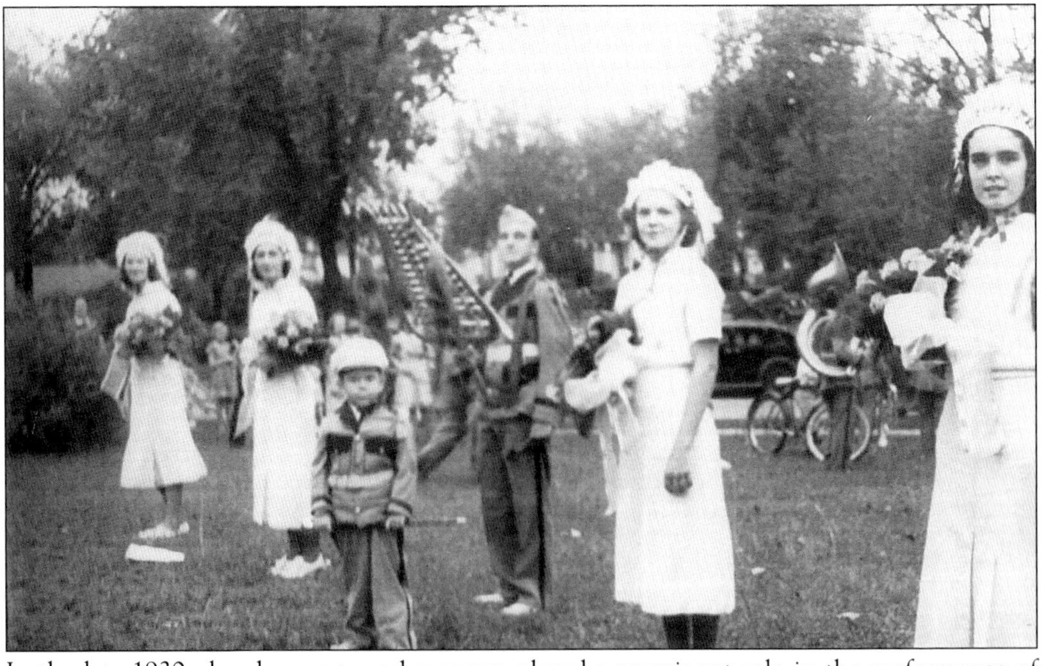

In the late 1930s, band mascots and sponsors played a prominent role in the performance of the Dobyns-Bennett Band. Among those pictured here are Barbara White, Nageba Haney, J.A. Hughes, Ruth Yancey, and Jane Lewis.

Eight

Religious, Social, and Cultural Life

Between 1917 and 1950, Kingsport achieved notable success as a community created within an established economic framework. Always considered essential to the realization of this economic plan was the presence of the "Kingsport Spirit," meaning a sense of community and mission. Fostering the "Kingsport Spirit" was a religious foundation encouraging a strong work ethic and a personal responsibility to the community. In addition to the sound religious base provided by the churches, local civic and cultural organizations were responding to national influences at the local level. With a broad sense of community and an attitude more cosmopolitan than parochial, civic and cultural activities in Kingsport became central to the community life of the town.

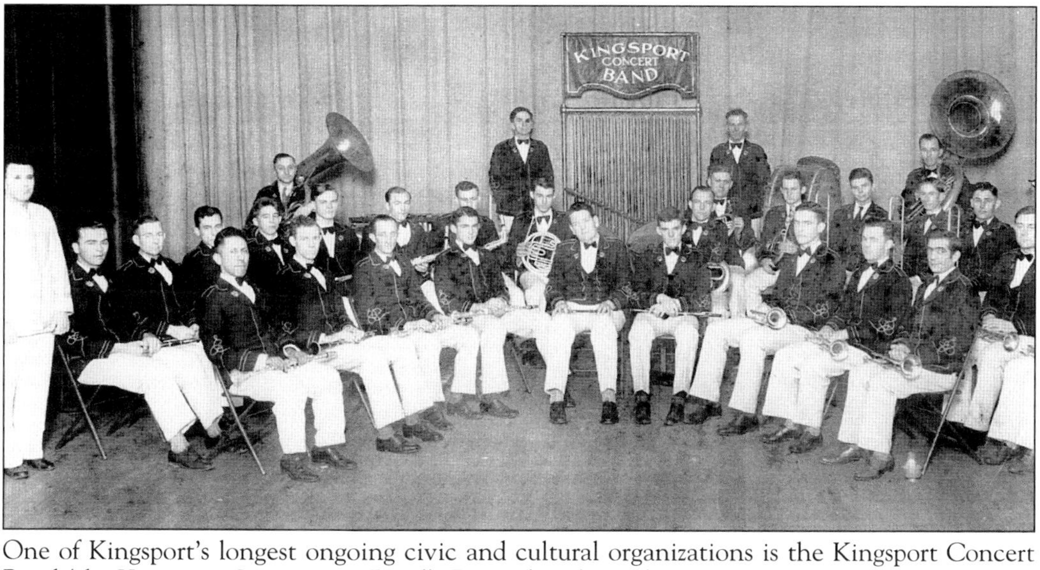

One of Kingsport's longest ongoing civic and cultural organizations is the Kingsport Concert Band (the Kingsport Community Band). Formed in the early 1900s, the band performed locally at Rotherwood and other locations. During the 1920s, the Kingsport Concert Band made regular radio appearances. For many years, the musicians' concerts were given on a downtown bandstand, located at the corner of Commerce and Center Streets. This 1924 photo of the Kingsport Concert Band features S.T. Witt (seen on the far left), the first band director at Dobyns-Bennett High School. Ray Witt, who became Lynn View High School's first band director, is seen on the front row, second from left.

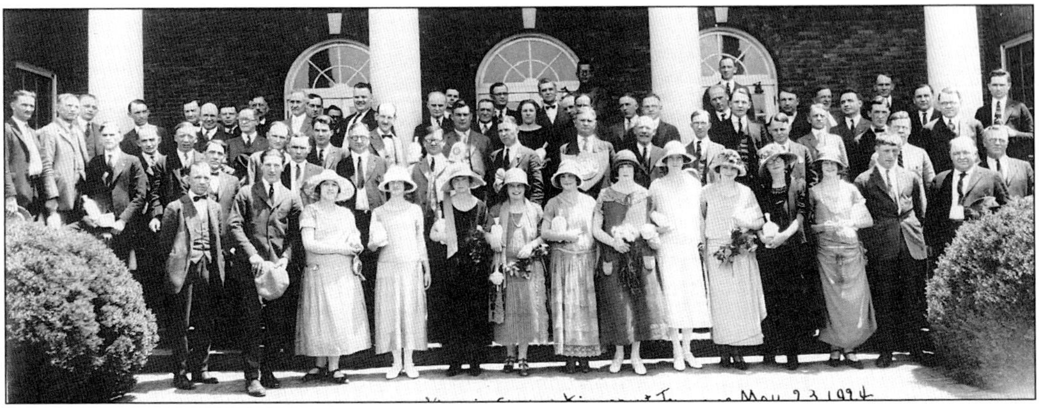

The Kiwanis Club was organized on January 8, 1924, with a membership of 58. The first-year officers and directors of the Kiwanis Club of Kingsport were Dr. E.W. Tipton, president; J.C. Stone, vice-president; G.D. Black, secretary; Glen Bruce, treasurer; A.D. Brockman, district trustee; and W.M. Bennett Jr., B.E. Dobyns, S.K. Lindsey, T.H. Pratt, C.E. Brooks, Reverend M.A. Stevenson, and J.R. Worley, directors. Guests of this meeting were graduating seniors of Kingsport High School.

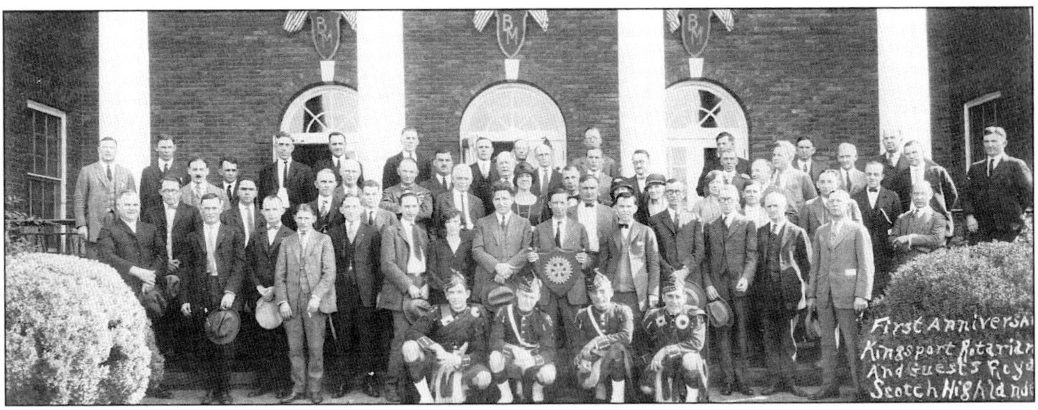

Along with the Kiwanis Club, the Rotary Club of Kingsport was active in the early history of modern Kingsport. Both groups continue to serve the community today. Dr. O.S. Hauk served as the first president of the Kingsport Rotary Club from 1923 to 1925, and Rotary president H.J. Shivell served until 1926 and was succeeded by E.W. Palmer of the Kingsport Press, Inc. J. Fred Johnson and William Roller were honorary members of the Rotary, which met at the Kingsport Inn each Wednesday at 12:10 p.m.

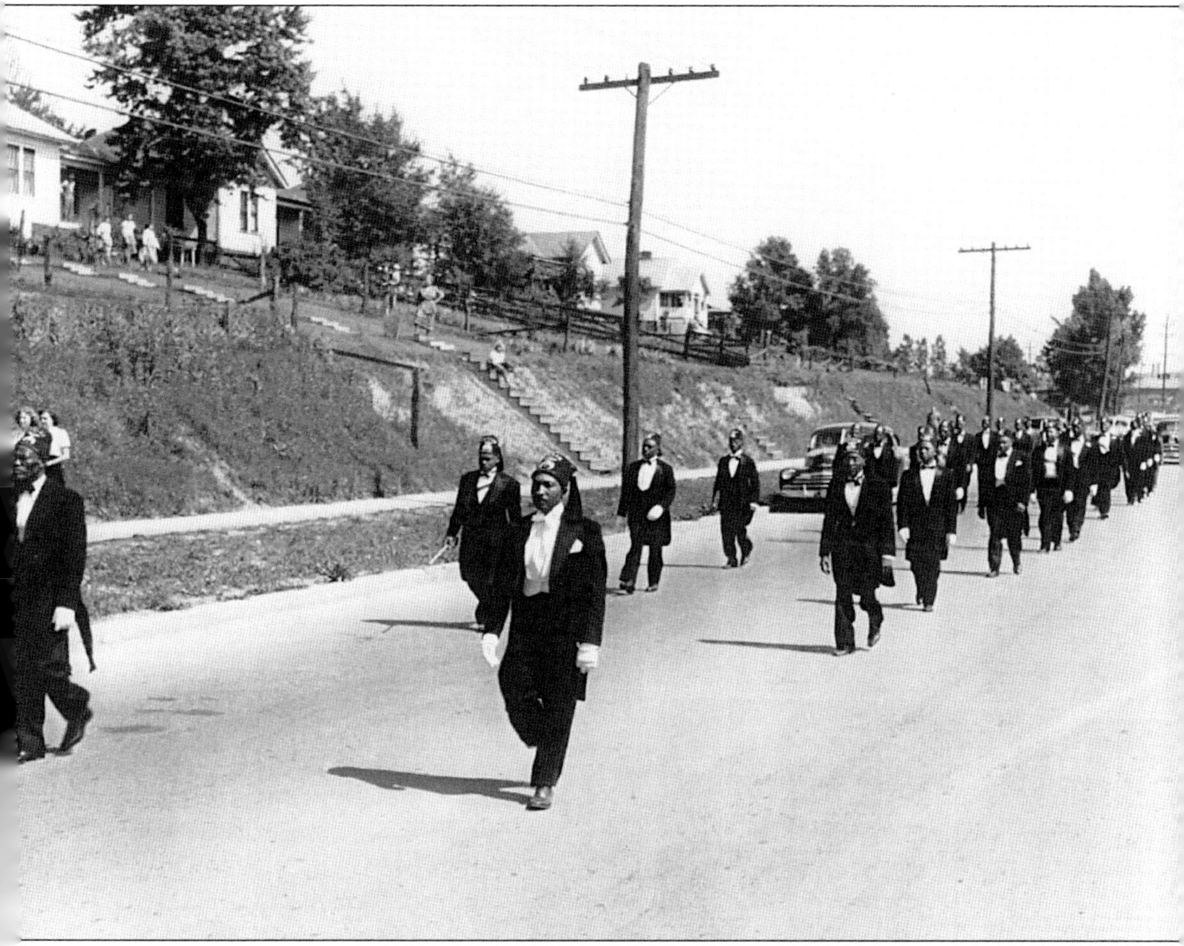

The traditional parade down Sullivan Street commemorated the state Elk convention in 1946.

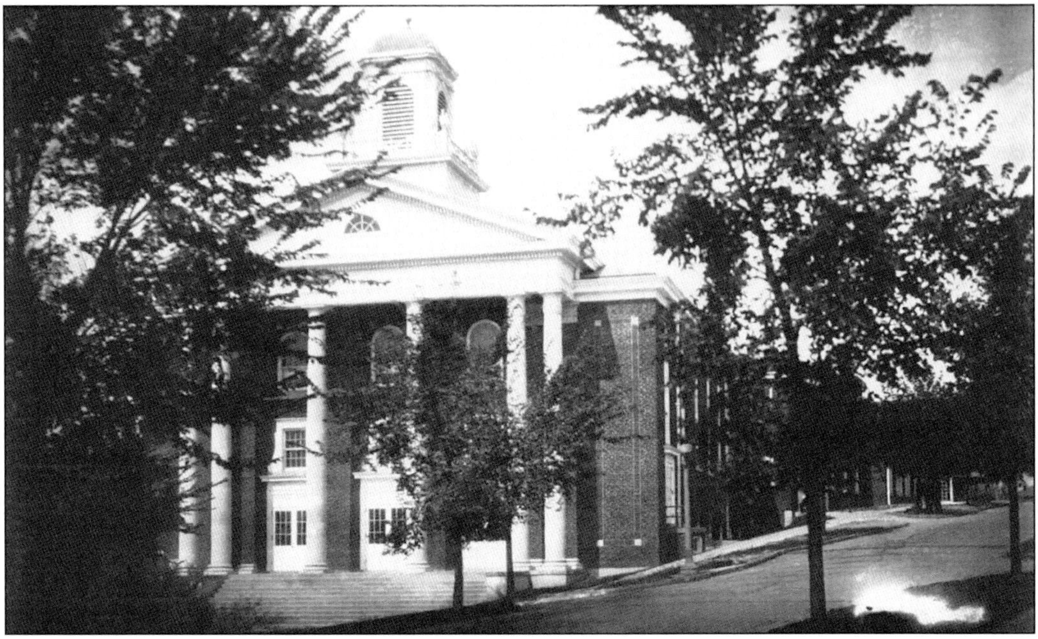

Organized January 14, 1917, the First Baptist Church of Kingsport met the need of the growing number of Baptists in Kingsport. Previously meeting in the Gem Theatre on Main Street, the congregation was given a lot on Church Circle by the Kingsport Improvement Corporation. The first building was built through contributions by William Roller, but by 1925 membership had grown from 91 to 401, and a new facility was needed. Designed by an architect from the Home Mission Board, the new building was completed in the fall of 1927. Church founders included the following: Mr. and Mrs. T.R. Bandy, Mrs. Howard Clifford, Mr. and Mrs. F.E. Mahan, Fred D. Booth, W.J. Hunter, Tom E. Hurst, W.D. Fuller, Mrs. George Rumbley, Mrs. G.W. Seaton, W.C. Yerger, Dr. David S. Yoakley, Mrs. M.L. Zimmerman, Mr. and Mrs. Guy D. Pitts, and Mr. Nunnerlly.

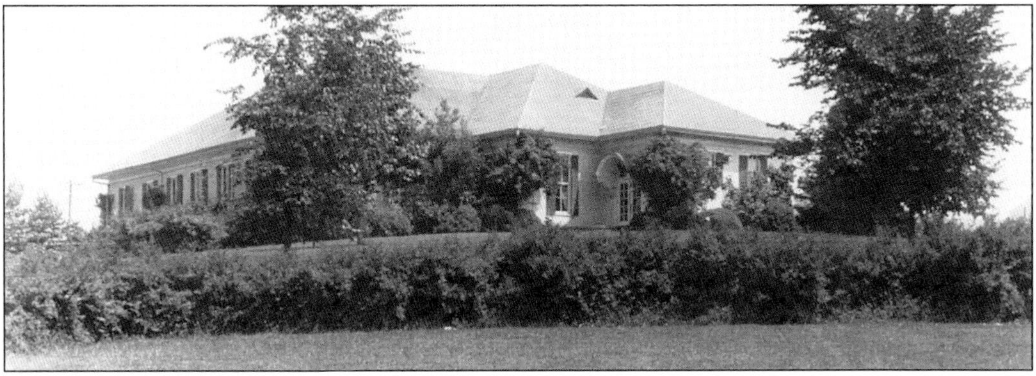

Beginning with 52 charter members, 6 elders, and 10 deacons, the First Presbyterian Church was organized on March 19, 1917, and met in a downtown tent and the old Gaiety Theatre before the Kingsport Improvement Corporation deeded a small schoolhouse to the congregation. Services were conducted in this structure until late in 1940, when the schoolhouse was demolished and a new church was constructed on the same site. Charter members included the Anderson, Angle, Barton, Bennett, Blair, Gorda, Hogan, Hoss, Hufford, Johnson, Kenner, King, Law, Lyons, McChesney, Nelms, Newland, Pierce, Pope, Porter, Russell, Smith, Steele, Vance, Wells, Westerman, Williams, Williamson, and Wright families.

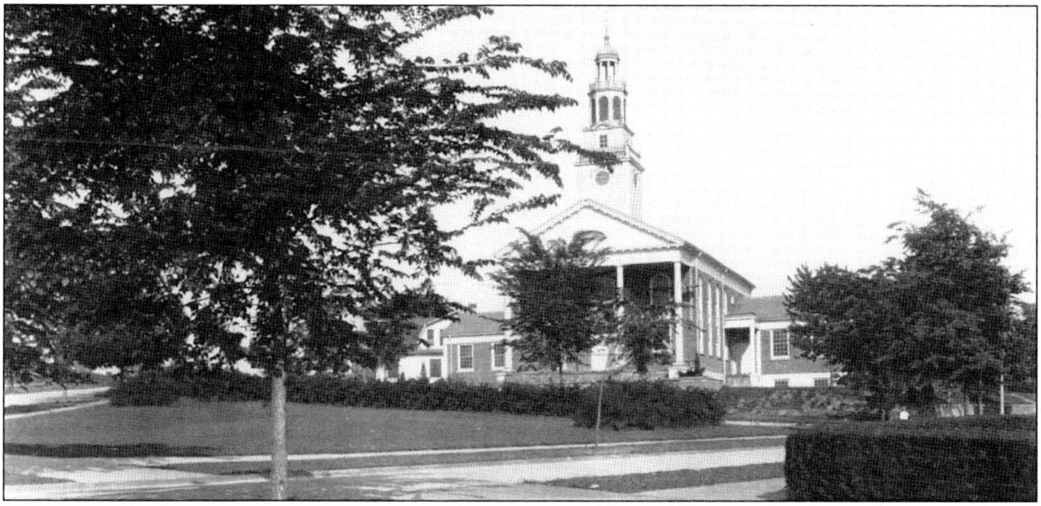

Three other Methodist congregations were involved in the formation of what is today known as the First Broad Street United Methodist Church. The old Boatyard Methodist Episcopal Church split during the Civil War into "Northern Methodists" and "Southern Methodists." Ultimately, members of these congregations moved to the "new" Kingsport. In 1916, the Kingsport Improvement Co. gave a piece of the Church Circle property to the Methodist Episcopal Church South, which was dedicated in 1917 as the Broad Street Methodist Episcopal Church South. The "Northern Methodists" organized their church as the First Methodist Episcopal Church and later obtained a Church Circle location in 1926. Charter members of the church include the following: Mr. and Mrs. Mel Cox, Mr. and Mrs. Guy DeVault, Bertie Lee Skeens, Mr. and Mrs. J.W. Harrison Sr., Dr. and Mrs. J.V. Hodge, Dr. and Mrs. George Keener, Mr. and Mrs. D.A. Pyle Sr., Miss Lydia Harrison, Miss Nora Harrison, Mrs. Mellie H. Keefauver, Mrs. Pearle Rogers, and Mrs. Effie Ketron Henderson.

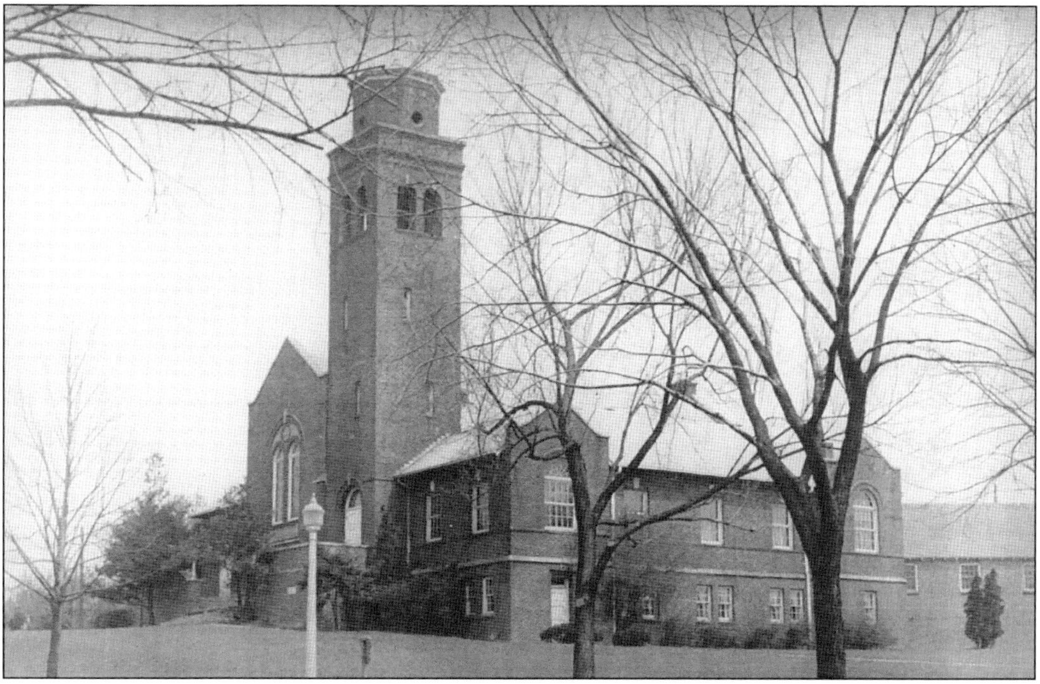

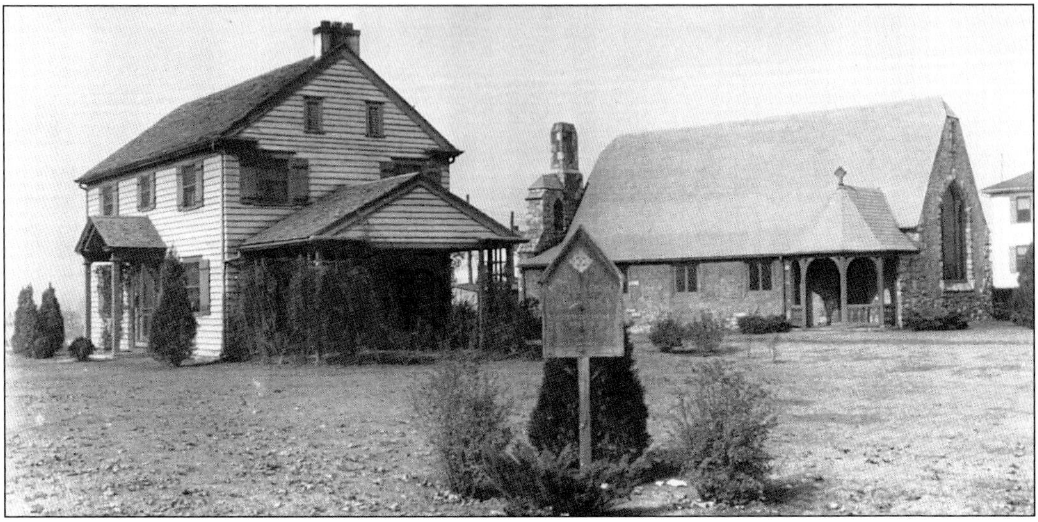

St. Paul's Episcopal Church began in 1916 as a mission of St. John's Church in Johnson City and became a self-supporting parish in 1931. In 1918 and 1919, property at the present Ravine Road site was donated to the mission by the Kingsport Improvement Corporation. Designed by architect Allen Dryden Sr., the present church building's construction began in late 1927.

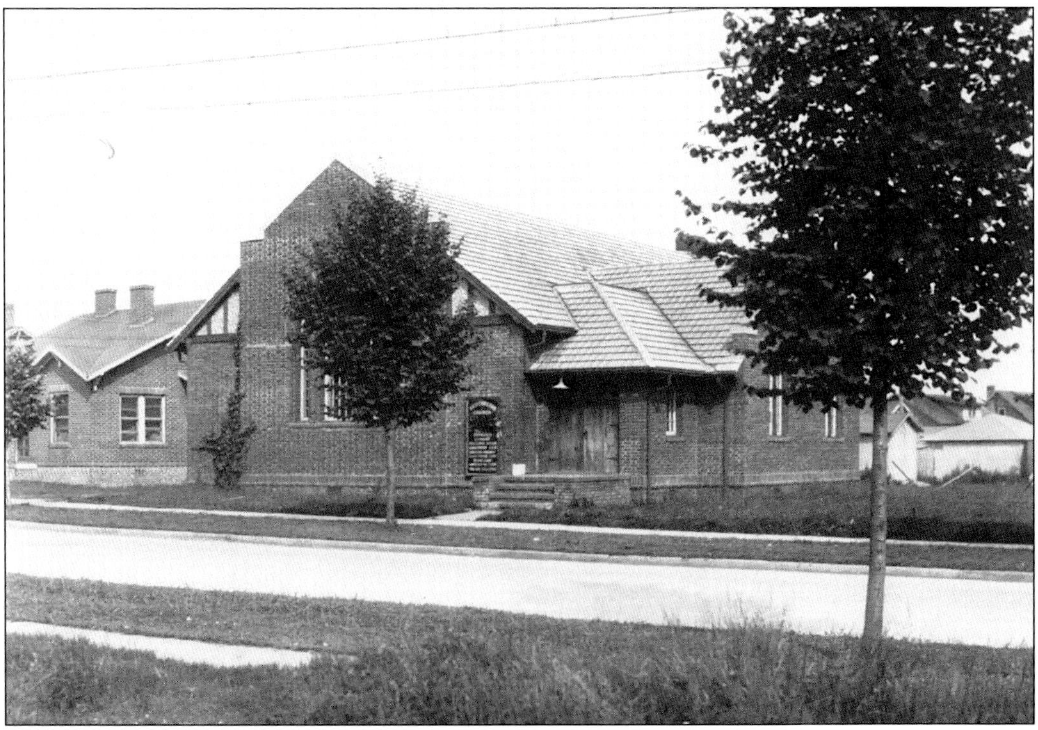

The Kingsport Hotel, located on Main Street, was the site of the 1917 organizational meeting of First Christian Church. Early in its history, services were conducted in the Gem Theatre, also on Main Street. Today, located near Church Circle on Charlemont Street, the church has created four newer congregations in Kingsport.

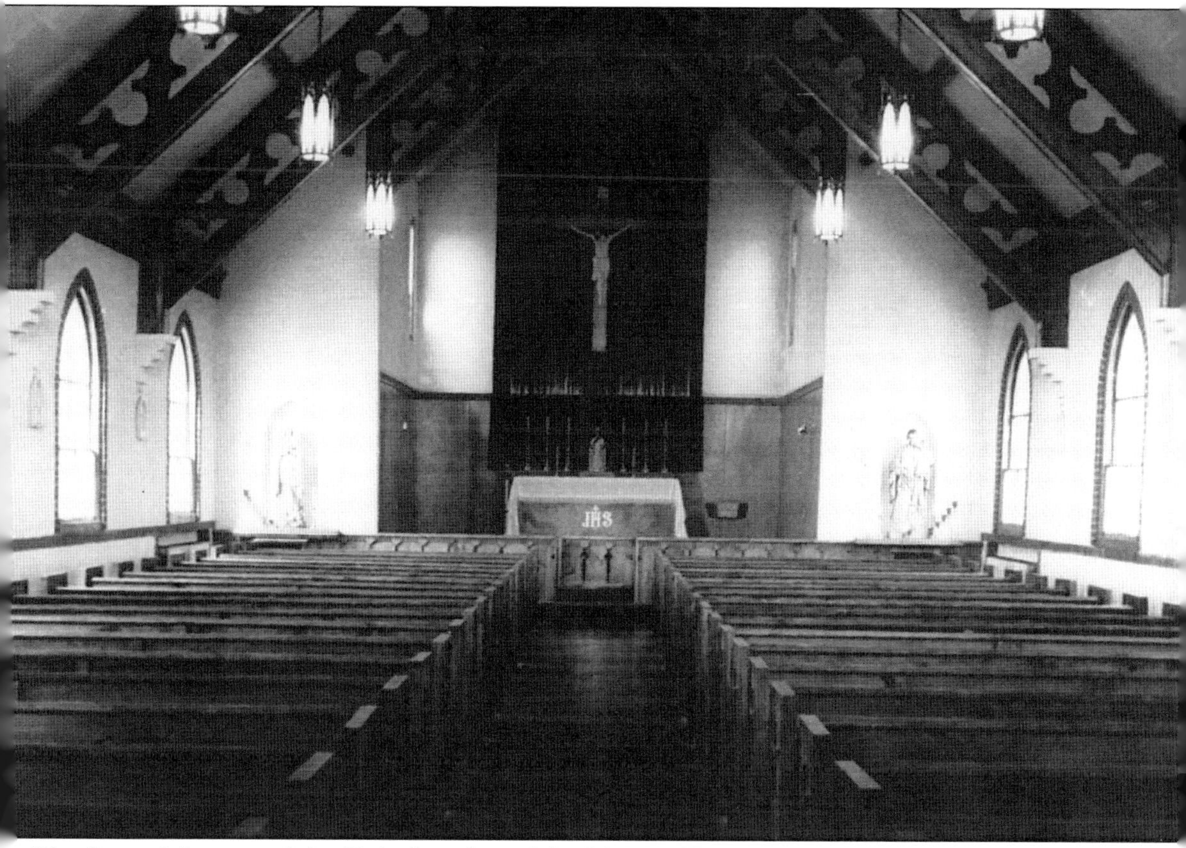

The first celebration of the Holy Sacrifice of the Mass in Kingsport was, most likely, held in 1914 by Johnson City's Father Callahan. He came to serve a Roman Catholic congregation who moved to Kingsport in connection with the construction and establishment of new industry. Mass was held at a variety of locations until St. Dominic Church, on Crescent and Center Streets, was dedicated in 1941. St. Dominic's, a mission of the Dominican Fathers, became a parish church of the Diocese of Nashville in 1945.

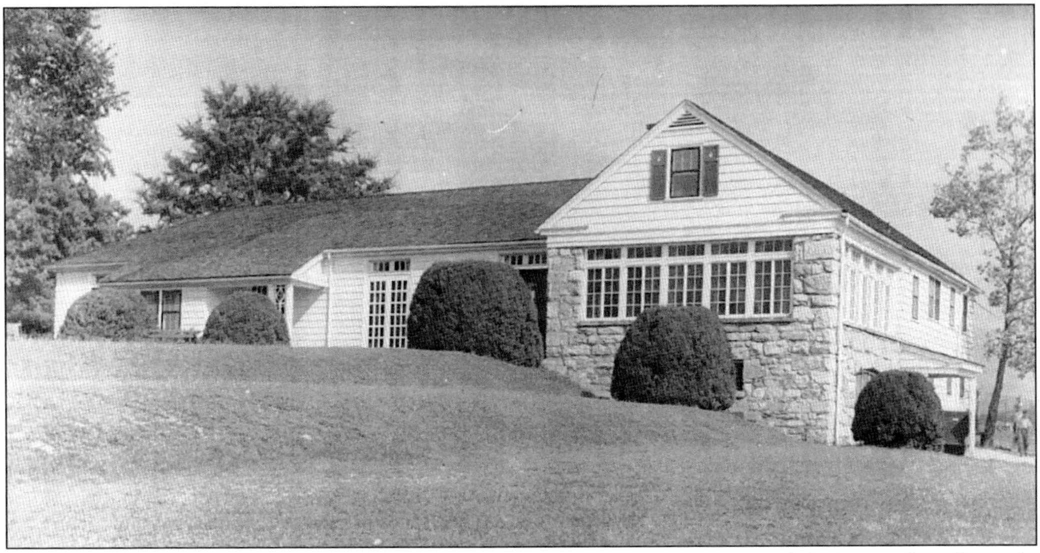

A center of Kingsport social life in this era was the Kingsport Country Club, located on Pineola Street. In the late 1930s, the club offered golf, tennis, and social privileges, and required a membership fee of $24 per year for a single membership or $36 for a family membership.

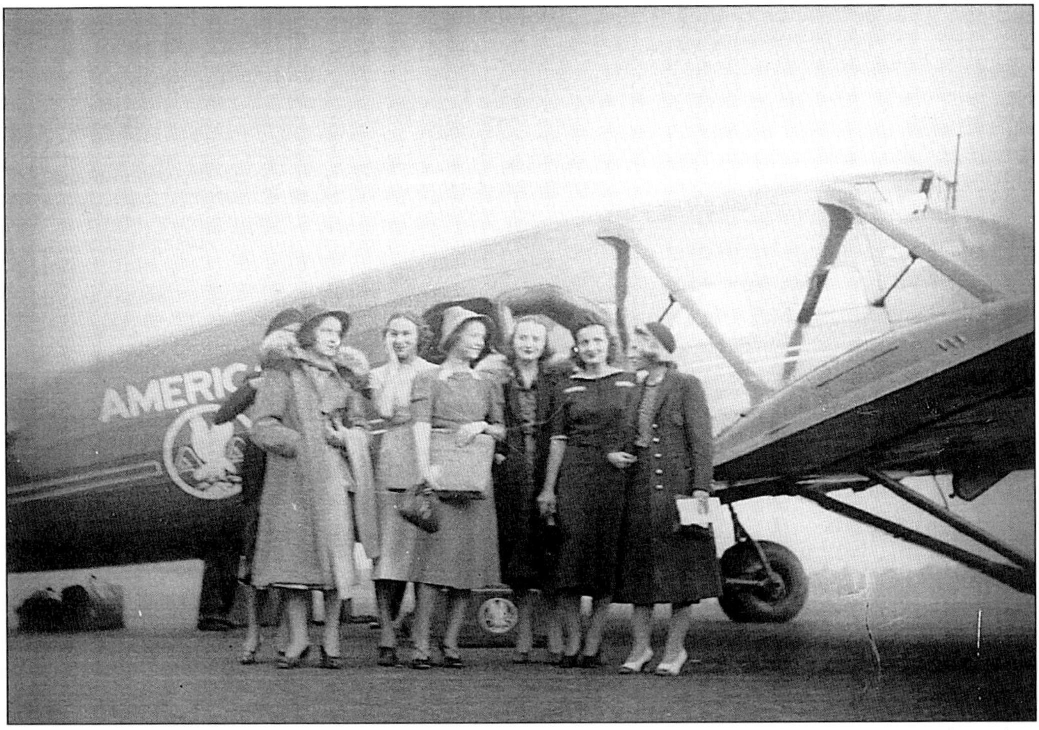

The inaugural flight of American Airlines to Kenneth McKellar Field was captured in this 1936 photograph.

Dobyns-Bennett High School's Graduates Day always included a variety of social and celebratory activities.

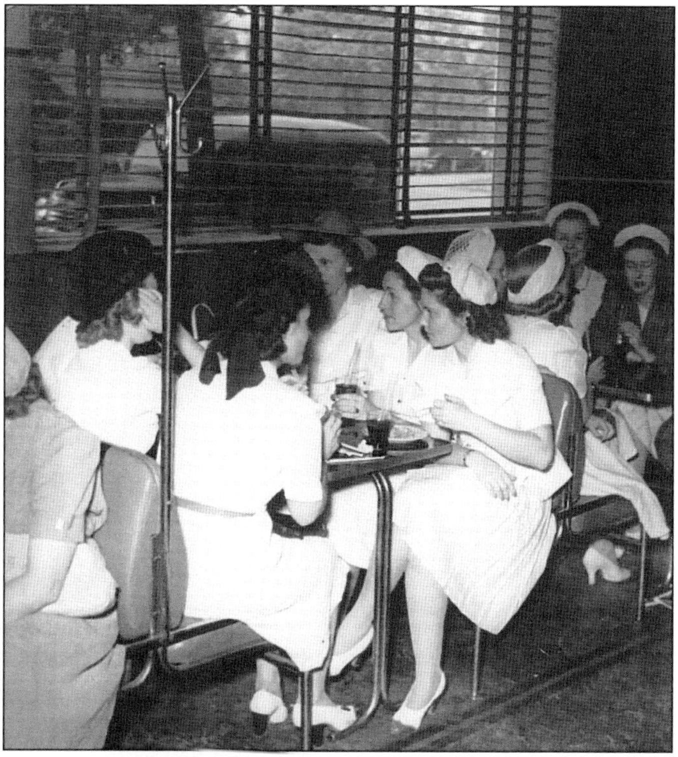

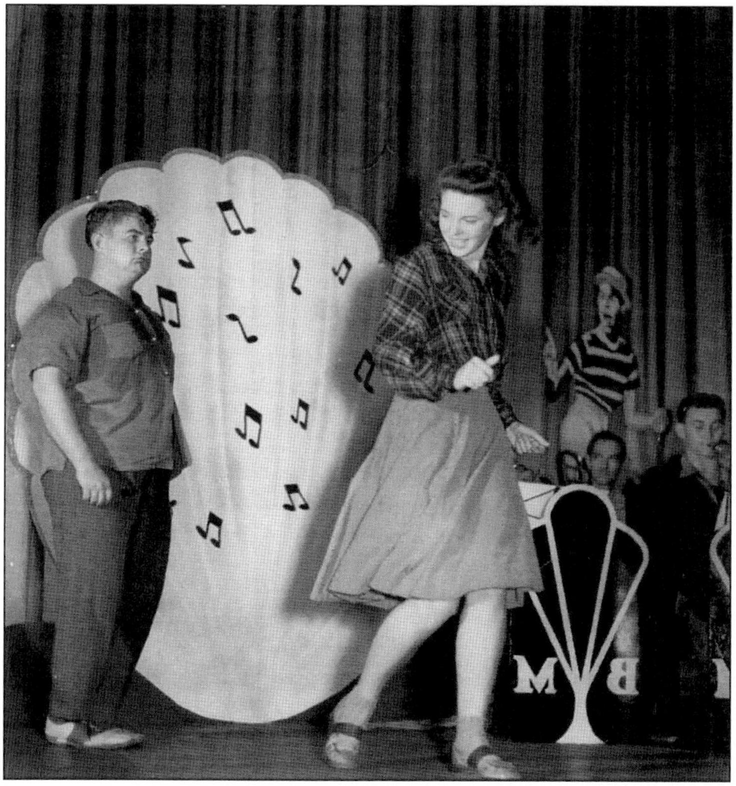

The State Theatre was the site of a 1941 Jitterbug contest. Pictured are Charles Aesque and Clara Dodd.

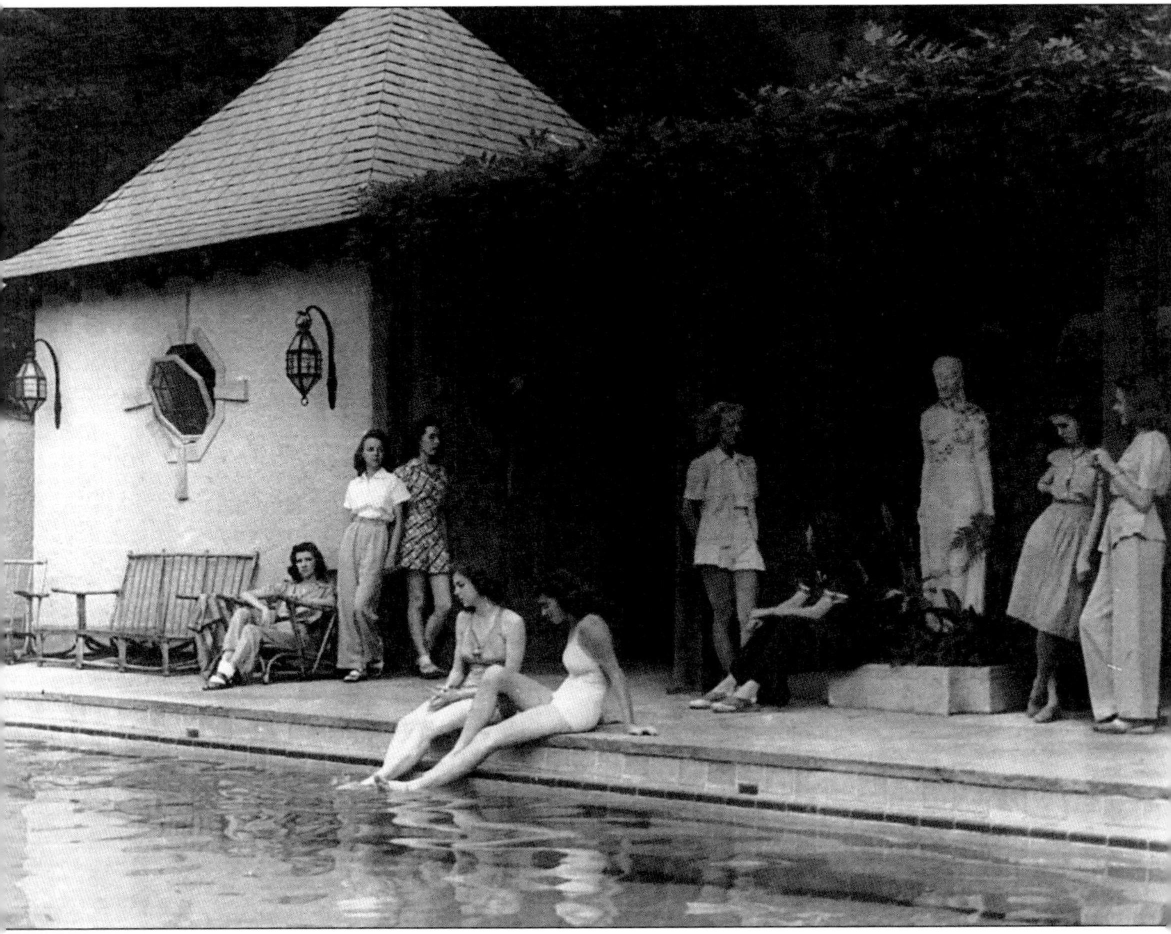

Meeting by the pool of the Perley Wilcox home, the Welfare League prepares for a 1940 fashion show. Originated in 1935, the Kingsport Junior Welfare League and the Kingsport Junior Auxiliary (1947) combined to create the Kingsport Junior Service League. Later, the Junior League of Kingsport was formed. Among the young women pictured here are Joyce Hammock (sitting in chair), Pauline Showalter, and Betty McAuliffe. Valda Stone and Ruth Von Bramer are seated next to the pool. Virginia Hawk is standing fourth from right with Patricia Fine, Jane Lewis, and Martha Corns.

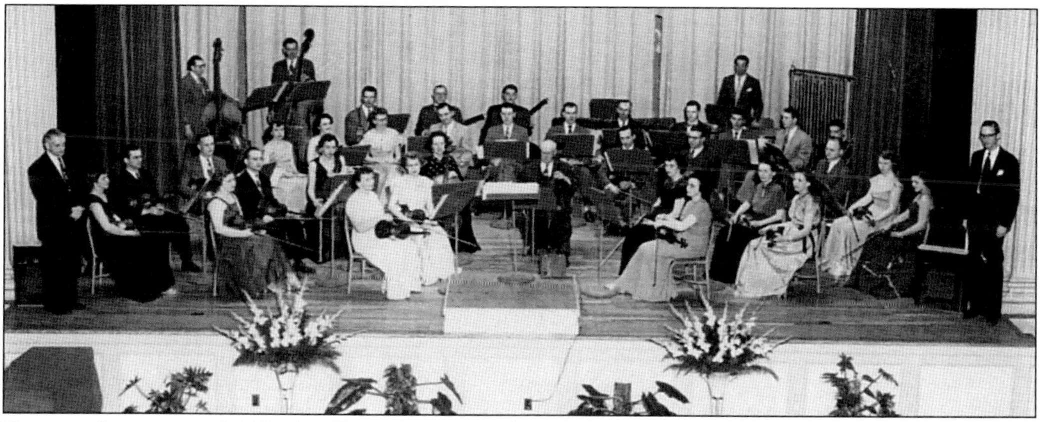

First performing in 1948, the Kingsport Symphony Orchestra (KSO) was under the direction of Roger Barrigar. Here is the KSO in 1951 performing in the auditorium at Dobyns-Bennett High School on Wateree Street. Orchestra personnel included the following: (first violins) Mrs. Vivian Parker, Mrs. J.W. Campbell, Mrs. Dave Wallace, Nick Drakos, Margaret Haygood, Pope Johnson, and N.C. Russin; (second violins) Mrs. Marjorie Pendleton (principal second), Mrs. Mary Leonard, Mrs. Helen Slemp, Brenda Goerdel (fifth chair), and Merle Pike (seventh chair); (violas) George DeCroes and Don Ross (principal); (cello) Elizabeth Alvey, Lois Perkins, and William Bryant; (bass) Tom Strickland and Paul Weston; (flutes) Elizabeth Barnes (principal, on right of group), Frances Earnest, and Margaret Barker; (oboe) Elbert Hurt; (clarinets) Luther Stapleton, Wayne McConnell, and John Jensen; (bassoons) Jitney (E.B) Blankenbecler and Bill Rucker; (horns) J.A. Hinkley and Dan Delius; (trombone) Joe Davy; (percussion) C.G. Jeremias; and (trumpet) Carl Archer. Conductor Barrigar is on the left of stage, and KSO board member Jim Welch is standing on the right of the D-B stage.

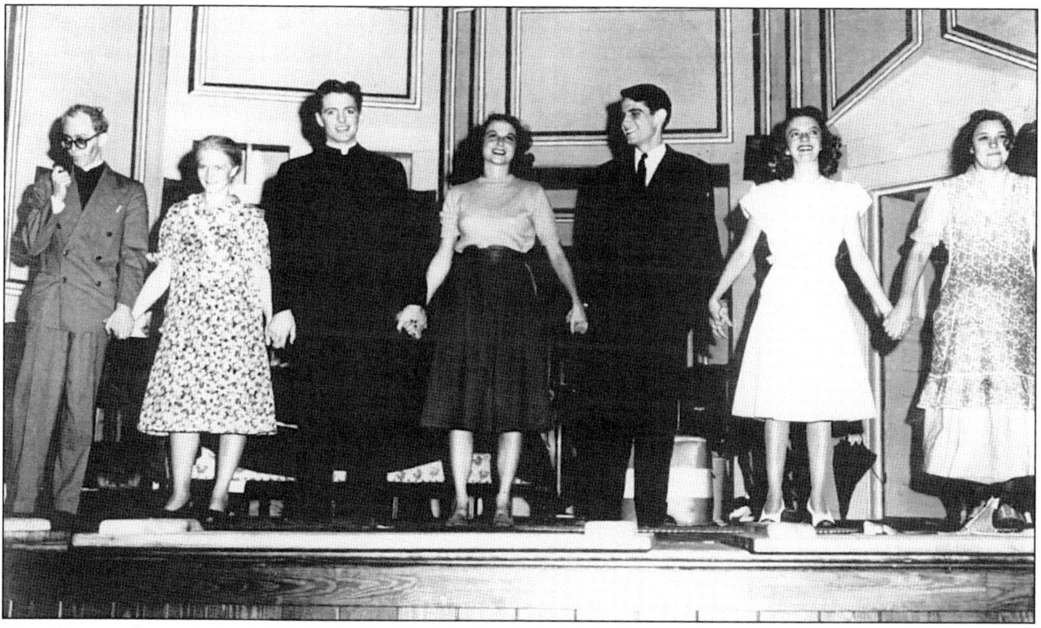

On September 22, 1947, the newly formed Kingsport Theatre Guild presented its first production, *Yes and No*, at the junior high school. The comedy was a hit with Kingsport audiences and featured, from left to right, Dan Anderson, Emma Straley, "Hezzy" Osborne, Elizabeth Hagemeyer, Ben Sargent, Margaret Throp, and Margaret Wimberly.

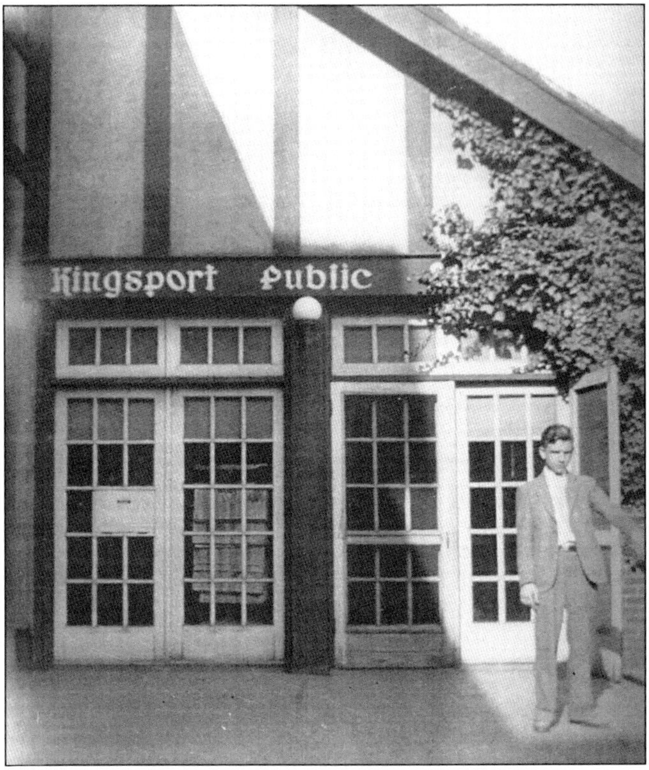

The first meeting of the board of trustees of the Kingsport Public Library was held on May 9, 1929, at the library, which was in the Municipal Building. Present were library organizers who then served as trustees: E.W. Palmer, Ross N. Robinson, E.W. Tipton, T.P. Johnston, Mrs. H.J. Shivell, Mrs. F.M. Kelly, and the librarian, Mrs. T.E. Hurst.

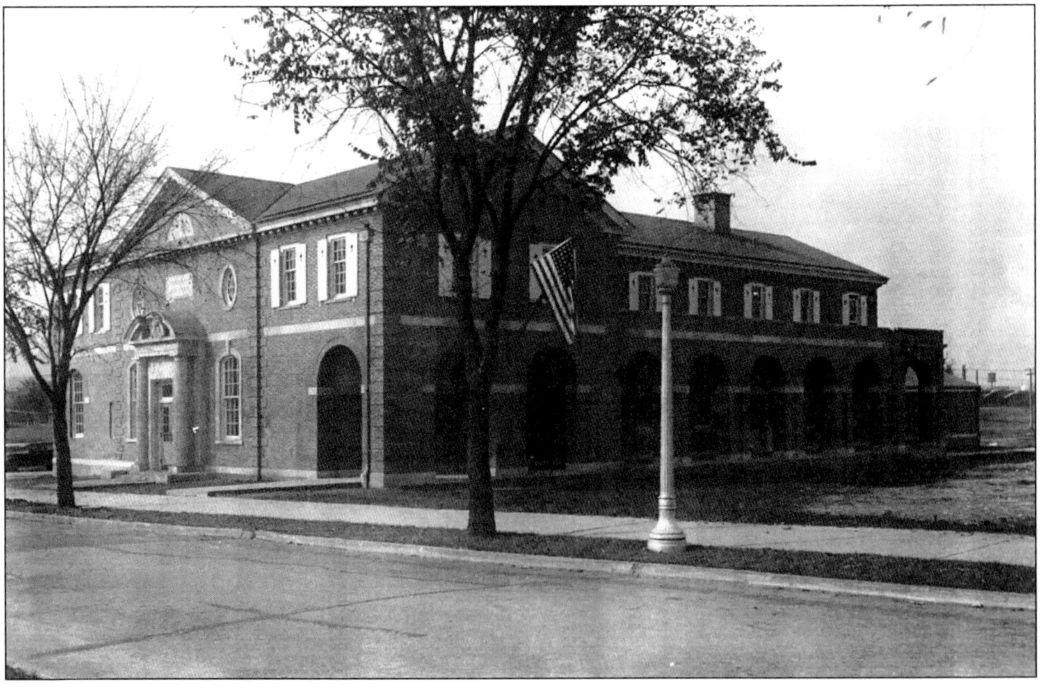

Later named the J. Fred Johnson Memorial Library, the facility relocated to a renovated post office building at the corner of Broad and New Streets and was dedicated on November 19, 1961.

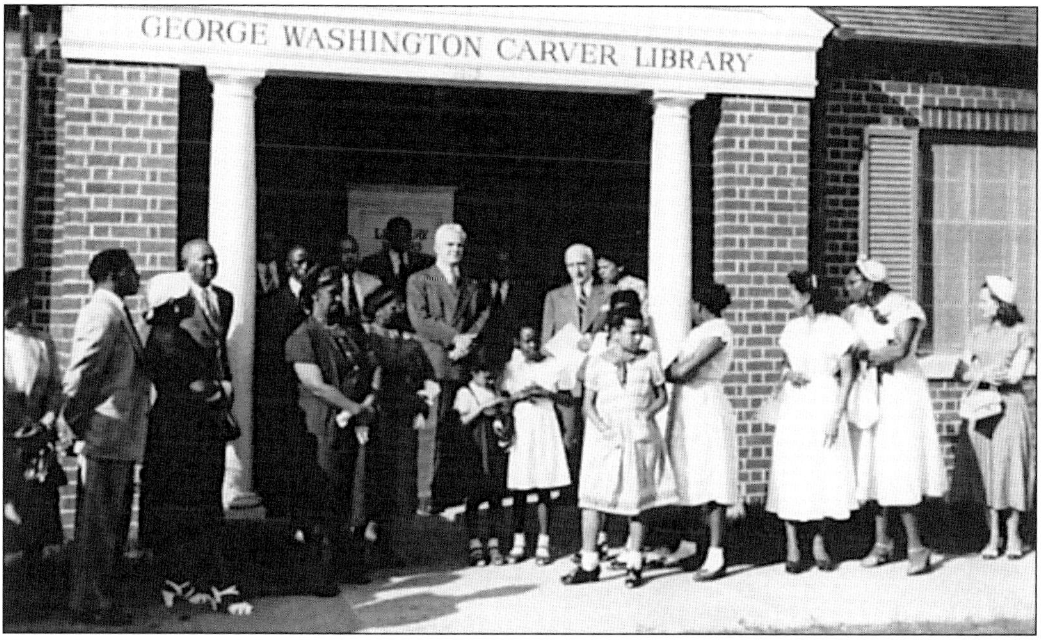

Named in honor of African-American scientist and educator George Washington Carver, a new Riverview branch of the Kingsport Public Library opened in 1951. The official opening was attended by library commissioner E.W. Palmer and interested citizens.

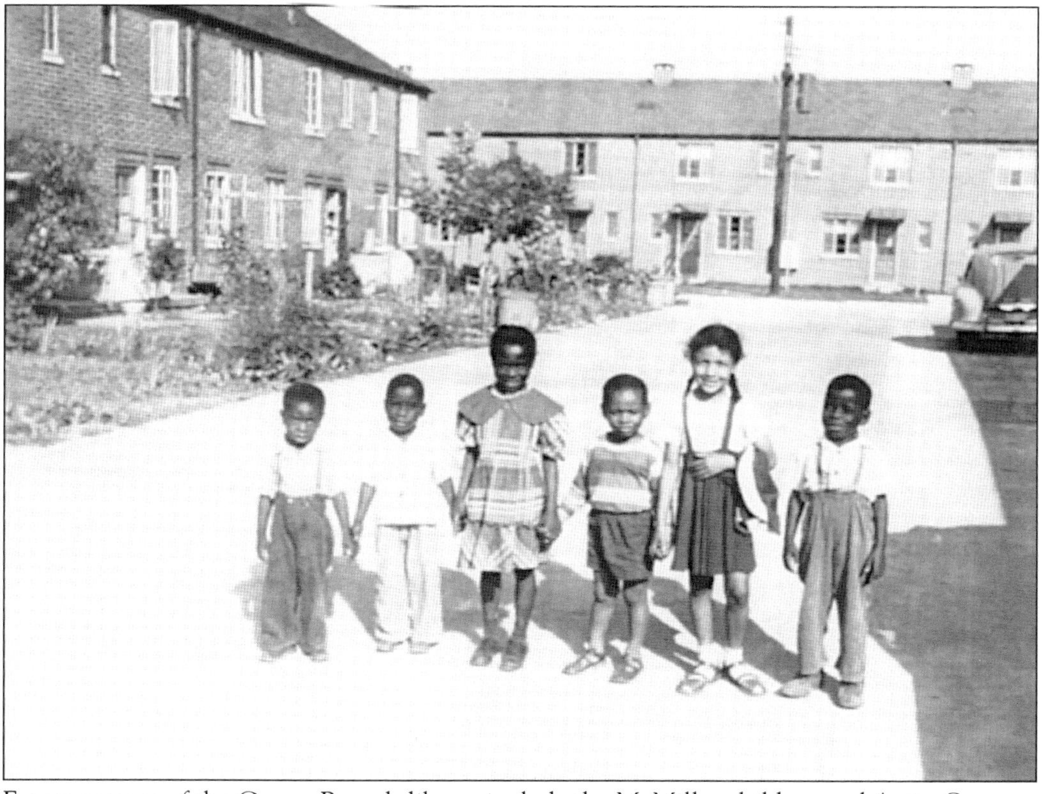

Future patrons of the Carver Branch library include the McMillar children and Anita Carnes.

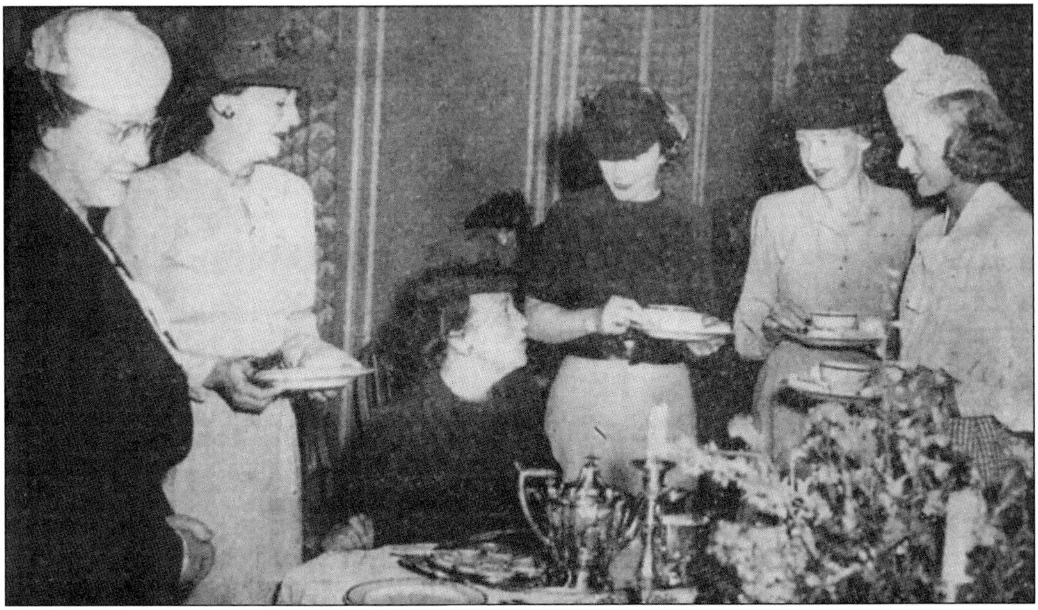

Reflecting project goals of the National League of Women Voters (LWV), Kingsport's group first formed in 1937. Its programs encouraging citizen education and encouraging governmental participation were regularly featured in the Kingsport *Times-News* section of the paper entitled "Society and Women's News." Pictured here is a membership tea with, from left to right, the following: (seated) Mrs. H.N. Horsley; (standing) Mmes. H.G. Gladson, L.J. Pepper, R.J. Sims, W.T. Trent, and Paul Wilson.

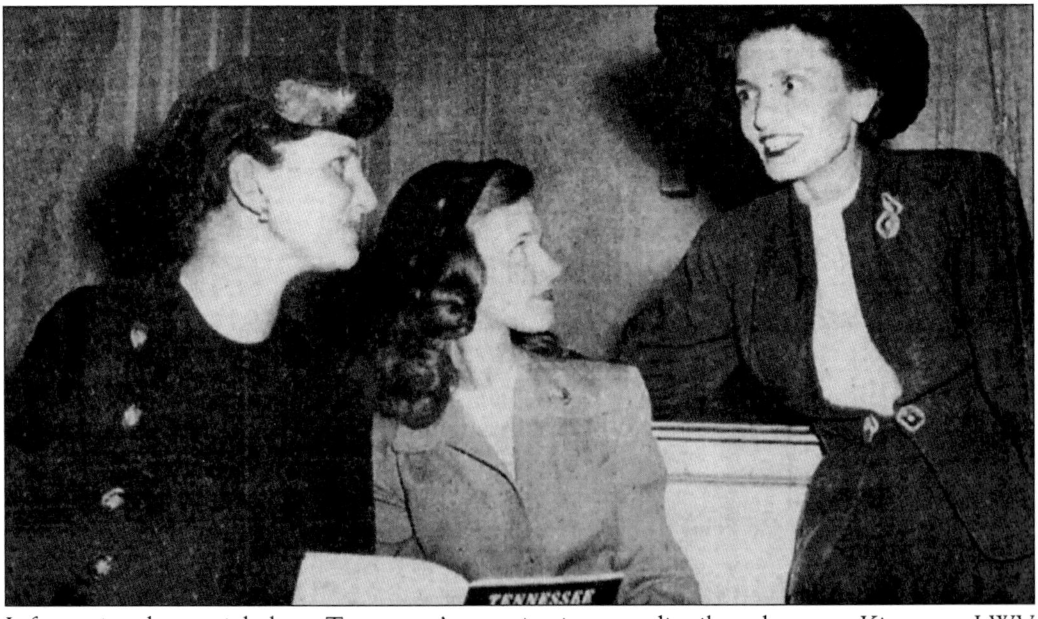

Informational material about Tennessee's constitution was distributed to new Kingsport LWV members. Mrs. T.M. Taylor, Mrs. James Mitchell, and LWV president Mrs. S.L. Showker were featured in this 1946 Kingsport *Times-News* story. Mrs. Showker's daughter, Selwa Showker (Mrs. Archibald Roosevelt, also known as "Lucky"), served as White House chief of protocol for President Ronald Reagan.

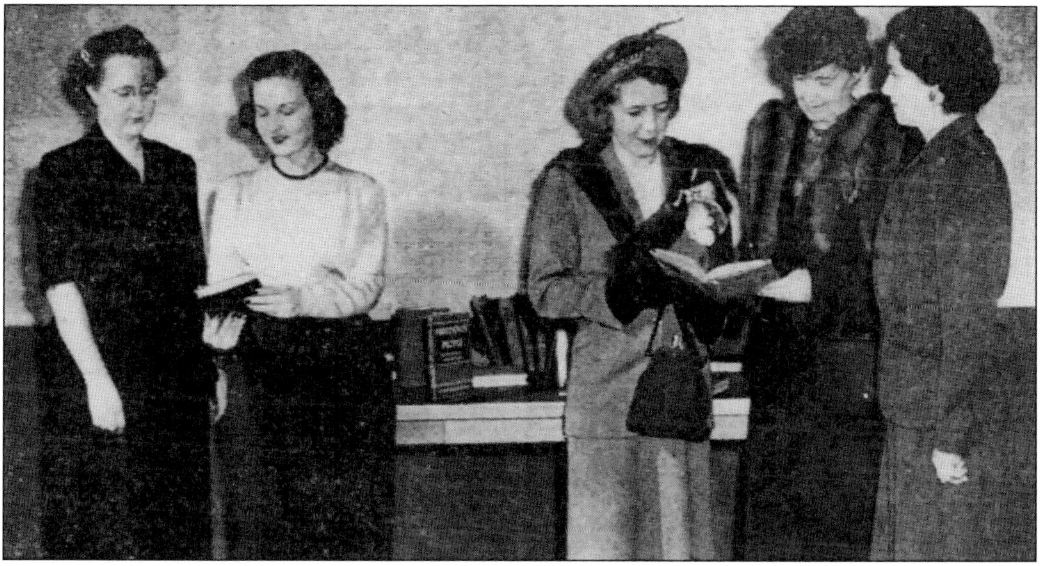

Providing programs and projects related to education, health care, and government, the Kingsport branch of the American Association of University Women (AAUW) formed in 1948. In this Kingsport *Times-News* photo from early 1949, the chapter meets with state officers for a program on Kingsport City Schools. From left to right, these members are Mrs. H.W. Dungan, membership chair; Miss Joanne Allen, Kingsport AAUW president; Mrs. Joe Phillips, state president; Mrs. C.D. Foree, state arts chair; and Mrs. L.G. Davy, education committee chair.

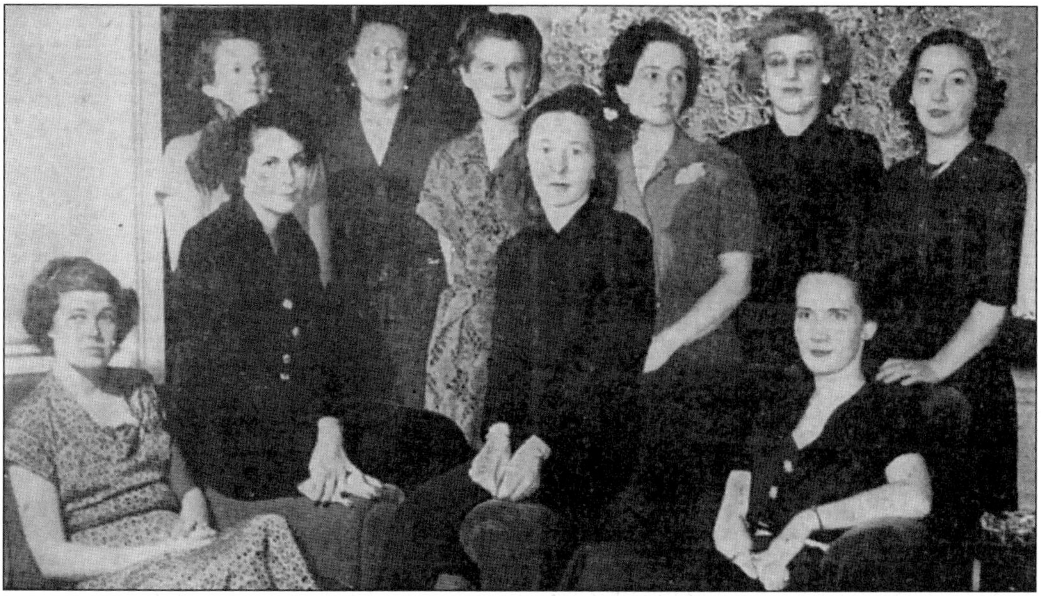

Meeting at the Kingsport Inn in December 1949 are AAUW officers and committee chairs. From left to right they are as follows: (seated) Mrs. Violet Addington, social studies chair; Miss Ruth Volcker, international relations chair; Mrs. Charles Lamkins, secretary; and Mrs. Howard S. Young, treasurer; (standing) Mrs. J.S. Hawkins, membership co-chair; Mrs. H.W. Dungan, vice-president; Mrs. C.S. Soe, legislation; Mrs. Lee Davy, education chair; Mrs. W.M. MacNaughton, arts chair; and Mrs. J.T. Jenkins, president.

BIBLIOGRAPHY

A. Primary Sources

Kingsport, Tennessee. Archives of the City of Kingsport, Kingsport Public Library and Archives. Historic Collections.

B. Books

Ackerman, Carl W. *George Eastman*. Boston: Houghton Mifflin Company, 1930. Reissued by Augustus M. Kelly of Clinton, New Jersey, 1973.

Brayer, Elizabeth. *George Eastman: A Biography*. Baltimore and London: Johns Hopkins University Press, 1996.

Boorstin, Daniel J. "The Businessman as City Booster." *American Urban History: An Interpretive Reader with Commentaries*. Ed. Alexander Callow Jr. New York and Oxford: Oxford University Press, 1982, pp. 94–101.

Chafe, William H. *The American Woman: Her Changing Social, Economic, and Political Roles, 1920–1970*. Oxford University Press, 1972; reprinted 1977.

Drewry, Henry. "Black Americans." *Academic American Encyclopedia*. Danbury, Connecticut: Grolier, Inc., 1995.

Dykes, Pete. *The Complete Kinnie Wagner Story*. Pete Dykes, Kingsport *Daily News*.

Egan, Martha Avaleen. "George Lafayette Carter." *Tennessee Encyclopedia of History and Culture*. Ed. Carroll Van West. Tennessee Historical Society and Rutledge Hill Press, 1998, p. 131.

———. "John B. Dennis." *Tennessee Encyclopedia of History and Culture*. Ed. Carroll Van West. Tennessee Historical Society and Rutledge Hill Press, 1998, p. 244.

———. "Kingsport Press." *Tennessee Encyclopedia of History and Culture*. Ed. Carroll Van West. Tennessee Historical Society and Rutledge Hill Press, 1998, pp. 503–504.

———. "Tennessee Eastman Company." *Tennessee Encyclopedia of History and Culture*. Ed. Carroll Van West. Tennessee Historical Society and Rutledge Hill Press, 1998, pp. 927–929.

Eller, Ronald D. *Miners, Millhands, and Mountaineers: Industrialization of the Appalachian South, 1800–1930*. Knoxville: University of Tennessee Press, 1982.

Goforth, James A. *Building the Clinchfield: A Construction History of America's Most Unusual Railroad*. Newell, Iowa: Bireline Publishing Co., Gem Publishers, 1983.

Grouff, Stephine. *Manhattan Project: The Untold Story of the Making of the Atomic Bomb*. Boston: Little, Brown, and Co., 1967.

Groves, Leslie *Now It Can Be Told: The Story of the Manhattan Project*. New York: Harper and Brothers, 1962.

Hancock, John L. "Planners in the Changing American City, 1900–1940." *American Urban History: An Interpretive Reader with Commentaries*. Ed. by Alexander Callow Jr. New York and Oxford: Oxford University Press, 1962, pp. 515–533.

Hoover, David Allen. *Dobyns-Bennett Football: The Sprankle Years, 1921–1934*. Johnson City, Tennessee: Overmountain Press, 1987.

Kingsport Retired Teachers' Association. *80 Years of Enlightenment: Recollections of Kingsport Teachers, 1996*. Kingsport: Collier's Printing Company, 1997.

Kingsport Rotary Club. *Kingsport, Tennessee: A Modern American City—Developed through Industry*. Kingsport: Kingsport Press, 1963.

———. *Kingsport: The Planned Industrial City*. Kingsport: Kingsport Press, 1937.

———. *Kingsport: The Planned Industrial City*. Kingsport: Kingsport Press, 1951.

Lay, Elery A. *An Industrial and Commercial History of the Tri Cities in Tennessee-Virginia*. Kingsport: Lay Publications, 1982.

Long, Howard. *Kingsport: A Romance of Industry*. Kingsport: Sevier Press, 1928.

Maurer, Herrymon. *In Quiet Ways, George H. Mead: The Man and the Company*. Dayton, Ohio: Mead Corporation, 1970.

Nolen, John. *New Towns for Old: Achievement in Civic Improvement in Some American Small Towns and Neighborhoods*. Boston: Marshall Jones Company, 1927.

Phillips, V.N. (Bud). *Bristol Tennessee/Virginia: A History 1852–1900*. Johnson City, Tennessee: Overmountain Press, 1992.

Ross, Charles D., ed. *The Story of Rotherwood from the Autobiography of Rev. Frederick A. Ross, D.D. in letters to a lady of Knoxville, (Mrs. Juliet Park White), Huntsville, Ala. 1882–83*. Knoxville, Tennessee: Bean, Warters & Co. Printers, 1923.

Spoden, Muriel C. and the Sullivan County Historical Commission and Associates. *Historic Sites of Sullivan County*. Kingsport Press, 1976

Spoden, M.C. Millar. *Kingsport Heritage: The Early Years 1700 to 1900*. Johnson City Tennessee: Overmountain Press, 1991.

Sullivan County Historical Society. *Foundations of Faith in Sullivan, 1777–1935*. Sullivan County: 1986.

Tindall, George Brown. *The Emergence of the New South, 1913–1945*. Baton Rouge: Louisiana State University Press, 1967.

Thackray, Arnold, Jeffrey L. Sturchio, P. Thomas Carroll, and Robert Bud. *Chemistry in America, 1876–1976: Historical Indicators*. Hingham, Massachusetts: Kluwer Publishers, 1985.

Way, William Jr. *The Clinchfield Railroad: The Story of a Trade Route across the Blue Ridge Mountains*. Chapel Hill: University of North Carolina Press, 1931.

Wolfe, Margaret Ripley. *Kingsport, Tennessee: A Planned American City*. University Press of Kentucky, 1987.

———. "Kingsport." *Tennessee Encyclopedia of History and Culture*. Ed. Carroll Van West. Tennessee Historical Society and Rutledge Hill Press, 1998, pp. 502–503.

C. *Articles, Reports, Theses, and Maps*

Ayers, Edward L. "Northern Business and the Shape of Southern Progress: The Case of Tennessee's 'Model City.' " *Tennessee Historical Quarterly* 39 (Summer 1980): 208–222.

Counce, Paul A. "Social and Economic History of Kingsport." M.A. thesis, University of Tennessee, 1939.

Egan, Martha Avaleen. "Islands of Industrialism: The Role of the Carolina, Clinchfield and Ohio Railway in the Industrialization of Upper East Tennessee, 1909–1925." M.A. thesis, East Tennessee State University, 1986.

Holly, John Fred. "The Social and Economic Effects Produced upon Small Towns by Rapid Industrialization." M.A. thesis, University of Tennessee, 1938.

Kelsey, Victor V. "Building a Complete Cycle of Industries." *Scientific American Supplement* 84 (20 October 1917): 250.

Mackenzie, Clinton. "Industrial Housing Development at Kingsport, Tenn." *The Architectural Forum* (March 1918): 78–80.

McNeil, Nellie. "Allen Dryden: Sullivan County Architect, Residences 1922–1940." Prepared for Sullivan County Historical Society Essay Contest, October 1981.

Page, Valda Stone. "Rotherwood." Unpublished article, 1998.

Patrick, Sherman. "Desegregation in Kingsport City Schools." M.A. thesis, East Tennessee State University, 1997.

Shuman, Isaac. "Kingsport, an Unusual City, Built to Make Business for a Railroad." *American City* 22 (May 1920): 471–473.

Smith, Samuel Boyd. "Joseph Buckner Killebrew and the New South Movement in Tennessee." East Tennessee Historical Society's *Publications 37* (1965): 5–22.

Spoden, Muriel Clark. "Kingsport, Tennessee: Historical Map of Long Island of the Holston." H.T. Spoden, cartographer; and Bob Hensley, illustrator for the Netherland Inn Association, 1969.

Stevenson, Charles. "Contrast in 'Perfect' Towns: Norris and Kingsport, Tennessee; Federal Showcase and Industry's Yardstick Town." *Nation's Business* (December 1937): 18–20, 124, 130.

Tindall, George B. "Business Progressivism: Southern Politics in the Twenties." *The South Atlantic Quarterly* 62, No. 1, (Winter 1963): 92–106.

Urbanism Committee of the National Resources Committee. "Urban Planning and Land Policies." Supplementary Report, 1939.

Veiller, Lawrence. "Industrial Housing Developments on America Part IV: A Colony in the Blue Ridge Mountains at Erwin, Tennessee, Grosvenor Atterbury, Architect and Town Planner." *The Architectural Record* 43 (June 1918): 547–559.

Whitman, Wilson. "Three Southern Towns III. Kingsport: They Planned It." *The Nation* 21 January 1939: 88–90.

Wolfe, Margaret Ripley. "Changing the Face of Southern Appalachia: Urban Planning in Southwest Virginia and East Tennessee, 1890–1929." *APA Journal* (July 1981): 252–265.

————. "J. Fred Johnson, His Town, and His People: A Case Study of Class Values, the Work Ethic, and Technology in Southern Appalachia, 1916–1944." *Appalachian Journal* 71 (Autumn-Winter 1979–1980): 70–83.